Roar of the Tigress

Roar
of the Tigress

The Oral Teachings of Rev. Master Jiyu-Kennett:

Western Woman and Zen Master

VOLUME I

An Introduction to Zen:

Religious Practice for Everyday Life

Edited and with an Introduction by

Rev. Daizui MacPhillamy

SHASTA ABBEY PRESS
MOUNT SHASTA, CALIFORNIA

First Edition—2000

© 2000 Order of Buddhist Contemplatives

Frontispiece: Rev. Master Jiyu-Kennett during an interview for the
Record Searchlight newspaper. This photograph first appeared along with
an article about her in the Redding Record Searchlight on December 28, 1983.
Reprinted with permission of the Record Searchlight.

The drawings on page 63 are by Shaun Williams. They were first published
in *The Next Step: Advice on continuing your practice*, 1997 and are reprinted
with permission of Shaun Williams. The photograph of Vimalakirti and his
wife on page 193 is reprinted with permission of the National Palace Museum,
Taipei, Taiwan, Republic of China. The photograph of ringing the great bell on
page 268 first appeared in the fourth edition of *Zen is Eternal Life* and the
photograph of Rev. Master Jiyu with her master, the Very Reverend Keido
Chisan Koho Zenji, on page 274 first appeared in the first edition of *Zen is
Eternal Life*. They are reprinted with permission of Shasta Abbey.

Printed in the United States of America.

ISBN: 0-930066-21-9
Library of Congress Control Number: 00-131505

Dedicated in grateful memory
to Rev. Master Houn Jiyu-Kennett.

"The Light of Buddha is increasing in brilliance
and the Wheel of the Dharma is always turning."

Contents

Introduction

ABOUT REV. MASTER JIYU-KENNETT*

Rev. Master Jiyu-Kennett was born in St. Leonards-on-Sea, near Hastings, Sussex, England on New Year's day, 1924. Baptized Peggy Teresa Nancy in the Church of England, she was the last child and only girl of a deeply unhappy marriage. Her first encounters with Buddhism came from a copy of *The Light of Asia* in her father's library and a statue of the Buddha, relic of the Empire, that for some unknown reason sat on a mantelpiece in the assembly hall of her first school. This statue gave her solace in the midst of the sorrows of home and school. Even earlier as a very small girl, on seeing a person in monastic robes in the street, she told her mother that this was what she wanted to be when she grew up.

In 1939 came World War II and the death of her father in December of that year after a long illness. Although evacuated to a safer part of England, she did not escape the trauma of war: her home town was heavily bombed; stray bombs fell near her even after evacuation; Peggy's best friend

---

* This section of the Introduction has been adapted from the obituary for Rev. Master Jiyu, which appeared in the Winter 1996/Spring 1997 memorial issue of *The Journal of the Order of Buddhist Contemplatives.*

ix

was drowned, caught in the barbed wire that had been strung for defense along the coast, and the girl's father died trying to save her. The sound of the bombs and the sight of the red night sky—London aflame—stayed with Peggy Kennett all her life and were the impetus to her spiritual search: why did people do this to one another?

These years also saw the beginnings of her professional career as a musician and her first encounters with Gregorian plain chant. This became a life-long interest and was put to excellent use in later years in the liturgy used by the Order of Buddhist Contemplatives, which she founded. During this time she also strengthened her connections with Buddhism. She received an excellent education in the basic teachings of the Theravada tradition, eventually taking the Refuges and Precepts from the Venerable Dr. Saddhatissa, a leading monk and scholar of that tradition who taught for many years in London, and earning a diploma in Buddhist doctrine from the Young Men's Buddhist Association of Sri Lanka.

In the years following the war, Peggy Kennett worked as a church organist wherever she could find employment. She also joined the Women's Royal Naval Reserve and worked for the Conservative Party as a youth representative. In 1954 she became a member of the London Buddhist Society, eventually becoming one of their lecturers and, in 1958, a member of the governing Council.

There being no money forthcoming from her family for her higher education, she put herself through university. She first studied at Trinity College of Music, London, where she was awarded a fellowship, and then went on to obtain the degree of Bachelor of Music from Durham University, specializing in organ and composition.

During her time at the London Buddhist Society, Peggy met and studied with the many Buddhist teachers who visited there, including D. T. Suzuki. In 1960 one of the Chief Abbots of the Soto Zen Church of Japan, the Very Rev. Keido Chisan Koho Zenji, visited London. He was on a tour of Western countries to investigate the possibilities of spreading the Dharma and to look for suitable Westerners to train as his disciples. He met Peggy Kennett, as she helped organize his visit, and invited her to come to Japan to be his disciple. She said, "Yes!" and began to make preparations. She worked at various jobs teaching music at several schools to help raise money, but in the end had to borrow the last few pounds from a friend to afford the boat ticket.

Around this time, the Buddhist community in Malaysia, led by the Ven. Seck Kim Seng, had finally succeeded in obtaining authorization from the government for the first public celebration of the Buddha's Birth. In commemoration of this, the American monk Ven. Sumangalo wrote the words to the anthem "Welcome Joyous Wesak Day", and an international contest was held to find a composer to set it to music. The contest was won by Peggy Kennett, and the Malaysian Buddhist community asked her to stop in their country on her way to Japan to receive the award and to give public lectures on the Dharma.

In the fall of 1961, Peggy Kennett boarded a ship for the East by way of the Suez Canal and India. Arriving in Malaysia, she discovered that, due to misunderstandings, preparations had been made for her ordination there. Because there was intense and often hostile coverage of her situation by the non-Buddhist press, she agreed to be ordained in Malaysia, rather than in Japan as she had planned, and asked the Ven. Seck Kim Seng to be her ordination master. This was because she thought that a refusal to be ordained in Malaysia might be used by the press to bring Buddhism into disrepute. On January 21, 1962, she was given Shramanera ordination into the Chinese Buddhist Sangha and received the name Sumitra (True Friend). At her request, she also received the Bodhisattva Precepts from Ven. Seck Sian Toh, assisted by other masters who were allowed out of China specifically for the ceremony. After several months in Malaysia studying with her ordination master, Rev. Sumitra travelled to Japan. On April 14, 1962, she was received by Koho Zenji as his personal disciple, and her ordination name was translated into Japanese as Jiyu (Compassionate Friend). At this time she also received the religious "family" name of Houn (Dharma Cloud), the family name that her disciples bear to this day.

There was considerable controversy in Sojiji, which was Koho Zenji's monastery and one of the two great training seminaries of the Japanese Soto Zen church, over his plans to train this foreign female disciple in what was to many minds a place for Japanese male trainees only. She asked him a number of times if she could go to one of the female monasteries, but he refused, knowing that unless she trained at Sojiji and did everything that the men did, it could be said in the future that things had been made easy for her.

Finally, the way was cleared for her to formally enter Sojiji as a novice trainee. Shortly before her entrance, the senior disciplinarian confronted her: what did she want? Many foreigners came to Japan seeking various things. Did she want to study calligraphy, flower arrangement, or perhaps tea ceremony? Rev. Jiyu looked him straight in the eye and said, "I want the perfection of Zen!" "So be it!" he replied, and from then on they understood each other. While he, and those like him, treated her with fairness and respect, many others did not, and she had to continually face discrimination for being both a foreigner and a woman. She took these tests of her sincerity positively, and her training soon bore fruit: after less than six months in the temple, she experienced a first kensho, a first understanding of Zen. This confirmed Koho Zenji's confidence in her and, in May 1963, he gave her the Dharma Transmission and, in later years, certified her as a Dharma Heir and holder of his branch of the Soto Zen lineage from Shakyamuni Buddha through Bodhidharma, Hui Neng, Tendo Nyojyo, Dogen, Keizan, and Manzan.

Thereafter Rev. Master Jiyu, as was Koho Zenji's wish, began to teach the many Westerners who came to Sojiji by serving as his Foreign Guest Master, ordaining Western monks, and eventually having her own temple, Umpukuji, in Mie Prefecture. She promised Koho Zenji that, no matter what, she would care for and protect his foreign disciples.

In the fall of 1965, in order to silence questions over the fitness of "this foreign woman" to inherit the Dharma, Koho Zenji sent Rev. Master Jiyu to the highly respected Soto Zen master Sawaki Kodo Roshi, who confirmed her understanding.

After Koho Zenji's death, and as a direct result of her promise to him, Rev. Master Jiyu left Japan with two Western disciples to accept invitations to visit the United States, Canada, and Great Britain. She arrived in San Francisco in November of 1969 and, although she made visits to England and Canada, decided to settle in the United States.

The next six years were spent simply doing her own training and trying to be of use to whoever came to her. Out of this emerged Shasta Abbey in Mt. Shasta, California, Throssel Hole Buddhist Abbey near Hexham in northern England, and eventually the Order of Buddhist Contemplatives with branch temples and meditation groups in North America and Europe. Many students came to her and stayed with her until her death; and many left, some perhaps because they did not understand what she was doing, and some perhaps because they did.

In 1976, worn out, ill, and having been told by her doctor that death was near, Rev. Master Jiyu went into retreat and experienced another kensho, this time a massive spiritual opening accompanied by visions and recollections of past lives. Having been prepared for this by the teachings she had received in Malaysia and Japan,* she knew what was taking place, but many of the people around her did not.

Her health recovered somewhat and she continued on, deepening her faith and practice in the basic tenets of Soto Zen and entering the most productive years of her religious life. Most of the lectures which form the basis of this volume were given by her between 1976 and 1990, when her health began to fail massively. The diabetes she had been diagnosed with soon after her arrival in America took a heavy toll on her body throughout the early nineties, eventually leaving her paralyzed from the waist down and nearly blind. Unable to continue giving public lectures, she nonetheless taught, working closely with her more senior disciples and providing a remarkable example of equanimity and all-acceptance in the face of ever-increasing disability. On November 6, 1996, Rev. Master Jiyu-Kennett passed away quickly and peacefully. It was, as she had wanted, as if she

---

* Such events are rare and not often discussed in the Zen tradition, but were well known to Zen masters of old. See, for example, Bernard Faure, *Visions of Power* (Princeton University Press, 1996); and Revs. Daizui MacPhillamy, Zensho Roberson, Koten Benson, and Hubert Nearman, "Yume: Visionary Experience in the Lives of Great Masters Dogen and Keizan" in *The Journal of the Order of Buddhist Contemplatives*, Vol. 12, No. 2 (Summer 1997).

had stepped out through a door: not an ending, nor even a new beginning, just a going on, going on, going on beyond.

ABOUT THIS EDITION

Over the course of her more than thirty years as a Buddhist teacher, Rev. Master Jiyu-Kennett gave many Dharma talks, public lectures, and informal discussions. Some of these were tape recorded, and the result is an archive at Shasta Abbey of over 1,000 tapes of her oral teachings. While a few of these have been reproduced and made available over the years,* most remain as archival material. Following her death in 1996, making more of these oral teachings generally available seemed a fitting activity for some of us who were her long-time chaplains (personal assistants).

Two of these, Rev. Kinsei Tower and myself, started working on this project in 1997, with Rev. Kinsei kindly taking charge of the immense task of selecting tapes and having them transcribed, and myself taking on the editorial function. Some of the tapes were incomplete; some contained her commentary on translations of texts copyrighted by others and hence were unavailable for publication; others were clearly intended for "in house" use by her monastic disciples alone; and a few were otherwise unsuitable candidates for publication. However, there were still many hundreds of

---

* A catalog of these may be obtained by writing or calling either Throssel Hole Buddhist Abbey Bookshop, Carrshield, Hexham, Northumberland NE47 8AL, United Kingdom, phone: +44 (0) 1434 345204, fax: +44 (0) 1434 345216; or Shasta Abbey Buddhist Supplies, 3724 Summit Dr., Mt. Shasta, CA 96067-9102, phone: (800) 653-3315, fax: (800) 653-1195, Int'l phone and fax: (530) 926-6682; O.B.C. website: www.obcon.org.

tapes to choose from. In consultation with various of her other disciples, and particularly with Rev. Zensho Roberson, then archivist of Shasta Abbey, Rev. Kinsei was able to select several dozen of the most promising tapes for potential inclusion in this first volume of Rev. Master Jiyu's oral teachings.

These tapes were then sent out for transcription to volunteers among the lay ministers and other long-term lay students of our Order. I would like to express here my gratitude to all, both monastic and lay, who have helped with this lengthy and exacting task: Supriti Bharma, Patti Brady, Scott Brant, Rev. Meian Elbert, Michele Feist, Linda Pitts, Jim Riis, Kate Schlapfer, Andrea Spark, Victor Stepan, Scott Tenney, and Margi Robertson. As these transcripts returned, they were converted to a standard word-processing format by Rev. Kinsei and then passed along to me to peruse. It soon became evident that their content was starting to clump them together into natural groups, one of which was composed of Rev. Master Jiyu's introductory talks on our Soto Zen, or Serene Reflection, tradition of Buddhist training. Since "beginnings" seemed a good place to begin, we then focused on these introductory teachings, and other tapes that seemed compatible with that theme were sought out, transcribed, and reviewed for possible addition to this first volume.

Several decisions had to be made in the editing process, and I would like to make those explicit here so that the reader will know exactly what it is that he or she is reading. The first decision was whether to edit the transcripts at all, or simply pick a compatible selection of them to be published completely unaltered. This would have had the obvious advantage of presenting Rev. Master Jiyu's words exactly as she had spoken them, with no danger of introducing any form of slanting or bias in the editorial process. That appealed to me, as I have a strong wish to offer the best of Rev. Master Jiyu as she was, not my interpretation of her. It soon became clear, however, that this very wish required of me that some editing be done. The spoken word is not the same medium as the written word, and what communicates well in one does not always work well in the other. Tone of voice, for instance, can convey continuity between phrases in speech, whereas in writing this function requires more reliance on grammatical construction and punctuation. Raw transcripts, for this reason, sometimes make for confusing, even bewildering, reading, and Rev. Master Jiyu placed a high value on clarity in her communications. In addition, certain words or phrases are typically added in speech to give a pause to the listener's ear, additions which become distracting in written form. Rev. Master Jiyu would, for example, repeat phrases or add the words "and", "so", or "now" at the beginnings of many sentences (to my chagrin, the transcripts reveal that one of my own favorites is the old standby, "well . . . um"). It helped me in making the decision to go ahead and undertake editing to realize that I was not going to destroy anything in the editing process: the original tapes, and now their raw transcripts as well, will be preserved in our archives for any who might have need of them.

Having decided that some degree of editing was advisable, the next decision was how extensively to edit. Initially, I tried to edit just enough to provide continuity and felicity of reading, to clarify ambiguity, and to correct the occasional obvious mistaken word, without altering the flavor or tone, and certainly not the meaning, of a passage. In this, I ran the risk of not doing as much editing as my master would have wished me to do. Over the course of my twenty-one years as chaplain to her, she would occasionally ask me to help her edit one of her lectures into written form. Her editing on these occasions was quite extensive: she altered sentence structure, grammar, word order, sentence order, and the order of major portions of the discourse; she altered numerous words so as to sharpen meaning, correct mistakes or ambiguities, and improve the clarity of the flow of thought; portions that were not directly contributory to the main thesis of the text were chopped out; she added entire new passages that covered points to which she felt she had given insufficient attention at the time of speaking. The result was a tightly-crafted and often grammatically complex work that tended to convey her meaning brilliantly, but bore little resemblance to the more easy-going style of her natural speech. I suspect that she had something of the same process in mind for some of the talks presented in this book, since when I offered to help her edit some of them herself in the last few years of her life, she told me that she was amenable to seeing them in print but no longer had the strength to undertake such a "huge task". At the outset, then, my editing was far less than she herself would have done.

In the early drafts of editing in my minimalist way, I also was scrupulous to inform the reader of any changes which I had made, so that they could know exactly what was Rev. Master Jiyu and what was Daizui's meddling. Thus each omission was marked with ellipses (. . .) and each addition was placed in brackets ([ ]). I even kept track of the reason for each editorial change and prepared a table of these, which was included in an earlier version of this introduction. The result of all this was then given to a number of her senior disciples to read, and their suggestions were solicited. The response was nearly unanimous and went something like this: "We're glad you're being so honest, but for goodness sakes, Daizui, lighten up a little. This is a book to be read; it's not an academic thesis. Take out those darned distracting ellipses and brackets, and don't be afraid to edit as Rev. Master would have wanted you to." So, I did. Well, . . . not quite. First, I didn't want to lose her informal style of speaking, which was part of the delight in listening to her, so I didn't do much editing in ways that would "tighten up" the style. Secondly, while I added a few sentences here and there where I felt she would have wanted clarification or "fleshing out" of her remarks, I just couldn't bring myself to make the extensive changes that she probably would have had me do, were she alive. Thus, to the extent that I have edited less than she might have wished, I must make my apologies, but I would rather err on that side, and present the reader with something that is relatively free of my own impositions and gives the feeling of what it was like to listen to her, than to create a polished written work at the risk of introducing too much of myself. And, to judge by the reactions of her senior disciples to the current volume, her "voice" does, indeed, come through loud and clear. I would like to thank all of the monks who have read the manuscript of this volume in its various stages of development and have offered me their wise discernment on how to improve it. I would also like to thank Rev. Hugh Gould for his assistance in researching the footnotes and checking the accuracy of scriptural quotations.

There is one area in which I did undertake systematic editorial changes, that of gender neutral pronouns. Rev. Master Jiyu was of a generation which referred to people inclusively by using what I call the "masculine neuter" form: "he" could refer either to a male person or to any person, the usage being inferred by context. This was the form that she used in speaking, occasionally stopping to note that she specifically intended it as gender neutral. In recognition of the underlying cultural bias of this type of usage, our language has recently evolved in such a way as to make this form somewhat problematic: "he" now is often understood to refer to a male person only. Thus, if I left the wording exactly as it appeared on the transcripts, to some readers it might seem that Rev. Master Jiyu was deliberately speaking only to and about men, which was clearly contrary to her intent. I have therefore altered some of the pronouns so as to make her gender inclusive intent clear in current English usage by sometimes including both masculine and feminine forms together, occasionally using them alternately, and frequently using the plural as a gender neutral singular ("When a person is hungry, *they* eat."). I have tried to do this in such a way as to keep an easy, natural flow of speech since, for reasons which the reader can discern from Chapter Five, Rev. Master Jiyu regarded self-consciously gender-neutral speech as almost as harmful as offensively gender-biased speech. To the extent that my editing has succeeded in avoiding either of these forms, I feel that I have done what my master would have wished me to do; to the extent that I have failed in this regard, I apologize to the reader.

Another editorial decision was whether or not to present each talk as a whole, or to combine portions of several talks into one book chapter. Again, the former initially seemed more straightforward and appealing, but I ended up doing the latter. Presenting every talk as a whole would give the most complete picture of her style of teaching and would be of value to students of the psychology of religious thought, in that it would shed light on changes in her approach to the same subject matter over the course of her life. But those aren't the reasons most of us are likely to read this book: we are more apt to want to know what Rev. Master Jiyu-Kennett had to say about a given topic, and what it was like to listen to her, without having to wade through a lot of repetitions or extraneous material. And part of her teaching style was that she didn't attempt to give a complete, highly organized, dissertation on all of her views on a topic in one talk. For example, when giving the introductory talks relevant to this volume, she often relied on a text of Dogen Zenji known as the *Shushogi*. In the talks she gave in July 1974, July 1982 and June 1989 she made extensive use of this work, but in the '89 lecture series she started part way through the first section of it and left out part of the fourth section, while in the '74 series she emphasized the first section, and in the '82 series she dealt extensively with the aspects of the fourth section that were omitted in '89.

I had three choices. I could use only one of these three lecture series, thus giving a complete picture of her approach at one time but failing to give a full view of her thought on this topic. I could include all three, thus avoiding any incompleteness but presenting extensive repeated material likely to frustrate the general reader. Or I could divide the material up and patch it together, in hopes of offering a reasonably complete presentation of Rev. Master Jiyu-Kennett's thought in a way that would be easily readable. I chose this third option. This volume, then, is primarily a compilation of the introductory lectures which Rev. Master Jiyu-Kennett delivered in July 1974, July 1981, July 1982, and June of 1989. Short sections of some sixteen of her other recorded talks have been added to "flesh out" the work, talks given as early as one in Singapore in 1966 and as late as one in the summer of 1989.

A related concern arose in regard to how to handle the questions and comments which occurred in these various lectures. I could have eliminated them altogether, concentrating only upon her more formal presentations, but Rev. Master Jiyu-Kennett often didn't lecture that way: these introductory talks were interactive, with the questions and comments of the audience and of her monks forming an integral part of their lively and informal nature. However, questions occur in random order, depending upon what was on the mind of whomever Rev. Master called upon next, and, if left in that order, questions on any given topic would be scattered throughout the book, again making for difficult reading. For this reason, I have taken the liberty of gathering up all of the questions and comments on a particular issue and placing them in the chapter wherein Rev. Master discusses that subject. As is inevitable in public talks, some questions and comments proved to be irrelevant to the subject matter at hand in a way that would be distracting to the flow of the chapter, and these were simply deleted. I have also taken the liberty of combining together some of the comments by the various monks who accompanied her to these lectures; thus these comments do not necessarily reflect the contributions or views of any particular monk.

When most of the editing for the first volume was completed, I had the good fortune to discover an old transcript of one of the same talks I had worked on, this one having been edited by Rev. Master Jiyu herself for possible publication. Although this was not one of the talks upon which the bulk of a chapter was based, it contained several passages which I had already edited and included in two chapters as part of the "fleshing out" process. These passages totaled some 1200 words, and, unable to resist the temptation to report at least a few numbers to the reader, I compared what I had done to those words with what Rev. Master Jiyu herself had done years before, thus generating an independent check on how closely my editing corresponded to hers. We both left 76 percent of the original transcript words unchanged. On another 6 percent of occasions we both changed the same words, often in similar ways. Of course, many of those were what one might call "editorial no-brainers" such as removing repeated words, misstarted sentences, and gratuitous introductory words such as "well" or "now". Another 16 percent of words were changed by Rev. Master Jiyu but left alone by me. This leaves only 2 percent of the original transcript where I made changes and she did not. The analysis of this fortunate discovery allows me to place more confidence in my subjective impression that, while I have not done as much editing as Rev. Master Jiyu might have liked, at least the reader is getting to hear her voice in these pages, not mine.

I would like to express my gratitude to all of those who have helped make this volume possible. In addition to the people involved in the selection and transcription of tapes, this would include the many senior disciples of Rev. Master Jiyu who read the manuscript for content. I also deeply appreciate the help given by Rev. Meiten McGuire, Rev. Oswin Hollenbeck, and Ms. Cate Lewis, who read it to help me find ways of expressing oral material in written form by using comprehensible forms of grammar and punctuation. Rev. Shiko Rom at Shasta Abbey Press undertook the mysterious tasks of turning the manuscript into a book, and without her kindness and persistence it would not be one. Finally, I would like to thank Rev. Master Eko Little, Abbot of Shasta Abbey, and Rev. Koten Benson, Prior of the Lions' Gate Buddhist Priory in Vancouver, Canada, for providing me with support, encouragement, and conducive places in which to do the work of editing.

BUDDHISM AS ATHEISM VS. BUDDHISM AS THEISM

The reader will notice right from the first chapter that Rev. Master Jiyu-Kennett is not afraid of using religious terminology, including the word "God", in teaching Buddhism. While this approach is one which has been adopted from time to time by other eminent Buddhist teachers of our time,* it may initially strike some Buddhists as strange, since one of the fundamental tenets of the Buddha's teaching was His rejection of the Hindu concept of a personal soul which seeks to unite with a Supreme Soul or God. Zen, in particular among the Buddhist Schools, is known for its use of negative terminology to describe ultimate things, making extensive use of words such as "emptiness", "the void", and "nothing from the first". And Rev. Master Jiyu herself both uses these terms and also notes in other passages in this same volume the problems with the notion of a Supreme Being. Well may the reader wonder what is going on.

What is going on are two things: first, Rev. Master Jiyu-Kennett was taught, and has passed on, Soto Zen as a religion; second, she was talking in these lectures to Western people with little or no background in the niceties of Buddhist doctrine. As to the former, Zen can be approached in several ways: for instance, it can be entered into as an almost secular philosophy with a supremely rational and self-determined way of life, or it can be seen as a deeply religious practice involving faith, ceremony, precepts, and spiritual intuition. While both approaches are viable, the more secular one has been prevalent in Western books on the subject and has

---

* See, for example, Ven. Thich Nhat Hanh, "The Practice of Prayer" in *The Mindfulness Bell*, No. 17 (Summer 1996), pp. 1–6.

given an impression of Buddhism, and especially of Zen, as being atheistic and even nihilistic. Such an impression, however, is an oversimplification and a distortion of the secular approach, which, like the religious approach, is actually attempting to point to something that is beyond the opposites of theism and atheism, eternalism and nihilism. Rev. Master Jiyu lived a Zen that was of the religious sort, and wished both to introduce this possibility to her listeners and to provide them with an antidote to the atheist-nihilist impression, so that they might have a better chance to move beyond the opposites.

But what words to use to describe That which is really beyond words? Since she was speaking to an introductory audience, she chose familiar words, religious words. In so doing, she was, in effect, saying, "Don't be afraid of religion; you can get beyond the opposites within a religious context. Maybe you have been disappointed by the limitations of religion up to now, but those limitations are imposed by us on ourselves; they are not inherent in religious training: *religion can free you.*" Since Westerners' backgrounds are in the Judeo-Christian-Islamic family of religions, our religious words will have a flavor of those traditions, and thus so did Rev. Master's words when introducing people to Zen. She also was not trying to convert her audiences to Buddhism: her sole desire was that they should be successful in the religion of their choice, whatever it might be. To this end she would speak at times of ways in which Soto Zen practice could assist in the religious endeavors of other faiths to "find God".

For the reasons mentioned above, when speaking of the ultimate things of Buddhism, Rev. Master Jiyu would often use words like "God", "the Eternal", or "the Lord of the

House", and she would sometimes use such terms in a very personal and familiar way: that does not mean she was an eternalist or a theist. This is somewhat parallel to what Shakyamuni Buddha Himself did in using terms like "the soul" when explaining His Way in common speech; while such usages have sometimes caused confusion over the centuries, they surely do not mean that He was contradicting His own teachings.* At other times she would use terms like "That Which Is", "the Unborn", or "the Immaculacy of Emptiness"; that does not mean she was a nihilist or an atheist. A full discussion of the linguistic and Buddhological complexities of speaking about ultimate things would require a scholarly treatise well beyond the scope of this introduction (and of this editor). Suffice it to say, then, that more is going on in Rev. Master Jiyu-Kennett's approach to this area than meets the eye: she is trying at once to introduce the religious approach to Zen, correct a common misperception, help people to get beyond the opposites, speak of what cannot really be spoken of, and, above all, let people know that they need not be frightened of religion. As to whether Buddhist scholars would criticize her for the possible doctrinal implications of all this (or of any other aspect of her talks), she frankly didn't give a darn. Indeed, I can almost hear her now, saying what she repeated to me so often, "Daizui, stop being afraid of words and get on with your training!"

Rev. Daizui MacPhillamy,
The Fugen Forest Hermitage
October, 1999.

---

* See, for example, S. Z. Aung and Mrs. Rhys-Davids, trans., *Points of Controversy* (Katha-Vatthu) (London: Pali Text Society, 1969), p. 27.

1.

Why Study Zen?

WHERE TO START

Before we discuss how to practice Zen training, I would like to talk to you about why one comes to study Zen in the first place. You have to start off on the "me" side, on the greed side. You see, somebody comes to religion not because he or she really wants to, but because they have nowhere else to go. You go to religion when psychology, psychiatry, and everything else breaks down, and you say, "Oops, where do we go from here?" Then you start saying, "Well, maybe there is something that I don't know very much about", and you start looking for a priest or a teacher. And, if you're lucky, you find one who knows their job.

So, what is it that primarily drives people to do this? A lot of people say that it is fear of death, but it isn't: it's fear of life. Far more people are scared of living than are scared of dying; they are terrified of living. They can put up with death: they know that it is going to come sometime, and there's always a doctor to put it off as long as possible, and then, with any luck, there are nice drugs that will make it easy. But tomorrow you've got to go and face the boss, you've got to go to work, you've got to drive on the freeway and there may be a maniac driving beside you: what do you do? The fear of life is what drives people to religion, what drives them to psychiatrists, what drives them to psychologists: "How do I act?" "How do I interact with people?" And when questions at that level don't give me the answer, I stop and I say, "All right, I must have a look deeply within me." And then you come to the most important thought of all, "Maybe it's not life or death that's the problem: maybe the problem is me."

The fact that most people fear life a lot more than they fear death is one of the reasons why so many young people are attracted to Zen Buddhism. Given what the world is like outside, I must confess I don't blame them. I probably would have done something totally different in life if I had not been a teenager during World War II, and at the age of twenty-one, after having had all the bombings and the like in England, I came to the conclusion that any life I had left was a bonus and that I'd better do something about using the bonus sensibly. I've never told people that, but that's the reason I went into religion. Who knows when somebody else was going to be an idiot? There just wasn't all that much time to spare, and so that is what I did, without realizing the reason why (because at that time in England nobody knew clearly what you did go into Buddhism for; they only knew you went into it "for enlightenment", and everybody had dozens of ideas as to what that was). When you know truly what it is to have unborn and undying Buddha Nature within you, then you do not fear life. And the older person usually comes to religion because, although they may not fear death, it is a very difficult thing and they want some help in dealing with it. Therefore, you find the young and the older person, and you usually do not find too many in the middle. They are usually "too busy doing other things" to look inside themselves.

This actually means that they have allowed themselves to lose sight of what is really important in life. And, indeed, most of us at any age are so self-satisfied with ourselves that we are content with just being able to "get by", which (forgive me because I know there are a lot of psychologists in the audience) is usually about as far as the average psychologist hopes to get you: so that you don't have problems with the world in general, so that you just get by without infringing on anybody. When you say, "That isn't enough, I want to go further than this", then you come to religion. When you say, "I'm not satisfied; there must be something more", and there is nowhere else to turn, where do you look? *Inside you.*

But before you are willing to do that, you've got to be really "fed up" with you. Which is why so very few people do it: there is much too much self-satisfaction. The most difficult person to teach Zen to is someone who's complacent. In fact, it is the only thing I know of that is going to take longer than twenty years to cure. Of course, it can only take a few minutes if the person really gets fed up enough, but that's the whole point of complacency: he's not fed up. So, complacency is the enemy, and you should know that it is the enemy. You should not be afraid of the word "enemy" because if you want to get somewhere, complacency is what is in your way: satisfaction with you as you are. If you are not satisfied with you as you are, then you will do something.

The great Thirteenth Century Zen master Eihei Dogen says at the end of the chapter from which I will be quoting today that none of us has more than one body during this lifetime, therefore it is indeed tragic to lead a life of evil as a result of wrong understanding, for it is impossible to escape from the consequence if we do that which is unwise, that which is "evil", on the assumption that if an act is not recognized by us as unwise, nothing bad can happen. How many of us have done this? How many of us have turned our backs, both on ourselves and on others, and said, "Well, I don't need to notice"? That is the other great enemy of doing something about you, of real, genuine religion: ignorance, not seeing. "Time flies as an arrow flies from a bow; birth and death are a grave event": you haven't got time to sit around and wait. You have to do it now. You have to sit down now, not tomorrow morning, not tomorrow night, or, "Well, I've got to wait until such-and-such", because that attitude of mind can go on forever.

Now a lot of people know that meditation is an important part of Zen Buddhist practice, and they ask, "Why do you do meditation?" "Why does Soto Zen (which is the form of Zen that I teach) meditate by sitting and looking at a wall?" Well, it is one of the main ways that we have of looking inside us, of facing life and death squarely. Have you ever looked at your own mind? In meditation, you sit and look at a physical wall, and after a bit you realize that you're looking at it with "bricked-up spectacles"; because when you meditate, you're really looking at what's going on inside you, and there's a lovely big "wall" in there which you've got to tear down, which you've got to do something about. Because it is that wall, which you have created to protect yourself from life and death, that is actually the problem. It's a problem because enlightenment is one and indivisible, so when you try to protect yourself from anything (and thus you separate yourself from it), you also separate yourself from enlightenment. And it is that separation from enlightenment which both perpetuates the fear of life and death and also causes you to sense that something is very wrong.

One of my students drew a cartoon which he put on the meditation hall wall: it showed a picture of him sitting there with a huge pair of bricked-up spectacles, and he was trying to peer around them and wondering why he couldn't. The next piece on the cartoon was two smashed-up spectacles and him with two blind eyes, because there comes a time when if you sit with bricked-up spectacles for too long, the darkness is so great you just cannot break through it: there is not enough time left. So, this is the main thing that a person learns when they come to meditation: how to do something about that wall inside them. That wall is as far as psychology can take you. The Zen master can take you from the wall to what lies behind it, if you have the courage to go. And understand me clearly: most people haven't. They are much happier to just be able to "get by": it's simpler, it's easier. But Zen does not accept that; there is much more to life than that. So, that which brings a person to religion is fear of life when they are young and fear of death when they are older, and you need to know that both are really the same thing: both are the result of that inner wall that separates you from enlightenment.

I would like to quote from the teachings of Dogen, the Patriarch* on whose work we base our teachings of Soto Zen. This is from the first paragraph of the *Shushogi*,† which is probably his most important teaching. It says simply this:

Scripture: "The most important question for all Buddhists is how to understand birth and death

---

* The Japanese term "*so*" is generally translated either as "patriarch" or as "ancestor"; Rev. Master Jiyu was not happy with either, but used both. The former has sexist connotations, the latter elicits associations of ancestor worship; neither implication is accurate.

† The translation of this work quoted here is by Rev. Master Jiyu-Kennett from her book *Zen is Eternal Life*, 4th ed. (Mt. Shasta, California: Shasta Abbey Press, 1999), pp. 94–103.

completely for then, should you be able to find the Buddha within birth and death, they both vanish. All you have to do is realize that birth and death, as such, should not be avoided and they will cease to exist for then, if you can understand that birth and death are Nirvana itself, there is not only no necessity to avoid them but also nothing to search for that is called Nirvana. The understanding of the above breaks the chains that bind one to birth and death therefore this problem, which is the greatest in all Buddhism, must be completely understood."

"Should you be able to find the Buddha within birth and death"—what is "the Buddha" for which you look? It is Buddha Nature, which lives within each and every one of us. It is that simple, quiet "thing" that is absolutely unmovable, completely free, which each one of us longs for and very few of us find, because we are afraid to pay the price that it takes to realize It. And the price that it takes is doing something about us. You come to your brick wall: "All right, books have got me this far; science has got me this far; where do I go from here? I must do something about me." And what is it that causes us to ask these questions, that motivates us to search for Buddha Nature? It is precisely Buddha Nature Itself, the "Higher Being", which patiently calls us from within. Thus, Zen says that the mind that seeks the Way is the Buddha Mind and that the merit of the mind with which we first start Zen training is fathomless. I don't know what psychology calls It, but I know what I'm talking about. It's Something that says, "Well, if you're satisfied, I'm not." Every one of us hears this every day of the week: "You're pleased with that? My goodness, you're easily satisfied!" I've had this discussion in my skull going on when I was younger many, many times. "Are you satisfied with this?" "Yes, I'm happy with it." "After all, a dog who sleeps in the sun is happy. You want to be a dog asleep in the sun?" Of course not; no one does. And so, "if you can find the Buddha within life and death, they both vanish. All you have to do is realize that life and death, as such, should not be avoided."

The first thing I have to teach you then, if you want to undertake serious Zen training, is don't be scared. Religion is a dangerous "game", because it is the "game" of living; it is to be able to be fully alive: alive, and vibrant, and worth knowing. If religion makes you quiet and sluggish, then you have got religion all the wrong way up. If sitting looking at the wall makes you go around in a half-dazed dream, then you are not meditating correctly. It should make you able to be a hundred percent better than you are right now.

Now, if life and death must not be avoided, this means that you have to accept them. Therefore, all-acceptance is the key to the "gateless gate" of Zen. You know, people often come to me and they talk about how beautiful it is going to be when they have this wonderful enlightenment experience, when the whole world is one, and how glorious. . . . And I sit back and I say to myself, "Yes, and when is it going to be that you're completely accepting the chap who is sitting beside you who's got body odor, and the one who's slurping his soup, and you're not complaining about any of it?" "Acceptance" means what it says: acceptance—no movement one way or the other. Either you accept or you don't. Don't play games with it: don't play games with religion. This is a serious business, and you can get hurt. If once you tear down that brick wall, if once you stare at that wall within you and you really break it up, then you must go the whole distance. So don't try meditating unless you want to get "grabbed by the Cosmic Buddha".

A certain gentleman from England, who had better be nameless, came to Japan once, when I was over there, and informed the abbot that he didn't want to go to ceremonies and he didn't want to do various things; all he wanted was the "true experience of Zen". And my master, who was the Archbishop of Tokyo, stretched, looked across at me, and then said to him, "Do you realize that anybody who meditates runs the risk of being grabbed by the Cosmic Buddha? Do you object to being grabbed?" The gentleman frowned and said, "And what is 'the Cosmic Buddha'?" And he got into this lovely little discussion of ideologies and doctrines, and he was still talking when suddenly he realized there was a snore coming out of the old abbot. If you tear down that wall, you will get grabbed by the Cosmic Buddha, you will be face-to-face with your Buddha Nature: there's no way out because that is what is there. And because of that, as Dogen quite rightly says, "If you can understand that birth and death are Nirvana itself, there is not only no necessity to avoid them but also nothing to search for that is called Nirvana."

Incidentally, I would warn you that atheists and agnostics are not safe from this "getting grabbed"; in fact, they're anything but safe. You see, they think that their refusal to believe will defend them, and they don't realize that, when they are "ripe for the plucking", the Cosmic Buddha just picks them off because they've got no ideological defenses up. Beliefs are not the issue; indeed, the man or woman who has the most problems is the one who suffers from dogmas and similar things in his head and is so busy running around with them that he can't see straight. So don't think that if you are a scientist and you just simply meditate, if you take notice of what I say and don't particularly query it, that you will be safe simply because you're a scientist: you won't be. If you sit down and look at a wall, and you don't get your mind in the way, and you don't theorize, then your Buddha Nature will pick you off like a ripe plum. I have seen it on a number of occasions. The Cosmic Buddha seems especially fond of psychological types who think they're safe; I think maybe they're a challenge. . . . (laughter) Anyway, where did I get to?

Nirvana, yes. In other words, Nirvana *is*: here and now. The Buddha Mind *is*: right here, right here in this room, within you. All you have to do is tear down the watertight door, the brick walls, and all the other things you have carefully locked It up in, to be able to live completely. You cannot live completely until you accept life completely; you cannot live completely until you accept death completely. You cannot know Nirvana until you recognize that it is here and now. You can make a mess of it or you needn't; you can get your own ideas in the way, or you needn't: it's entirely up to you. The Buddhas and Ancestors aren't going to turn a hair whether you are with Them or you are not, because They *are*. They are as "iron beings". One of the things you are told when you are Transmitted by your master is that to know the Buddha Mind is to become an iron being: absolutely immovable. And it is iron: the Buddha Nature within you cannot be pulled over, toppled, by anyone. This is why you can't brainwash a Zen master; it's physically impossible. She or he cannot be controlled, cannot be held. You can physically kill them, but you cannot harm their brain or their mind. It is impossible because they have touched the Iron Being within. One of the reasons why there is so much beating done in monasteries in Japan is to see if you are scared, or if you are really willing to sit as an iron being, and no matter if earthquakes or anything else hits you, you will still sit. "I will get rid of this wall; I will realize enlightenment; I will know. I don't care what happens: I'll lay my life on the line, but I'll do it!" Then, and only then, will you know the

Unborn. So if you haven't got the courage to do that, don't try it. Just stay happily with your psychology; it's a lot simpler and a lot easier. You can get by: "Nice, we can go and play golf on Sunday; we can go to the country club; we can do all the other things we do." But if you want to live, and I mean *live*, then you have to do something about you.

Every one of you can do it, if you want to. But you're not going to do it until you get fed up enough with being the dog asleep in the sun: there is no way that you will manage it without that. Because if you train thoroughly, your whole lifestyle will have to change. You cannot take anything for granted any longer. Enlightenment will not bring you happiness, but it will bring you complete peace and the ability to live utterly and be unafraid of life. But the price is that you will have to change everything you do, and in so doing you will change everybody else around you, because there is no way you can avoid it. Doing something about you also does something about the world, because there is no way you can do something about you without having an effect on everyone else around you. This is the main way you deal with the problems of the world: you don't go out to deal with the problems, you go out to deal with you. Having dealt with you, other people (when they come up against you) say, "This one is different; I like what I see." And so, perhaps ten or twelve people reverberate off you, and they start doing something about themselves. Ten or twelve do it off each one of those: that's how you cure the world. We'll talk more about Zen and social action later, but the point here is that you don't go out to cure the world, you go out to do something about you.

There were a lot of problems when I was first leaving Japan in that several people over in England were terrified that I was coming to the West to take over their Buddhist organizations, and then they got very worried when they discovered that I wasn't interested, because they were convinced that meant I was going to convert the whole world. (laughter) They had missed the whole point of Buddhism: I went to Japan to do something about me, I didn't go to Japan to do something about England. However much other people didn't like me, I liked me a lot less; so I went to convert me, I did not go to convert the world. In converting me, I helped a lot of other people, but that was by accident. It's that simple. That is how Buddhism's spread, that is how Zen works: you neither "get something", nor do you not "get something", and the signs of enlightenment spread. Charity, benevolence, tenderness, sympathy: the four signs of enlightenment (which we will look at in detail a bit later), and if a Zen master does not exhibit them, then they are not a Zen master. But don't expect the master to exhibit them in the same way as you understand the terms, because sympathy is not saying, "Oh, I'm sorry that the cat was chased by the dog." It is understanding how the cat actually felt when the dog was behind it, which is a very different matter, and therefore making quite sure that the door is not left open so that it happens again; responsibility comes into it too. The signs of enlightenment are not making pretty noises about religion; they are acts, actual acts.

At some level we're all at least vaguely aware that we need to do something about that brick wall inside ourselves. But most of us don't want to do that just yet, and this is why people who undertake serious Zen training both benefit many people and also tend to lose all their friends. Your friends will wonder what on earth is wrong with you. Now, you may take a few with you: it's just possible, though you may not. But you will pick up with the next group that is on a stage higher. That's an atrocious way of putting it: "a stage higher"; we're all marching along the same road. But you will catch up with the next lot, who will be a lot better than the previous bunch—a lot more enjoyable, a lot more interesting, because they'll be people who have done the same thing you have done. They took a look at themselves and said, "Yeah, I'm not content with 'getting by', because I know that I can do more, much more, than just 'get by'."

And you may not just catch up to them but you may pass them, because an awful lot of people get satisfied part way along the way—"Why, it's great here!"—and they sit down and they picnic on the road of life, and before they know what's hit them, it's evening. Over the meditation hall door in a Zen monastery hang the words "Time flies as an arrow from a bow: I wish to obtain the Lord's teaching. Birth and death are a grave event: time flies as an arrow from a bow." I have only now in which to live. Am I going to sit and waste it? Am I going to run away from it? Or am I going to lay my life on the line and say, "Right, I don't care what happens, I am going to do something about me."

Thus do you start on the road of getting rid of that huge blockage that most of us have, of the watertight door that we set between the serenity of the years before we are seven and the time that comes after. It is interesting that the Buddha did not find peace of mind, did not find understanding, until He went back to doing that which He did as a child. At the age of seven, He achieved the first understanding through simple meditation. When he was older, He left His palace and He went off in search of truth. He went around going through all sorts of harsh disciplines, every imaginable torment that the body could stand, and He only found that He was making life worse and He was getting hallucinations. One day he got really fed up with this and said, "I know what I am going to do. I can remember, when I was small, when all I did was just sit, I got incredible peace of mind. Why don't I try that? I know: I'll go off, I'll have a bath, I'll get a meal, and I'll try that. And I'll go on doing that until it works." And He did just that, and that was the night that He got His understanding. He had to go back, in other words, to the naive mind of a child. He had to drop out all these silly ideas of hanging himself upside-down, and walking around on hot coals, and various other things He'd employed. He had to go back to the naive mind of a child and just sit with His mind still. There, in that stillness, he found the Iron Being within Himself. He had pulled down all the walls he had built: walls with his ideas and his concepts, his notions of right and wrong, good and evil, how it is done, how it is not done, what is wise, and what is not wise. He had dropped all that stuff, and He just sat still, completely still, and found enlightenment.

ENLIGHTENMENT: IT'S NOT WHAT YOU LOOK FOR; IT MIGHT BE WHAT YOU FIND

What, then, is this "enlightenment" that He found? Understand that the Buddhist world has been stuck with the word "enlightenment" for two-thousand-odd years. That has been very unfortunate, because the Buddha did not go out to look for enlightenment; He was not trying to "get a spiritual experience". He went out to find the reason for birth, old age, decay, and death. In other words, to put it in Zen terminology, he had the first koan* in existence: "Why is there

---

* Koan: a statement or story of the catalyst for an ancient master's enlightenment which is used by a Zen master as a teaching device to help

misery in the world? Why is there suffering? How do I get out of it?" He was trying to escape from life instead of accepting that life exists and being able to rise above it. In trying to escape from it, He could find nothing; in accepting it, He found all. His koan is the same koan, which we dress up in various ways, that every one of us brings to Zen training: "How can I escape living? How can I escape dying?" The same koan appears at every turn. We can call it what we like, we can use what terminology we like, but it is the same question as Shakyamuni Buddha's. And we have to solve it by the same method: by first accepting it and then transcending it.

As I said, Shakyamuni Buddha did not go out to look for enlightenment; He went out to look for the cure of suffering and, by accident, He found the Eightfold Path,* which was the method that got over the problem. By accident He got something else: He got peace of mind. The only way I can describe it accurately to you is by this story: supposing you've got a caveman who wants to break a stone, so he goes on slamming it with another stone and nothing happens. One day, by accident, he has a bright idea: he fits the second stone to a piece of wood, and so he makes a hammer with which he breaks the first stone. He did not set out to make a hammer, he set out to break a stone. By accident he got the hammer—that is, enlightenment. That's how you "get" it,

---

a disciple realize her or his True Nature. By extension, it means any spiritual barrier or fundamental question in one's training which one needs to face, penetrate, clarify, and transcend. In Rinzai Zen, formal koans are used in meditation practice; in Soto Zen the emphasis is on the naturally arising koans of everyday life.

* The way to transcend suffering as taught by Shakyamuni Buddha in the Fourth Noble Truth. The eight aspects are right understanding, right thought, right speech, right action, right livelihood, right effort, right mindfulness, and right concentration.

and that's what it is: it's the bonus you get for doing something about you.

If all you're looking for is the bonus, you're not going to get it, because the thing that matters is doing something about you, doing something about the inner wall. You built it: you pull it down. You made the mess of you: you have to clean it up. If the pond is muddy and you can't see the moon of Zen, it is because you polluted it. In this day of environmental concern, you should get the point of that loud and clear. If you pollute the water, it will not reflect the moon. We put all the daft ideas into our own skulls: we have to throw them out. Shakyamuni Buddha tried all sorts of ways; He had to go back to the naive mind of the child to find the purity and the stillness, and the iron, with which to live life.

And when you realize the true extent of this purity and stillness, you realize your position in the scheme of things and you know the awe-fullness of the Unborn. You "see" the world as if through an ever-changing kaleidoscope that can see the Buddha in everything. This is what is meant by the line in our Morning Service scriptures which says, "The wooden figure sings and the stone maiden dances." And the fence posts sing and dance: they all glorify the Eternal. To be able to see Buddha Nature in all things, to be able to see the spirit in all things (for it exists in all things), this is what is meant by enlightenment. It is not something that will make you a better ballet dancer, or a better writer, or a better this, or a better that, although it may very well do that. That's a bonus; that's not what you've done it for. Bonuses exist, but they must not be taken as the purpose for which you train. That's not what you go to study Zen for, or what you go to study any religion for. You go there because you are so fed up with you that you are ready to give up everything in order to know the Eternal, to know God!

I can remember saying, many years ago, to a Christian monk who was asking why I wanted to go into monasticism, "Well, at least it will help me get rid of my sins", and I was sixteen or seventeen at the time. He said, "You think that's what you go into a monastery for—you've got another 'think' coming!" Yes! I thought it might help me to be a better person, but when I really analyzed it out, I discovered that this did not go nearly far enough: what I wanted was what at a later date I came to call "the perfection of Zen". I was willing, eager, to give up "me" completely, which *is* to want to know God, or the Eternal. And when you sit in meditation, that is what you sit for. If you sit down to meditate today, know that that is what you are sitting there for. There are ways and ways in which you can be helped in doing this, and later on we hope to show you how they work, but you need to know why you are sitting there.

ZEN PRACTICE: ACTIVITY WITHIN STILLNESS

After you have been meditating awhile, you will come to sense that meditation alone is not enough. If you ignore that inner prompting, there will be a tendency to fall into what I call "quietism", a sort of "love and light" attachment which says, "Oh, I will just sit and meditate, and if I make myself perfect, everything will be fine", which is what it looks like on the surface. But there is a whole other side to Zen training: there has to be activity. Therefore, there are both sitting meditation and active behavior in Buddhism. Indeed, temples in the Far East are set up to teach people exactly that: how to look for signs of the Eternal, how to find the Eternal, what to do to find the Eternal, and how to help others. So, trust the willingness, the willingness not to stay permanently looking at a wall but to go out and try to help others to see the advisability of learning to train, of trying to find the Eternal. For example, I am always overjoyed when we are asked to go along to prisons to help people with the meditation group in prison; I am always overjoyed by that. We have a lot of people, several of them on death row, who correspond with us. It is important not to cut yourself off from the rest of the world: one must "live in the world as if in the sky", one must try and emulate the Eternal (which is Pure Love) in the world, whilst knowing that, although I am *not* the Eternal, there is nothing in me that is not *of* the Eternal. And all activity which is done with the heart of benevolence does that, and thus is teaching, although it must not be done with the intention of "teaching", for that implies superiority and judgment: simply it is done because it is the next thing to do, simply it is done because it is what must be done.

So, for the first two to five years in a monastery a person is "left to sit looking at a wall" (is encouraged to do lots of formal meditation), to take a thorough look at themselves, and be fed up with it, and want to do something about it. After he or she has been doing that for some years, at the abbot's discretion, he will then be asked to take an active part in ceremonial. Now a properly done ceremony is an interrelated act with another human being, and it's amazing how someone who has been "sitting looking at a wall", when he suddenly finds he's got to twist and turn and move things around on the altar, drops things, gets embarrassed, gets worried, and says, "Why should I be doing ceremonial?" What he's really saying is, "Why do I have to do anything other than just look at me? Why do I have to get back into the world?": embarrassment, fear. You don't know if someone has really done something about himself until you put him in the hondo, which is the ceremony hall, and make him carry incense and offerings and the like all around, and do all the necessary movements, and be really tough with him if he leaves any out, and watch him become embarrassed in front of other people. Because he's not found the Iron Being within himself until, whatever he does, the Iron Being is still. The use of ceremonial is quite incredible in Zen. Monks generally are not allowed to take major roles in it until they have been at a monastery for at least two to five years, because they are going to get completely the wrong understanding of what it's all about. It is how to put the stillness into activity and remain still without being pulled off center.

From that you can carry it out into the world: how to put the stillness into the world outside when you are dealing with troublesome people, when you are dealing with the boss in the office, when you have a class that's unruly—how to remain truly still. Because the world is just a ceremony. Dealing with your next-door neighbor is a ceremony of acting and reacting as they do things. Ceremony is the last stage of meditation before you go back into the world and are able to handle the world. If that part is left out and you go back into the world after all you have learned is how to look at a wall (i.e., how to clean up the mess within yourself)—if you cannot go back into the world and remain still within activity—you are going to be useless. Zen training is not something that you do in order to be able to run away from the world. A Zen monk goes into the monastery as a novice for anything from two or three to five years or longer with the sole purpose of truly living, i.e., going back to live, to make use of themselves, for all beings. What is the use of having the four signs of enlightenment all cooped up in a monastery? The world needs to see them. Therefore, he or she has to learn to live. It is just that simple: unless you can learn to live, you have wasted your time in the monastery.

So, two years, five years, just "looking at a wall". And that is only the beginning!

I say "just" looking at a wall, and I know that the Zenists present are going to jump up and down all over me for saying it, but I am trying to get you to understand that the two pillars of the Mahayana School of Buddhism (to which Soto Zen belongs) are Great Compassion and Great Wisdom: Mahakaruna and Mahaprajna. Many years ago, when I was in my early twenties, the late Dr. Daisetz Suzuki was in London and I was acting as his interpreter at several lectures he gave. I heard him speak on the pillars of the Mahayana, Mahaprajna and Mahakaruna, and that what was wrong with the West was all it wanted was Mahaprajna, Great Wisdom. They didn't want to have to *do* anything; they wanted to be able to "have" it and talk about it. They wanted to sound learned, and he made the point then that unless you *did*, you were useless. You were a Pratyekabuddha,* that which sat upon its throne unseen by any save itself (except that it got dusted now and then, and that was when somebody came by and thought it was decorative). But a real Buddha gets out there and gets "at it".

And two to five years or more after you have been in the monastery, that's exactly what you do: you get "dumped into it", with a vengeance. You have to get into the ceremonial, you have to be able to get into the "debates", the Hossen Ceremonies.† You have to be able to move: you have to be

---

* A general term referring to one who is enlightened as a result of his own efforts but does not share his understanding with others.

† The ceremony in which a trainee completes their term as Head Novice by answering, from the place of meditation, spiritual questions asked of them publicly and formally by the other novice trainees. Such Dharma Ceremonies are not debates in the normal sense of the term, as

able to get out in the garden and dig the septic tank in the same mind as you carry the incense around the altar, the same still mind, the same Iron Being. There is no difference between digging the septic tank and carrying the incense stick. If there is a difference, you have not understood what Zen is trying to teach, and you will not be able to deal with various things in the world outside, because there will always be something you are holding back and therefore you will not know what true freedom really is.

ZEN IS A RELIGION

I am sure you've noticed by now that I've been talking about Zen as a religion, and yet some of you may have heard that all of Buddhism, and especially Zen, is atheistic. It is not. You've heard this due to the fact that the Christian missionaries who brought back the scriptures from the Far East either did not know of, or deliberately steered clear of, one particular scripture spoken by the Buddha. In the *Udana Scripture* He says very clearly, "O monks, there is an Unborn, Undying, Unchanging, Uncreated."* This is what He found in meditation and which gave Him His enlightenment. In other words, He found That Which Is. What the Christians call "God" and Mohammedans call "Allah", the Buddhists call variably: That Which Is, the Lord of the House, the Cosmic

---

there is no competitive aspect, being instead a sharing of the Truth in a way which stimulates both parties to move more deeply into It.

* F. L. Woodward, trans., "Udana: Verses of Uplift" from the *Minor Anthologies* of the Pali Canon, Part II, Chap. VII, sec. iii (London: Oxford University Press, 1935), pp. 97 & 98.

Buddha, the Eternal, Amida Buddha, the Immaculacy of Emptiness, Vairocana Buddha, the Unborn, etc.*

The terms we use for It don't really matter: they're just labels, just concepts. Don't waste time thinking about what God is like. Whatever you imagine that It is, I assure you, is not what you'll—how can I say this?—I was going to say, "is not what you'll know", when you get self out of the way. That's not strictly true; what it comes down to is this: we always place upon ourselves our own personal concept of God or the Eternal—something that is much better than us. But we usually stop short at Something that just is *there*, and is such perfect love It can tolerate everybody in the world. I don't know if you ever saw that really great old comedy "The Night They Raided Minsky's". There was a lovely line in there where the old Jewish vaudevillian is speaking to the dour Amish father of one of his girls, and they both decide to pray together because, as one of them points out, "Only a God that could tolerate me could possibly tolerate you." (laughter) Now you have to keep this in mind. How can you imagine Something that doesn't just love, It *is* unquestioning Love? It makes the rain of compassion to fall on the evil and the good. What is evil; what is good? They are concepts in our minds. It is all right for us to have these concepts as long as we don't try to put them on the Eternal. You cannot be judgmental: the most important thing for a Buddhist is not to judge other people. In other words, love God, do your own training; love the Cosmic Buddha, do your own training;

---

* At various times in her career, Rev. Master Jiyu used many of these terms to describe the ultimate aspect of our religion. For a discussion of her apparent identification of these terms here with the concepts of God and eternalism, please read on and also refer to the Introduction.

love Allah, do your own training. Don't worry about other people.

And do not suffer from the notion that Zen training will make you anything other than a human being. Accepting our own humanity is one of the hardest tests of all-acceptance. There is a great difference, you know, between thinking you *are* God and knowing that what is in you is *of* God. "I am not God, and there is nothing in me that is not of God" is the way in which one has to think about it. The reason for Zen practice is to find the Eternal. On finding the Eternal, we call it "enlightenment". To know the Eternal (and you really do know It once you have had this experience) is to know how infinitesimal you are in the scheme of things: to know that you are "no-thing": even a grain of sand is miles too big. When you forsake self in this way, then you *are* the universe, and, if you've done it right, you might even behave like it. In *The Light of Asia** by Sir Edwin Arnold are the words "Forsaking self, the Universe grows 'I'." What a lot of people do not know, by the way, is that in Hong Kong there is a huge temple with probably the most famous secondary school in all of the Chinese area. That temple is dedicated to Sir Edwin Arnold, and his portrait is the Buddha upon the altar. When he went back to England and wished to publish *The Light of Asia*, they would only do it on the condition that he would pay lip service to Christian doctrine first, because there was this funny little bit in the law in England that since the King or Queen is the Head of the Church of England, if you don't believe in that, then automatically you have committed treason. It is one of the rather more peculiar little bits of British law that isn't talked about much nowadays; in those days it

---

* Sir Edwin Arnold, *The Light of Asia* (Los Angeles, California: The Theosophy Company, 1977).

was. And so the copy of the book has this introduction wherein he implies that he doesn't really believe in Buddhism. But he was actually a Buddhist; he is regarded as a Buddha in the Far East. His temple is magnificent, and he was a pioneer in girls' education, and it is still the finest school in English-speaking areas in the Far East. So, "Forsaking self, the universe grows 'I'." Do you get the difference between that and the notion that "I" become "God"?

Perhaps it will help if I explain a bit about another foundation of our religion: all things change, the doctrine of anicca in Buddhism. Everything changes. There is a famous story of Winston Churchill who, although he had an excellent wit and got half of his response right, didn't make it fully so. A lady came up to him, when he appeared at a meeting somewhat tipsy, and said, "Sir, you are drunk; you are very drunk; you are very, very drunk." And he replied to her, "Madam, you are ugly; you are very ugly; you are very, very ugly. And I shall be sober in the morning." (laughter) He understood change, but he hadn't seen that, however ugly she was, there was the spark of the Eternal in her, the Buddha Nature, and that is the important point. It sounds funny; it is funny; but he should have been able to see the next bit on. If you would really study religion and understand the meaning of perfect faith, that's how you've got to look at people. He may be, or she may be, what you would call a "louse" right now, and tomorrow there could be an incredible change, there could be a total conversion. There could be a finding of the Eternal. Are you still going to carry around the fact that, once, he or she was a louse?

Not only do you look at other people with the awareness of continual change, you look at everything in this light. Everything is always changing; nothing stays the same. At first this is rather scary, because if you think deeply about it, it means that there is no constant, separate thing you can call "me": there is only an ever-changing flow of space-time-being. But soon it becomes enjoyable because it means that you are not alone in the universe, and that is a great relief. Do not think that anything whatsoever is separate from the Eternal: do not think, for example, that there was a time when the Eternal was Kanzeon (the Bodhisattva of Compassion) and another time when It was Buddha; indeed, there is a time when the Eternal is Kanzeon and a time when It is Buddha, but there was never a time or place when the Eternal was not present as the whole of the Eternal. If you think of Kanzeon as separate, of the Buddha as separate, of the mountain as separate, of the river as separate, and of yourself as separate—if you think in that way, you cannot understand the Eternal. If you know that you are the whole of the Eternal, and that Kanzeon and the Buddha are the whole of the Eternal, and that the whole of the past is present now, and the whole of the future is present now, that there is no other time than (and there will never be any other time than) now, in the real sense of the term, then you understand the eternal now, you understand the Eternal. Otherwise, you become a separate being in a body that is not the Buddha's body, in a body that is not Kanzeon's body, and the Eternal becomes a separate Being that is not your body. So you can see how the Eternal is thought of as flowing; It is the eternal flow; It is not static, nor can we truly say It is changing. The whole world must be seen as the Eternal, and not only must it be seen, it must be known to be the Eternal; the Eternal must be able to be felt, seen, smelt, tasted, touched in everyone and in everything. It is not a thing of yesterday; It is not a thing of today; It is not a thing of tomorrow. The Eternal *is* the eternal flowing, the non-static eternal, the "universe growing 'I'".

So this is what the Buddha found, and He explained It by what in religion is called the *via negativa*: He explained It by what It is not. It isn't born, because It has always been there; It doesn't change, because It is Eternal; It is not created; there is nothing greater than It. The Buddha goes on in this scripture to say if this were not so, then there would be no hope whatsoever for humankind. Now, it's just as good to say, to explain, what you know to be true by saying what you know the thing isn't, as it is to say what you know to be true by saying what you believe that it is. You can know what it is not; you believe what it is.

This approach is rather similar to the one taken by what I believe is known as Moravian Christianity. In Moravian Christianity, there is no God and no Christ until you know them; there is merely a Christian way to follow. Now, that is pure Buddhism: there is no Cosmic Buddha until you know the Cosmic Buddha, the Lord of the House. Because so few people take the trouble to get to know Him/Her/It, Buddhism has often become an atheistic or a non-God religion: just a way of life. But in the East they look at you: "Oh, you haven't met the Lord Buddha yet? Good heavens, you're an undutiful being! You're merely following the Buddhist way?!?" They look down on you, you know, almost withdrawing the hem of their garment from you, because you have not got to know That Which Is. Buddhism in its real setting is an incredibly uh . . . "theistic" is dangerous, because the word "God" is wrong . . . uh, "Supreme Being"-oriented religion, let's put it that way. And once you know the Lord of the House, then you can speak of It. So, Buddhism has a Supreme Being. Except that It's not a Supreme Being in the normal sense: It is That Which . . . *Is.* It's not a big daddy God who spanks you when you do something wrong. And "Being" isn't quite the right word either.

Now, since about the 1500s there has been an attempt on the part of the Shin, or Pure Land, School of Buddhists to say, "Let's not do it by the way of meditation because so few people ever bother to get any further than the 'way of life' attitude of mind." They decided to start a school of Buddhism called "Shin", which means the True Heart of Buddhism, which placed faith in and worshipped the Amida Buddha, the Amida Buddha being the equivalent of God or the Cosmic Buddha. Now, this has always confused and confounded Christians and others who say, "Half the Buddhists are worshipping and half aren't; what on earth is going on?" It was merely that one bunch said, "It's useless to try and go on with people not really trying to get to know the Lord of the House, because Buddhism has just turned into a way of life, so why don't we start saying that It really does exist and letting them worship It from that point of view?" And the other bunch said, "This is completely wrong, because they will enter into belief and worship rather than recognizing they have to find the Lord of the House within themselves." And these two factions have warred for about four hundred years, and in 1924 in China the two of them came together and, since then, all the Buddhists in China became one big school: the Zenists openly admitting, "Yes, we place faith in the Amida Buddha" and the Shinists openly saying, "All right, we go by meditation." Now, since I was ordained and did some of my training in Chinese Buddhism, you see the background from which I come to this.

This brings us to the importance of understanding the difference between perfect faith and absolute belief. In these little booklets we have for you there is an article on perfect faith which I want you to read over carefully because it is one of the best ways I ever put it, and I don't want to detract from that.* Perfect faith is a very different thing from absolute belief. Absolute belief insists that it's right, and sometimes burns people at the stake and does other things to prove it, as we know from the Middle Ages. Perfect faith, because it is perfect, does not have to insist upon itself. Real truth does not have to insist upon itself; real trust does not have to insist upon itself: there is an incredibly beautiful interplay. It's like a kaleidoscope: the faith is always there, the trust is always there, the certainty is always there, but you don't have to beat each other up or damage other people to make them believe as you do. In order to have the courage to leap beyond the opposites, to let go of everything we have, want, and know, perfect faith is necessary in Buddhism—perfect faith in the fact that there is an Unborn, Unchanging, Undying, Uncreated: That which I call the Eternal, and what unfortunately has been very badly translated in the main scripture of Zen Buddhism, *The Scripture of Great Wisdom*, as "emptiness".

It is not Nietzsche's kind of emptiness. In recent years, we have seen the translation and publication of many of the original works of those who took Buddhism to China, and these are making it very clear that the "emptiness" they are talking about is something that is so full it cannot be described. In that sense it's very like the Jewish concept of God: That which you can't put a hand on, you can't feel, you can't grasp. It's beyond everything; It is Unborn, Undying, Uncreated, Unchanging. You know It's there, but when somebody says, "Show It to me", you can't show It to them. Again, I am afraid it's our Christian missionary friends who

----

* See Rev. Master Jiyu-Kennett, M.O.B.C., "Perfect Faith" in *An Introduction to the Tradition of Serene Reflection Meditation*, 5th ed. rev. (Mt. Shasta, California: Shasta Abbey Press, 1997), pp. 37–40.

decided to first have It translated as "emptiness", which turned Buddhism for many, many people into something that was very little more than a way of life, instead of a very, very great religion based on perfect faith, and you need to know this.

The fact that there is an Unborn and there is a role for faith in Zen upsets many Westerners, because they think that it means that they are required to have the same blind belief which they feel was required of them in their own religion. I can remember a British professor in Japan getting madder and madder by the minute because he felt that Zen training was deliberately putting him into a double bind so as to get him beyond the opposites, which he believed to be impossible. And I recall Koho Zenji looking at him and saying, "My good man, don't you realize that there is Something that is beyond the opposites?" "Oh no, I'm not going to believe in a God!" "You are not required to" was the answer, "but there is a third position." You are not required to believe in an "entity", but there is That which is unborn, unchanging, undying. And in that Place one can take genuine rest and, there, one can get beyond the opposites. People try to flee from God, they try to escape from the "golden body of the Buddha", but it is only because we do not know what the golden body of the Buddha really is, only because our minds have been raped by theories, that we are afraid of It. When we know what It is not, we can then be free of concepts of what It is, and we do not have to escape. And, even when we are trying to escape, we are still in the flow of the Eternal.

I can remember being infuriated about the same thing when I was first in Japan, in Sojiji. I had gone over like every other Briton I'd ever met, "Oh how wonderful, I will be completely free; I will be supreme, you know; and there's no God that's going to be over me, nothing of this sort!" And the first thing I was told was "Well, of course, Shin Buddhism and Zen Buddhism are exactly the same; they're the two opposite ends of a tunnel." The point is, which is the "right" end of a tunnel? If you go all the way through, then does it matter which is the entrance and which is the exit? And I remember almost jumping up and down like a baboon with fury at that one, because, I mean, I'd gone fifteen thousand miles to avoid that sort of "Supreme Being idiocy"! And then I had a kensho* and I saw they were right, and between joy and annoyance at having been proved wrong, I spent a very interesting week. (laughter) I was really annoyed at having been proved wrong, and that is one of the reasons you hear about people who have had kensho laughing and crying and getting furious and throwing things, because yes, there they were, sitting in the Buddha's hand all along and He was grinning at them. You can call it "God's hand" if you like. It doesn't matter what you call it, but in the end it's rather enjoyable just to be there.

Unfortunately, our concepts and beliefs have taught us that we, and time and existence, are somehow apart from the Truth, and thus we think that the golden body of the Buddha is not our body. And so we spend our lives trying to free ourselves from this very fact of being the golden body of the Buddha. We try to run away from the Eternal because we think of It as the golden body of the Buddha, with which we have nothing whatsoever to do and from which we must get free. But that is wrong: if you know of the Place of the Eternal—which is beyond all opposites of right and wrong, past and present, etc.—if you know of That, then there is no need whatsoever to try to escape. One of the

---

* Kensho (Japanese): to see into one's own true nature. The experience of touching enlightenment; satori.

tragedies of so many Zen books is that they talk about getting beyond the opposites, but they do not explain that this is the Place of the Eternal, the "third position" beyond the two opposites.

Now, if you would study Soto Zen, or for that matter any form of Buddhism, you need three things. You need perfect faith in That Which Is, the Eternal. You need to know, to have the faith in and the willingness to go hunting for, that which will tell you about the Eternal. And you need to know that when you can't get the answers, there are people whom you can trust to help you. In other words, when you yell, "Help! I'm stuck", there are people who are willing and able to help. These three things are what we in Buddhism call the Three Refuges: "I take refuge in the Buddha; I take refuge in the Dharma; I take refuge in the Sangha." These three things are absolutely essential: perfect faith, the willingness to study, and trusting someone who says, "Well, let's talk; maybe I can help; maybe we can help each other; maybe I have a bunch of experience which I am willing to put at your disposal and see if it's any use." Those are the three things you'll need if you are to study Soto Zen or any other form of Buddhism.

All the rest are beliefs which you have to prove true for yourself. The Buddha said very clearly, "Do not believe anything because I tell you. Only believe it when you have made it true for yourself."* Therefore, enlightenment is the making true for oneself of the reality of the existence, and the experience of the existence, of the Unborn. Again, remember that the word "enlightenment" has got muddled as a result of not understanding the importance of the *Udana Scripture*. When that scripture was first translated, incidentally, a

---

* See F. L. Woodward, trans., *The Book of the Gradual Sayings* (Anguttara-Nikaya), Vol. I (London: Pali Text Society, 1979), pp. 171 ff.

number of people tried to pull it down saying, "Oh, it couldn't possibly be that the Buddha had found the Eternal!" You read a bit more, and if you do, you discover that this is the only interpretation that makes sense in Buddhism. He definitely did, and it makes it into a real religion and not just a way of life.

Faith, study, and trust: if you think of the word "refuge", what does it actually mean? To take refuge in something that you can neither see nor grasp nor feel, you have to have faith in it. When you start, perhaps you believe it, but you have to go on beyond belief: belief does not go nearly far enough. So often in religion people get stuck with belief. They think that is enough: it's not. It has to go on to the certainty of faith, which is an absolute certainty but one which leads not to absolute belief and the hard-fisted type of certainty; it leads to perfect faith, which can allow everybody else to have their beliefs and not interfere with them, and know that when those people find perfect faith, whatever they happen to call the Eternal will be all right. You do not have to insist on call-ing the Christian God "the Eternal". You do not have to force the Mohammedans to call Allah "the Amida Buddha". In perfect faith, they are all found to be one and the same thing.

Now, there is a big difference between taking refuge at this level and what is frequently taught as either Christianity or Buddhism. In recent months I have been reading the thir-teenth or fourteenth century works of an English woman who has recently been established as a Christian saint, Julian of Norwich, who, interestingly enough, was at that time preaching what I would have called pure Zen Buddhism with Christian terminology. And I have had a number of conversations with Christian monks, one of whom I corre-spond with fairly frequently, who agree with me that most of what is taught as popular Christianity doesn't go nearly far enough, because in actual practice and experience both the deeper, contemplative Christianity and Zen Buddhism are almost identical with the exception of one or two doctrines. This has been a great joy to me, an incredibly great joy, and one of the other things that I found out was that Hasidic Judaism is almost identically the same, which just proves that if you go into the really deeper reaches of these things and do not get caught up in externals, dogmas and doctrines, you can find a Place where we can all be at one together. When going up Mount Sumeru it is delightful to discover that the people climbing Mount Carmel and the people climbing Mount Sinai were coming up the other side, and we all meet on the top and sort of shake hands like our friends on Everest. That's quite a joy to discover.

The big impediment to this is, of course, the baggage that comes with every religion. I flatly refuse to believe that what Eve got up to is my problem. It isn't: what I get up to is my problem; it's got nothing to do with Eve. But there are people who say, "You are born in sin." That is one theory; Buddhists simply say, "We are born." And there is a pile of karma that sort of sits around and just waits to "glom on" to us when we are born. There was a lovely argument not too many years ago as to how that karma "glommed on". Does it sit on the end of the male organ at the time of conception; is it already inside the woman, knowing that she is about to conceive? Who the so-and-so-heck cares?!? What matters is there are things we need to clean up that we have both done in this lifetime and perhaps have inherited from another. Who knows? The point is: it doesn't really matter. What you need to know is that you are looking for the Eternal, there are ways of finding It, and there are people who can help. The argument they had on how the karma got there was, to my mind, almost identical to the medieval Christian one where they argued about how many angels could sit on the head of a pin. Who cares? It's not important. What matters is that you find the Unborn, that you study, and that you ask for help when you need help. And you also learn how to ask for help in meditation, which is another reason why meditation is so terribly important. You absolutely must be willing to ask for help and not be too proud to do it. There are always people who can help and who will. What is fundamental is the finding of the Eternal; at a later date, as things come up, you can prove the doctrines true in the books. I've done it. If you get cluttered with doctrine at the beginning ("I must believe this . . ."), then such things can rise up almost like ghosts in your meditation and make life difficult. But if something happens in meditation that you can't understand, have a look in the doctrine books and you will probably find that it's explained in there. Thus, you prove things true for yourself.

Now of all this stuff, of all this baggage that we lug around with us, judgmentalism is one of the "heaviest". One of the purposes of meditation is to become as close as possible to the Pure Love of the Eternal. To become close to That, you have to be rid of judgmentalism, you have to stop worrying about what other people do, you have to pay attention to your own training. Sadly enough, because we live in the world, because there are people who do not train at all, we are constantly having to do things to other people that we'd rather not do, because we do have to consider the rest of society. For instance, we have to have a legal system because there are those who are not yet ready to be responsible; we have to have ways of safeguarding other people. If we can do this without vindictiveness, without judgmentalism (in the sense of "Look at how good I am and how bad he is or she is")—if we can do that, it will not drag us out of our meditation. We do live in the world, and as the Buddhist teaching says, "We live in the world as if in the sky. . . ." We aim for the ideal. The motto of Buddhism is "Hope for the best; do the possible." If you can keep doing that, keep up your meditation, and avoid getting into judgmentalism (whether judging yourself or judging others), you can make progress in Soto Zen. For that matter, you can make progress in any religion.

The old koans frequently speak of things like this, and they teach people the dangers of holding on to baggage that is not important. There is the story of two monks out journeying who found a young woman who couldn't get across a sort of large puddle or shallow pond. One picked her up, carried her across, and put her down on the other side, and they both went on together. The one that didn't pick her up was fuming, thinking, "I mean—what are we doing?!? He touched a woman! It's completely against the rules! Lust must be raging in him: he's this, he's that, and the other!" After two or three miles, he couldn't contain himself, and he asked the other monk, "What do you think you did picking this woman up?" And the other monk said, "Why, . . . are you still carrying her?" (laughter) You have to put the stuff down and stop looking with this sort of discriminatory eye. Because the more you look at such things in this way, the less you will understand how true love, pure love, works.

The danger of holding on to things that are not ultimately important is why I am not going to get into an awful lot of the baggage that goes along with Zen Buddhism (as it does with everything else). You can read up in any good book on Buddhism (and we can give you a couple of names) what the doctrine, the baggage, is. And if you've proved it true for yourself, that's great, and if you haven't, then neither say it's untrue nor force it down your throat. Imagine you've got a sort of cooking stove (being female, I'd think this way, wouldn't I?). Imagine you've got a cooking stove with a couple of slow burners on the back. Any aspect of the teaching that you can't accept now, put on the slow burners and wait. I've done that with an awful lot of stuff that I could not believe in the beginning, and I've only got two tiny things that I learned from my master that are still cooking on the back burner. I probably won't be able to prove them till I'm dying, you know. That's all right: they can sit there till then. So, trust. Don't say, "I can't accept this because I have learned such-and-such." Allow yourselves to look at these things and say, "Well, it's another way of looking at something; why don't I leave it and one day it might be useful." Just leave it sitting there: don't fight it, don't force yourself to believe, and don't argue with it.

This is also the reason why Buddhism does not discuss such things as creation, where the world came from, where it is going to, what happens after death, and the like. What matters in Buddhism is that you find the place of the Unborn and Undying while you're still alive, and you work on that as hard as you can. And then you find that none of these "problems" are actually a problem at all. I've found that for myself and so have a lot of others: if you don't worry about them, but instead get on and find the Place of the Unborn, then when you've found It, these questions don't really matter. Speculating on them may be very amusing on a cold winter's night if you've nothing better to do, but if you make that your religious practice, then you are not going to have any real understanding or any real peace of mind at the time of death.

And this leads us to the realization that true teaching, the Dharma, is not simply to be found in the trappings of religion: it can be found everywhere. I can remember being very concerned when I didn't seem to be getting much help in the Far East from various people, and I said, "Well, why aren't you teaching me on a regular basis?" you know, sort of thinking there'll be classes and there'll be this and there'll be that. The person who was teaching me said, "Surely you can learn from everything." There are ways these things are done, you know, and they are done like that. Then I realized, fortunately very soon, that every single thing is teaching at every single time and at every single moment: all you have to do is have a mind that is open enough to look.

This brings us to the third refuge, trusting the Sangha. Now, of course, as you go through life, if you are a Buddhist or whatever you happen to be, you will meet with priests or teachers or fellow Buddhists who are less worthy of their calling than perhaps they should be, and some who are far more worthy. Whichever way it goes, if you wish to truly learn, you must trust, and not get upset if someone does not live up to your expectations. There is a very famous Buddhist story of a woman trainee who was the disciple of a really (even the Buddhists were willing to admit to this) useless master, who trained so well that she gained full enlightenment, full knowledge of the Eternal. She never looked at him as unfit to serve and work with. She did her own training. It wasn't her problem what he did; her problem was what she did. You understand what I mean by that? It's terribly important not to worry about other people's training, but to do your own. In this way you learn how to really trust others and learn from them.

I made that mistake when I was first in the Far East. I can remember trying to be such a really, really fine monk, and coming back dead tired from about four hours of meditation with just a quarter of an hour break between each one (and probably feeling a little pious about it), and finding three fellow juniors hiding in a cupboard playing Ma-jong. I was fuming: how dare this happen; what sort of example is this?!? I told the person who was teaching me and he said, "Hmm, in this world there are various sorts of monks." I didn't think this was nearly good enough, and I went off the next day and I bought a beautiful goldfish and took it as a present to my master, the abbot of Sojiji, and I handed it to him and I told him the story. He said, "I see." Then he looked at the goldfish and said, "Well, I've got a bowl over here. This fish, I think, is too good to go into the pond, so we'll put it in the bowl for the time being; it will probably be a bit lonely, but that's all right." The lesson was very clear: my training was my training; their training was their training. They would get the karmic consequence of what they did; I would get the karmic consequence of what I did. If I felt proud of myself and a bit pious because I thought I was better than they were, then I was just as bad, because I was wasting my time and so were they.

So, the next lesson to learn from Soto Zen is: don't worry what other people do, worry about what you do. It's not your problem that the master is, or is not, what you think they should be. If he teaches the truth, learn from him and don't get upset by him. There is a chapter in the *Shushogi* here, which we will be studying tomorrow, which says, "When you meet someone who teaches the Truth, don't worry about his color, don't worry about his caste, or his sex, or his shortcomings: learn from him." What he gets up to, he'll pay for: what you get up to, you'll pay for. If you would study Soto Zen and meditate in Soto Zen, don't sit there thinking about what everybody else has got up to.

This is another aspect of what is meant by trust and will: the trust that there is a grain of truth in everything, the trust that whatever the teacher you are with may or may not do, they possess the Buddha Nature whether or not you can see it, and you can learn from them. There are a number of ways you can go on this. Again, you have to be very careful of the baggage that goes with it, the doctrinal baggage. You have to have the trust that That exists—the spark of God, the spark of the Eternal—in every single person. That you cannot see it in the teacher or your fellow trainees at the moment is either due to your own incapacity at the present time to see what is actually going on, or due to the fact that you personally have some sort of a blockage between you and that teacher, or that the teacher has got a sort of "storm cloud". You've seen those cartoons of storm clouds going along over the top of somebody's car? There are people like that who have a sort of "storm cloud" going permanently over their heads, and you can't really see their Buddha Nature, but it's still there. So you need to know that, whatever is going on, the Buddha Nature is still there. That doesn't necessarily mean you decide that you'll go and study with that teacher, but you have to have your mind open that the Buddha Nature is there. We had a very heavily drunk man come to Shasta on one occasion, and we told him he could come back and study when he wasn't drunk. We weren't putting him outside: we were putting out the results of the bottle. This is how you must think of all people: respect them, learn from them, and do not copy their mistakes.

Finally, let me say some more about the use of the will in Zen training. It is not easy to give up attachments to everything, to accept everything. But this is exactly the sort of willingness that is required throughout Zen training. There is a very fine little book which is used by many to teach the role of the will in Soto Zen, called *Beyond the Pale of Vengeance*,* which is the story of a famous thief (it is a true story), a very famous thief and murderer, who would go out with his wife, and they would murder people and steal their jewelry. On one occasion his wife was yelling and screaming at him because he did not take the tortoise-shell combs from the last person he'd murdered. He was looking down at the body and he was looking at the wife, and he was suddenly, utterly, totally revolted with disgust at himself and her. He leaves her; he goes to see a monk, a very famous monk, whom he tells he wants to go to the authorities: he needs to be tortured and killed for what he's done. The monk looks at him and says, "That will be a terrible waste. Now, I'll tell you what: around the corner from here there's a mountain on which thousands of people have died because the passageway around it is so narrow and they get swept into the ravine. Why don't you try widening it?" This mountain exists, by the way, and through it there is a tunnel, dug by this one man by himself, with a hammer and the equivalent of a chisel. I have pictures of it. He goes to the mountain and he sets himself the task of literally going all the way through the mountain in order to save lives. It takes him his entire life. And one day the son of one of the people he murdered finds him and decides he's going to kill him. The former murderer says to him, "Yes, by all means kill me, but

---

* For a version of this Work currently in print see Kan Kikuchi, *Beyond the Pale of Vengeance*, trans., Rev. Jisho Perry, M.O.B.C., and Kimiko Vago (Mt. Shasta, California: Shasta Abbey Press, 1998). Historical records suggest that the story is loosely based on fact, although some of the aspects, as told in the story or as recounted by Rev. Master Jiyu-Kennett here, may not be exact. The religious significance of the tale, nonetheless, is as described.

will you let me finish the tunnel first?" So in order to get his vengeance sooner, the son decides to help him finish. The son ends up his disciple as the tunnel is finished. There is a lot of teaching in that story, and the pictures exist, and the tunnel is still used in Japan. That is the exact way in which the will is used. The easy way would have been to have gone and been tortured and executed. Just think, what an incredible waste! The will is not heroic, not spectacular: it is the willingness to accept everything and to do the very best we can at all times.

You can also learn from this story by thinking about the son: ask yourself, when you think like he did—when immediately up comes "Well, what about revenge? What about . . . ?"—who wants revenge? What is it in you, or me, that wants to hurt those people who have hurt us? Who benefits from that? That is simply to retreat into judgmentalism, to hurt ourselves further, to continue the pain. Now, obviously everybody doesn't convert. Obviously, therefore, we have to have prisons and the like to put such people. But how about helping them to convert; how about making such places positive instead of negative? That would be the Buddhist way. Obviously, you can't leave somebody who's running around with a hatchet slaughtering people on the street! That would be totally un-Buddhist and irresponsible. And there is, again, a piece in the *Shushogi* that speaks of that. You can't do nothing on the impression, "Well, since I must not judge others, then it would be wrong for me to do anything." Because if you do that, it's worse than doing something; which means, of course, there's no way you can escape karma or karmic consequence. But you can separate it from judgmentalism; you can separate it from revenge. Obviously, the Zen master in this story had seen, from the position of an incredibly fine, pure kensho (as it's called, or "enlightenment experience") that this man had truly converted, realized the horror of his deeds, and, as such, could be made very good use of in society. So a great use was made of him, and everyone has benefitted down the centuries. How would the Buddhists look upon those whom he murdered? Obviously, they are victims, but it was their deaths that made this conversion possible; therefore, they are regarded as "saints" in the Buddhist Church. This is the great difference in the way to look at victims, and the way to look at criminals. The purpose of putting someone in prison obviously is to deter them from doing more harm, and also to teach them not to continue. But revenge won't do it: hate begets hate. It was the man's will, coupled with his purity of intent, all-acceptance, and deep love, that converted the vengeful son and brought them both to peace.

So, the will plays a crucial role in this, and that brings us back to where we began, because whether we recognized them or not, it was our faith and our will that got us started in the first place. The trust in that little inner sense that "there's got to be more to life than this", that dissatisfaction with skating along on the surface of life, is actually faith in the Buddha Nature. And the willingness to do something about it, to actually sit down and meditate, to come to a lecture like this, to enter into religious training—that is the operation of the will. Therefore, do not believe that Zen training is beyond you; the fact that you are here today is proof that you have everything it takes to make it all the way. The only question is: will you do it?

Now, having talked about what Zen is, let me say a few words about what it is not. First, the dangers of asceticism. People think of the term "asceticism" as meaning beating themselves up, wearing hair shirts and a few other interesting things, or getting thrashed with a kyosaku.* Asceticism in its most subtle form is getting stuck with ideas. For example, "I must sit in meditation for forty-five minutes. If I don't sit forty-five minutes, the Eternal will abandon me." So no matter how painful it is, or how bad the meditation is, you force yourself to do it. Don't do that: learn to do it properly and accept your humanity. If you can sit for five minutes, try pushing yourself to six the next day. If you can sit well for six, try pushing yourself to seven the next day, always presuming you are not getting a conflict in your mind with "I should be doing this" or "I should be doing that." Because as soon as that comes up, whatever happens after, it's a waste of time. If you are terribly busy, then use your will just to sit down, maybe on the edge of the bed when you get up, and just be still. For a minute, or thirty seconds, just be still: put your mind in a still place and, after a bit, you'll enjoy it so much you'll want more. Never make yourself hate meditation or any other aspect of Buddhist training. I saw so many people made to hate meditation in the Far East. I got really frightened by it. And, afterwards, young monks would go back to their temple and they would "dine out" for the rest of their lives on how many times they got flogged and how many hours they sat looking at a wall. But they didn't get any further than that. You're not there to show how

---

* The kyosaku or "awakening stick" is a slender, flat piece of wood traditionally carried during meditation periods by an assistant disciplinarian. It is used by striking the shoulder muscles of meditators in a way that massages away stiffness and encourages alertness. The kyosaku has been misused frequently down the ages as a form of ascetic practice or as corporal punishment; Rev. Master Jiyu abolished its use in our Order soon after arriving in the West.

brave you are; you're not there to be a superman. You are training to find the Eternal, and finding the Eternal is the all and only important thing. The person who's willing to get up a minute or two early in the morning, or, even when they are late, just to take a few seconds when they are sitting in their car at a red light, just putting their mind still, can do true meditation, true training.

Another aspect of some religions which is a major obstacle to Zen practice is guilt. "Oh dear, I didn't meditate this morning; the Eternal will turn His back on me." I mean, of course He won't! That's you attributing to the Absolute the way you think about somebody who didn't do for you what you think that person should do. Don't put your little-minded ideas on the Eternal: It is far too huge for that. Don't blame the Eternal for your shortcomings. The Eternal *IS*. It waits, and waits, and waits . . . for eternity. It is pure love. And when all conditions ripen, It and you will be one. Do the very best you can, and know that it is enough. Remember that motto: "hope for the best, do the possible", and then do the best you can.

Have you ever thought how huge that phrase is: "the best you can"? It was the best bit of teaching I ever got from my master. I kept saying, "I can't do all this; I can't do this." I was expected to run the foreign guest department; I was supposed to do six dozen other jobs. And he kept saying, "You just do the best you can." I was so afraid I'd be in serious trouble because it wasn't all done, I felt so guilty and worried, and then one day I discovered that it just sat there and it got done as it got done. I gave the Eternal Its due, and I gave the guest department its due, and I gave my studies their due, and I stopped worrying and feeling guilty, and my blood pressure went down and everything was fine. *You do the best you can.* And if one morning you don't come to meditation at all, the

Eternal won't hold it against you. The Eternal doesn't work that way. So, know what guilt is and do not try to put on the Eternal what you think. And know what asceticism is: it's forcing yourself to do something against your will. There has to be total free will, total freedom of mind. There is no brainwashing in this, no forcing of theories, no forcing of doctrines. At all times you have free choice. And at all times you will take the consequences of what you choose.

QUESTIONS

Right, on that note let's stop and take some questions. Yes, friend, go ahead.

> *Question:* "I still don't understand about why the Unborn sometimes gets translated as "Emptiness".

Partly this is because of the difficulty of trying to describe in words That which cannot really be described and partly it is a problem of translation. For example, when the missionaries first went to the Far East and studied Buddhist texts, they encountered the character "mu" being used to describe the ultimate. And they thought, because the term "mu" represented nothingness, emptiness, immaculacy, that Buddhism was atheistic. But if you look very carefully at the Chinese character, you will see that it symbolizes a fire that is blazing up, that there is nothing left and, as and when one has an actual experience of the Eternal, it is as a fire that blazes up within. So the character "mu" is very graphic and very true, but if you were asked what it means in English, it is . . . well, what can you say it is? It's "nothing" or "emptiness".

I have been criticized by some people over here who are not perhaps as well versed in the scriptures as others, in that I have translated what has been called "Emptiness" in *The Scripture of Great Wisdom*, which is the main scripture of Zen, as "the Immaculacy of Emptiness" or "Purity". Now, "Purity" is a term used for this by Bodhidharma,* the founder of Zen in China, and I think it fits rather well, if you understand that Purity is not a "thing". If you call It a god you get involved very much with the Judeo-Christian sort of thinking, but if you say It is the Immaculacy of Emptiness, That Which is Eternal, you are getting very, very close to the truth, because "the Immaculacy of Emptiness" implies the fullest emptiness possible. It is an incredibly full thing. You "know" It when you "have" It, and "having" enlightenment is to "know" It. And there is no-thing to "have" and no-thing to "know" and no-one to "do" either.

Which, of course, brings us back again to what in the world is enlightenment? Now, a tremendous number of people have tried to explain this. The reason they have not succeeded is because, as it were, the chief piece of information, the chief piece of instruction, was missing: that Buddhism really is a faith; you have to trust that there is something greater than you that is unborn, undying, unchanging; and when you find out for certain that it is so, then you are enlightened. And enlightenment is knowing for certain— without a shadow of a doubt, without the possibility of the thought of the possibility of the thought of a doubt coming in—that there is That which is beyond all things, and it is

---

* See J. C. Cleary, trans., *Zen Dawn: Early Zen Texts from Tun Huang* (Boston, Massachusetts: Shambhala, 1986).

That that the Buddha found out.* He was no different from any one of us: He lived and He died. He was an extraordinary person perhaps, but no different from any one of us.

> *Question:* "You mentioned not doubting, but what do I do about doubt? I have a lot of doubts, about everything: about myself, about what I'm doing . . . ?"

Doubt is extraordinarily valuable: doubt turns into faith, and faith turns into certainty. Without doubt you can get nowhere. I would be very grateful, if I were you, that you have doubt. You have something to work with. The person who is in the biggest hole is the person who doesn't have any doubts, who doesn't have any problems, who's feeling fine. There's "nothing wrong with them". And you look at them, and you can see the "mouse within a cage", running around. Remember what it says in the Morning Service scriptures, "If outwardly all calm we do appear and yet within disturbed should be, we are as if a mouse within a cage or as a tethered

---

* This and similar statements by Rev. Master Jiyu on certainty can be interpreted as meaning that certainty itself is the goal and doubt is always a hindrance. This is not my understanding of her intent. Indeed, see the next question on the value of honest doubts. As to certainty, I understood her to mean that certainty is not an end in itself but rather a consequence of something much more fundamental: the direct experience of the Unborn. If one seeks certainty, one will no doubt find it, but it will more than likely be based on one's ideas and opinions, or even on rank delusions. The certainty of which she speaks is not a hard certainty; it is, instead, a soft but solid sort of thing which does not insist upon itself and does not "know" anything. It is this type of certainty which, for example, allowed Dogen Zenji to say on one occasion that "about the only thing I'm certain of is that on a face there are two eyes and a nose."

horse." I have seen monks in Sojiji sitting there looking incredibly beautiful, and if you looked a little deeper you saw this thing like "eeeeek" inside. No way! Good honest doubt is valuable. They have a saying in Zen, "Small doubt, small understanding; moderate doubt, moderate understanding; great doubt, great understanding." But don't try to make the doubt any bigger! (laughter). I knew somebody who tried that once, when I made that comment.

> *Question:* "What are some of the dangers for people when they enter Buddhist training? How can this go wrong?"

Well, of course, it depends on the person concerned. You can have someone who will meditate to a certain extent, and be contented with what they've learned, and go away, and get into a "power trip", with a vengeance. That's the first and biggest danger, which is why I say that anyone who comes to us as a monk has got to guarantee to stay at least two to five years as a novice so that I can get them out of that. If you get into a "power trip", you're in real trouble!

The next one is someone who has done what we call "guru hopping": you know, they've tried it here, and they've tried it there, and they've tried it all the way around. You name it, they've been there. And they've got all these techniques kicking around in their head. They've picked a little bit from each, which they like, and they've thrown away the rest, and they invent something which does a lot of damage to other people. It may or may not do damage to them, but it does an incredible amount of damage to other people if they go around teaching it. There is such a thing as ethics with this, and a really good Zen teacher or master will not accept someone who has given allegiance to another teacher.

They can come and spend time in the monastery: there'll be no problem on that, but they will not be accepted as a student. We have a form which we send out saying, "Have you an allegiance to any other teacher?" Now you obviously can't have a hard and fast rule on that, because there is going to be somebody whose master has died, or somebody who genuinely, either by his own stupidity or by sheer accident, chose the wrong one. But you have to make it so they do not run from one place to the other, because then they never discipline themselves either. They take what they want and they run off. So that's the second danger: the danger to other people of making a "mishmash" of the thing, which isn't going to work. I'm not saying that the other teachings or the other methods are wrong: all paths lead to the goal, walk which one is best for you. This one happens to be best for me. What I am saying is: don't muddle them. Dogen, himself, warned against that. When you do one practice, don't mix it up with another: do that practice, finish it completely, then go to another if you must; don't mix them.

A third problem is people who have done an awful lot of certain types of practices in which they have got into trance states, because you have to get them out of that. They can be a problem because they keep trying to turn meditation into another sort of trance state, which it is not. There are all sorts of individual problems, too, of course; it depends on the person concerned.

> *Question:* "Does a person have a sudden awareness of reaching the state of Nirvana, or is there a recognition of enlightenment, so to speak?"

A sudden awareness? When it happens, it's like nothing you can imagine, and you'll know. But it may not necessarily happen terribly fast, and it may not necessarily happen terribly slowly. It's like a light bulb: sometimes when you flick the switch it goes on immediately, and sometimes there's a dimmer on it and it comes up slowly. And thus we have what are known as the sudden and gradual enlightenment schools. Now, there are teachers who try to make you do it one way or the other. From what I know, there is no way in which you can make anybody do it any one way: they do it whichever way they're naturally set up to do it. But, believe me, you'll know when it happens! But you won't "know" in the way we usually use that word, because that implies a division, a separation.

One of the beauties, I've discovered, in studying the more advanced stuff that Dogen himself wrote is that he was very much against calling his school the Soto School of Zen (as opposed to the Rinzai School of Zen), because in the ancient days there was no such thing as a separation. The ancient masters were very much like brilliant artists: they took each person as an individual and helped him or her to train in whatever way was best for them. And this was the way that Koho Zenji, who was the person who taught me, liked to do it. And it is the way he said that I should try to teach people, if I were doing it: not try to insist on one specific way or another. Now, we've got a lot of problems with that, in the West, in that so many books have been published on various ways that people say, "Well, which is the best way?" And, of course, immediately you are stuck in a pair of opposites. What you are really trying to do is find the Unborn, and whichever way works for you is the way to go. As I say sometimes, "the truth, the whole truth, and anything else that works." (laughter) There are even some Buddhist schools which will make a trench of hot coals, and the master will stand with a knife, and if you don't run across them you'll get the knife in your back, and he's going across the coals with you. There's nothing like that to concentrate a man's mind very, very fast. (laughter) If that's the system that works for somebody, that's fine. It certainly wouldn't work for me; to me it is asceticism and I've just warned you to be careful of that. But no true Zen Buddhist will criticize those for whom such a system works, nor will he be against any other system that really gets you to find the Unborn. But anything that makes you unnatural from what you as an individual are, anything that places an unusual strain physically or mentally on you, will be asceticism for you and will stop you from finding It. Now, I guess there are people who love to be miserable by running across hot coals, people for whom this is natural, and the beauty of the Unborn is that It loves so deeply that It doesn't care what method you use: if that works, that's fine. So there can be no complaint against other religions or other systems: that's the system that works for you. I have found the one that works for me. Those with me, I believe, have found the one that works for them. Something else may work for another person. Because it works for them does not mean that it will work for me or you. You have to find the way that is right for you. That's the best advice I can give to anybody. Go ahead, friend.

Question: "What is a minor enlightenment?"

A what?

Questioner continues: "A minor kensho, a minor satori?"

Enlightenment is enlightenment. Sometimes the glimpses are big and sometimes they are small, but it is still one and the same thing. Don't think that the enlightenment is greater or smaller.

> *Questioner continues:* "I had the impression that once you got enlightenment, you got it."

Once you have realized it, you will always know it. But if you don't keep your training up, heaven help you: you'll be worse off than you were before. It's not something that you "get"; it's not something that you "keep" for eternity. Training, as Dogen says, *is* enlightenment. This is why Shakyamuni Buddha always carried His begging bowl and always wore His robe. A lot of people think, "Why didn't He just sit back and enjoy it?" Enlightenment isn't something you have: it's something you *are*, something you *do*.

> *Questioner continues:* "But if you've 'made it', you've 'made it', right?" (laughter)

There's an old Zen saying, "They travel fastest who are not there."

> *Monk's comment:* "The moment you think that you have it, you've lost it. And the moment you think that you've lost it, you've lost it. There's nothing to have, but you can lose it when you don't train."

You only "know" when you are not enlightened; you never "know" when you are.

> *Questioner continues:* "But. . . ." (laughter)

The question he is actually asking is the question that was asked of a Zen master, who was fanning himself, by a novice monk. The novice said to him, "Since the nature of air is forever with us, why do you fan yourself?" The master answered, "If I do not fan myself, how do I know that the nature of air is with us?" Yes, the air is always present, but if I do not stir it, how can I feel it? These are not his exact words, but that is the meaning of what he was saying. You can be sitting with air all around you and be awfully hot. If you fan yourself, you can be cool because you know that the air exists. You can be fully enlightened, but if you do not practice that which causes enlightenment, that which *is* enlightenment, you will not manifest the signs of enlightenment.

> *Question:* "I've heard you say so often that if you don't want to go all the way, don't start. Why is it necessary to say it? Because we wouldn't be here if we didn't want to go all the way, isn't that right?"

Well, there are a number of people who don't know that. I've known people who do it for two or three years and then they say, "Well, I decided I wouldn't meditate any more; I didn't seem to be getting anywhere." I've had that happen, and I just want to warn anyone here who may decide to take up meditation and see what it is like that there can be problems down the line if they take it up for a period of time and then stop. I'm not expecting you to stop.

> *Question:* "Do we have a responsibility here if we are encouraging friends to try meditation, if we don't know fully what we're getting into?"

This has been the argument against having lay people meditate in the East. In certain areas in China, for example, monasticism became so much a sort of ivory tower for the monks that the laity, in the end, didn't see why they should provide food and lodging for them. The answer to your question is: each person has to decide for themself whether they feel it is wise to get friends involved. I take the risk, but I always tell them what the risks are, which is what I'm doing right now. I think we have a responsibility to do that. I definitely do not think you should just tell a person to meditate without telling him what may happen. Remember that meditation tends to make one more aware of oneself and of the things we have buried from our past; if you get that process started and then stop half way, you may be more unhappy than if you had never started. Go ahead.

> *Monk's comment:* "One of the main problems in this country is that some people meditate strictly for what, from a religious point of view, are the 'side effects'. Some people want to meditate solely to increase their physical vitality, or want to meditate solely to gain more ability to concentrate, etc., and someone coming from that motivation could get into a lot of trouble if they specifically do not want some of these spiritual things and they don't want to get into making fundamental changes in how they live their lives."

Yes, because not only will you become much more efficient and the like, you'll go right on past becoming more efficient into all the other stuff. Remember what we said: anytime you sit down to meditate you are beckoning to the Unborn and the Undying. You are saying, "I want to find You." That you have sat down to meditate thinking, "Well, maybe it will make me more efficient", is neither here nor there. What the Cosmic Buddha hears is, "Ah, you want Me!?! Right . . . you can have some efficiency, but you're coming all the way as well." So, it's very dangerous to do it by any other means. I have often read these articles on "Become more efficient! Become more competent! Be able to concentrate better!" Two hundred and fifty dollars for a meditation weekend, or something of the sort. They call them "enlightenment intensives" and the like; I'm sure you've seen them. And I get really scared by such things, because the people who are doing that, I have to believe, cannot know fully what they are doing. And I feel that as a responsible person, I have to tell somebody that if they meditate, these things may happen. And if you once start the process going, then it's really going; it's not going to stop.

Well, friends, I see that we need to end for today. I hope that you have a better sense now of what you may be getting into if you take up Zen training seriously. And if I haven't scared you away completely, the rest of these lectures will be devoted to exploring how to do this training: how to meditate, how to live the life of Buddha, the fruits of that life, and the two forms which it may take—the way of the householder and the way of the monk.

2.

How to Do Serene Reflection Meditation

Now, because I am going blind and I want to do some meditation with all of you, I am going to ask one of the monks here if he will read the *Fukanzazengi* or *Rules for Meditation*,* and then we'll try to do some, and he can explain as we go along. I'm going to have to rest for a second.

> *Scripture:* "Why are training and enlightenment differentiated since the Truth is universal? Why study the means of attaining it since the supreme teaching is free? Since Truth is seen to be clearly apart from that which is unclean, why cling to a means of cleansing it?"

> *Monk's comment:* "Another way of looking at that is 'Since we are taught that we are already inherently enlightened, why do we need to do anything about it? If we are already in our hearts at one with the Eternal, why do we have to do something like meditation or religious practice in order to know that?'"

---

* See *The Monastic Office*, trans. Rev. Hubert Nearman, O.B.C., with Rev. Master P.T.N.H. Jiyu-Kennett, M.O.B.C., as consultant and editor (Mt. Shasta, California: Shasta Abbey Press, 1993), pp. 77–80.

Scripture: "Since Truth is not separate from training, training is unnecessary—the separation will be as that between heaven and earth if even the slightest gap exists for, when the opposites arise, the Buddha Mind is lost."

Monk's comment: "This is the answer to the previous question. Indeed, training and enlightenment are one thing, not two. And whenever discrimination and judgment enter into our minds we lose sight of the Eternal, of that Oneness that is always there."

Scripture: "However much you may be proud of your understanding, however much you may be enlightened, whatever your attainment of wisdom and supernatural power, your finding of the way to mind illumination, your power to touch heaven and to enter into enlightenment. . . ."

Monk's comment: "No matter what you've done in your life, no matter how advanced or rudimentary you believe your spiritual understanding and practice to be, no matter how good or rotten a person you may think yourself to be. . . ."

Scripture: ". . . when the opposites arise you have almost lost the way to salvation. Although the Buddha had great wisdom at birth, He sat in training for six years."

Monk's comment: "He wasn't just born with that, with the understanding that He had. He had to cultivate it, and, because He did that and realized the

Truth, we can do it as well. It wasn't something that just He could do, something that is not available for anybody else. Any woman or man, no matter what state of life they are in, can do what He did."

He was an ordinary person, you must remember that.

Scripture: "The Ancestors were very diligent and there is no reason why we people of the present day cannot understand. All you have to do is cease from erudition, withdraw within and reflect upon yourself. Should you be able to cast off body and mind naturally, the Buddha Mind will immediately manifest itself; if you want to find it quickly, you must start at once."

Monk's comment: "This writing puts emphasis on the word 'naturally', because it is not something artificial. We have to allow it to arise of itself, and know it for ourselves, through Zen practice. One analogy to that is if you don't know how to swim and you read a book on swimming: you can stand on the edge of the pool or the beach, and you can do everything you want—practice breathing, go back and forth, go back to the book, get all the moves right— and there is nothing that will prepare you for the first shock of hitting the water."

Not least of which is, it's cold!

Monk's comment: "After you begin to understand the instruction, you realize that swimming, or anything else that is familiar to you in this way, is a very natural thing to do. Meditation and religious training are exactly the same thing: the Truth appears naturally when you get in there and do what needs to be done."

Scripture: "You should meditate in a quiet room, eat and drink moderately, cut all ties, give up everything, think of neither good nor evil, consider neither right nor wrong."

Monk's comment: "Now, one of the things that really worries a lot of people is the phrase "give up everything". Rev. Dogen in this writing, and we also here today, are not suggesting that as soon as you leave this class you go off and sell all your clothes, give your money to the poor, and head up the nearest mountain in rags. What he was asking people to look at was the necessity of finding this oneness with the Eternal in everyday life. This is the priority of religious life."

And throwing out the concepts and notions you've got in your head, and just being still to find the Eternal.

Monk's comment: "And, as well, seeing that everything in this world, because it is subject to change, is insubstantial. If we hold on to something that is insubstantial, in the end it will cause suffering for us. But when we don't hold on, we see that the flow of change itself is none other than the Unborn, Undying, Uncreated, and Unformed."

At this point, let me mention a few things in more detail. This passage also speaks of eating and drinking moderately, which is to be taken as general advice and also applies in particular to eating prior to meditation. Eat moderately, and don't sit down immediately after you've eaten a meal: you will have the most horrendous things happen. Everything is going to tip upside down; you're going to get murderously hot, then murderously cold; you're going to shiver, you're going to sweat; you're going to complain; things will tip sideways; and above all you won't digest your meal! Give it forty-five minutes, at least. The very best time to meditate is just before a meal, which is why we do our meditations just before lunch or just before supper or just before breakfast. That's the time when the body is doing least work, physically, and has time to just be still. The "works" inside one have rights, and if you've just filled them with various substances, you should not complain that they wish to get on with their job. And you will only hurt yourself if you try to do anything different.

From a general consensus of the finest Japanese and Chinese masters I have found and met, and from the corroboration of the words of the ancient masters Dogen and Keizan themselves, what matters is that you do not force yourself to suffer from the "three lacks": lack of food, lack of sleep, and lack of clothing (lack of warmth). You should have adequate clothing, but not too much. Six hours sleep is required, as a minimum, in the best temples. Now, there are some people who can't get away with less than eight or nine, and some who can't get away with less than seven. Again, I try very hard in Shasta to find a middle ground. This is the most difficult one for me to deal with, because the majority of people are happy with six hours sleep, but there is a fair swatch of them who can't do it with that, and the only way I can deal with that is to let them go to bed earlier. So, don't feel dreadful if you can't make it with the six, but don't overdo it either.

The same is true of food. Food should be good and simple, without a lot of highly spiced things. After you have been meditating awhile, very spicy things tend to become hard to digest: it would seem they are somehow too coarse. Be sure that your food is simple and nutritious: simple things that you can do a lot with, and thoroughly enjoy, and which will not interfere with the digestion very much. But above all remember, as Dogen himself pointed out, "six parts of a full stomach support a man and the other two support his doctor." Don't go and feed yourself to such an extent that you're glutted, because then you're going to have to take longer than forty-five minutes before you're finished digesting; you'll probably sleep, you'll probably be very lethargic. Be careful how much you eat. And whatever you do, make sure it is very nourishing. Eat for the food—for the quality of the food, for the food value itself—and not for the taste. Make sure you have plenty of fruit and fresh vegetables, but not too much in the way of harsh "scrubby" greens in your salads: there's plenty of good things you can have in salads, but do not use stuff that is going to do damage or cause the interior to overwork too much.

So, remember the "three lacks". There is nothing wrong, if you are cold, with putting on a sweater, but don't make yourself too hot. There is nothing wrong with going to bed a half an hour or hour earlier, if the rising time is something your particular metabolism can't cope with. But it is better you go to bed a bit early than you get up a bit late. And be very careful about how you eat, so it is for the food value, and not just because, "Ooh, how wonderful to have this or that."

> *Scripture:* "Control mind function, will, consciousness, memory, perception and understanding; you must not strive thus to become Buddha. Cling to neither sitting nor lying down. When meditating, do not wear tight clothing. Rest the left hand in the palm

of the right hand with the thumbs touching lightly; sit upright, leaning neither to left nor right, backwards nor forwards. The ears must be in line with the shoulders and the nose in line with the navel."

These are not instructions that are given when somebody says, "Well, I've got a slightly curved spine; I suppose I can't meditate." This is the ideal. But the Eternal made some of us short, some of us long, some of us fat, some of us thin: you sit the best you know how with what you've got. So, the important thing here is having your spine correct for you. There are a lot of people in this world who've damaged their backs and can't sit in the absolutely ideal position (I didn't know how many until I ran a monastery). Meditation is not supposed to make you unnatural, strange, weird; it is not supposed to make you ill. Have a straight spine, yes; if you are in perfect health then your spine should be as a perfectly healthy spine should be, which is slightly "S" shaped. That is, for the sake of the books, a "straight spine". If you have a fused spine or a damaged spine, hold it as perfectly as you can.

One of the beauties of the Eternal is that It does not hold against us the fact that we've done damage to ourselves. And, remember, the purpose of this exercise is to find the Eternal, it is not to look good sitting on the floor. There are those, I know, in the East (and I've met some of them) who insist that everybody sits like a bunch of ramrods. It looks terrific, but you should feel the atmosphere in there: you can almost cut the pain with a knife. Maybe that's good for some, but certainly in Soto Zen we didn't find it worked, and we knew what we were trying to do: we were trying to become one with the Eternal. That being so, find the way that it is right for you to sit.

As we get older we have to face the fact that our bones don't twist up nearly as simply as they did when they were younger. There is a beautiful piece, often neglected by present-day teachers, in the instructions for every single ceremony involving both lay people and monks, which says very clearly that if trainees are old they should be allowed to sit as is best for them. For example, if a trainee is coming to be ordained, and he or she is old, they do not necessarily have to do all the bows or all the actions listed in the ceremony. The accent is always on compassion. You are there to find the Eternal, to do the finest you possibly can. That's your purpose. That it makes a neat and beautiful ceremony is nice when you've got a twenty-year-old who's got the world's prize figure and can hop up and down and look good; that's great. I'm sure the Eternal loves it. (laughter) But when you're in your sixties and your legs don't work so good, the Eternal is just as overjoyed.

Now, speaking of legs, you do not have to sit in a cross-legged position, twisted up like a pretzel: find a comfortable chair, or manufacture a meditation cushion or bench. You don't necessarily have to have it high up in the air; you can have it just sitting on the floor, but make it a comfortable thing to sit on. In China sometimes the Zen monks sit in a sort of chair; I tried to get some made once, for Shasta for Morning Service, but it was going to cost us too much and we ended up with benches. But benches will do if you don't want to manufacture chairs.

Now, having found your comfortable place to sit—a place where your spine is comfortable, a place where your feet are comfortable—the next thing is to make sure that there are no tensions in the shoulder area. If this gets tense (there are big muscles here that tend to get very tense), you will be in a lot of pain and have a lot of trouble sitting. Some monks use a stick, called a kyosaku, an "awakening stick", to remove the

SOME MEDITATION POSTURES

On a chair with a wedge-shaped cushion.

On a kneeling chair.

On a meditation bench.

In full lotus—front view.

In full lotus—side view showing traditional round meditation cushion.

In half lotus.

In Burmese posture.

tension in those muscles. The real art of meditating, however, is not to let the tension get there in the first place, and the way to prevent that is having the arms in the correct position. Find where they are correctly comfortable, along with the comfort of the head, so that nothing feels heavy or weighty. It's very important not to be heavy or weighty, just very loose and comfortable. If you are not trying to maintain a position that somebody has forced upon you because that's the way they sit, but instead have found a position that is the right way for you because that is where your head is correct and weightless, if you are in that sort of position, the chances of your messing up your shoulders are very small. Because once your spine and head are correct, your hands and arms can find the correct place, too. Here, however, there is a problem because a lot of people don't have long enough arms for them to rest comfortably on their lap. So as to prevent pain in the neck and shoulders, what you need is a pad of some sort—a rolled up sweater, something of the sort. If your arms are too short, place the pad on the knees so the hands can rest on it comfortably without tensing. Place one hand on the pad and the other hand on top of the first, with the thumbs touching lightly. The reason for this position is very important. When you tense up, you tend to push your thumbs together; and if you do that, you'll soon feel the muscles in the neck and shoulders get in terrible pain. So the person whose thumbs are just lightly touching each other has got it dead right. And then this cycle of pain and tension does not start up, and you don't have a problem with it.

So remember, when monks go around showing you how to put your hands or hold your head, they are not trying to say, "This is the way I do it and this is the way it's got to be done." They are saying to you, "I don't want your neck tensed up; I don't want you in pain. I want you to be able to do it the best way possible." And that is the sole purpose for the position of the hands and arms, that, and making a "circuit" out of the whole body, which is flowing—simply and very lightly. So remember, if your arms aren't long enough, it doesn't matter: just make a nice wedge or something nice and soft, and put it on your lap, and put your hands on top. Monks do that, too. Those who need a pad roll up their huge sleeves, put them on their laps, and that's enough to make a nice pad for the length of the arms—very simple.

> *Scripture*: "The tongue must be held lightly against the back of the top teeth with the lips and teeth closed. Keep the eyes open, breathe in quickly, settle the body comfortably and breathe out sharply."

> *Monk's comment*: "You'll see that—to condense these instructions—it's saying basically, 'Sit there quietly with your body and mind in a posture of relaxed attention.'"

Whatever is the most comfortable posture, if you will just sit with your mind right, is the right one for you. Remember that your eyes will be somewhat open; you do not want to go off into trance. If you wear spectacles, do not take them off. You are not supposed to make yourself feel weird because you can't see; if you wear spectacles, keep them on. What you do is find any area (the East says at a distance of about a meter, which is fine if everybody's got 20–20 vision, but everybody doesn't have 20–20 vision) on the floor in front of you where your eyes are comfortably focused for you as an individual. And then let them rest there, comfortably. You do not want anything making you feel dis-ease: that is the best way of putting it. Find the comfortable place for the eyes to rest, and let them stay there. They will then blink very little because they will be comfortable.

> *Monk's comment:* "And breathe naturally: don't do anything weird with your breathing. Breathe the way you would normally breathe."

Apropos of that, I'd like to mention in regard to breathing exercises: unfortunately an awful lot of people have been taught that you need to count your breaths. Now, counting of the breaths is extremely useful if you can't keep your mind from wandering: it keeps the mind doing something. If you have a mind that is constantly running off and chasing its own thoughts, then it can be very useful indeed, especially if you've got a mind that is very, very active that way. Then what you need to do is count the breaths up to ten, and when you reach ten, start from one again. If at any time during those ten, a thought comes in (that is, a discriminative thought, one where you are discussing things inside yourself—not a natural thought, they're harmless), start at one again. Really all you need is ten: "1 out, 2 out, 3 out". Some people argue you should count the number on the in-breath, and some say you should count it on the out. Knowing what I do, I think the "outs" have a slight preference over the "ins", but it really doesn't matter all that much. What matters is you slow the mind down enough that it doesn't spend its entire time talking to itself; that's the main thing. So just take it up to ten, start again, take it up to ten, start again.

But once the mind does not constantly wander, counting of breaths will damage your meditation.* It is a means of

---

* These comments pertain to the Soto Zen form of meditation, known as shikan-taza, "just sitting", or "serene reflection", and are not a

concentration, learning to concentrate; it is not a means of meditation, and there should be a very clear distinction on that. Sir Christmas Humphreys many years ago actually wrote a book on that which was very valuable.* There is a tremendous difference between concentration and meditation. To focus on one thing and, every time your brain wanders off, to bring yourself back to it, is concentration. There is a difference between that and just sitting still in meditation: the one is getting one-pointedness of mind so that your brain isn't scattered, the other is just sitting still. And counting breaths can be a bridge from one to the other. For example, just now that car siren went off. You can be sitting in meditation and you can notice, "A car siren went off" ('cause your ears aren't stuffed up). And that won't harm your meditation at all. But if you say to yourself, "A car siren went off and it's ruined my meditation; I wish it hadn't happened", that's when you count your breaths. Bring your mind back to not discriminating and being annoyed by what's going on outside. A dog barks: so . . . , a dog barks; so . . . , something happens; this happens. I can remember being very annoyed when I was first studying in the East because of certain things that went on: they rang bells, and did this-and-that-and-the-other, and I wanted to be totally quiet. You know, I was still the gorgeous goldfish in the bowl at this time. My master eventually called me in to him, by the way, and said, "Let's put that goldfish in the pond"; that was after I played Ma-jong with one of the monks. He made a very important point for me to learn: there is no

---

criticism of other traditions in which the counting of breaths sometimes plays a central role.

* Christmas Humphreys, *Concentration and Meditation* (Santa Fe, New Mexico: Sun Publishing Co., 1981).

problem with trying to understand other people, but you still shouldn't encourage them in such things, and he told me I shouldn't have done it, but at least I was fit to get back into the pond. So, you have someone like me complaining about the noises in the temple, and my teacher said, "Well, this morning under my robe a flea was walking; just I noticed it had strong legs." That is how you must notice things that go by in your meditation. They will mess up your meditation if you let them, if you allow the discriminatory mind to think. There is an actual statement in here later on which says, "Don't think and don't try not to think. Just sit." The Japanese words for that are specifically: "natural thinking" and "deliberate thought". Because your ears are open, you will hear things; because your eyes are not totally closed, you will see things on the carpet or on the wall. You will have this happen. They will only mess up your meditation if you deliberately start thinking about them.

I've gotten a little ahead of myself here. Back as to how one does one's breathing when one meditates: first of all, be very careful with a lot of books that you read on how to do this, 'cause what the person is talking about is almost always the method that worked perfectly for him or her. The main thing is not to become unusual in your breathing. Now in the *Fukanzazengi* it says to take two or three deep breaths, and that is to clear the air passages if you've got a stuffy nose or a bad throat, and also to set up a "circular" pattern of breathing. Take two or three deep breaths, feeling or visualizing the breath coming up the spine to the top of the head on the in-breath and going down the front into your belly on the out-breath. Then settle down to a natural rhythm of breathing without noticing that it is happening. Do not try to continue to follow the breaths, count them, or do strenuous breathing, heavy breathing, because then your mind will be constantly stuck on your breathing. One or two people have sometimes made it by heavy breathing because that was the normal way they breathed. Whatever is the normal way for you to breathe is the way in which you personally are going to find the Unborn. So don't try to do something unnatural to your body. But do, definitely, clear your throat and clear your nostrils, settle down, and clear your head as much as you can. Following the breath in the circular pattern for two or three good breaths will usually do that. Definitely blow your nose beforehand. In the East monks are required to go to the toilets and blow their noses loudly into them before meditation. That was something else I decided one could do sensibly into one's own handkerchief in one's own private room; one did not need to make it into something that was required. So, just breathe normally, and eventually the breathing gets quieter and quieter until there seems almost no breath at all. It's incredibly beautiful at that stage, so don't try forcing breathing out, forcing breathing in. I've seen so many strange things go on, I'm amazed that half the people I have looked at haven't had heart attacks! But, never mind. . . . Go ahead, friend, I'm sorry: I didn't mean to get into that.

> *Scripture:* "Sway the body left and right then sit steadily, neither trying to think nor trying not to think."

> *Monk's comment:* "Neither pushing away your thoughts or trying to hold on to them, not thinking 'This is a good thought or a bad thought, or a good feeling or a bad feeling'—just sitting still."

Do not deliberately try to think of anything, and don't try not to think because that sets up another pair of opposites. Natural thoughts are going to come and go: you're going to feel a breeze, you're going to hear a few noises, you are going to see a few things because your eyes are going to be

slightly open. None of these things will upset your meditation or damage it unless you chase after them. For example, you can hear a bird sing outside (there's one doing it
now). So, "a bird is singing": that thought is going to go
through your head because it is impossible and even unwise
to try to turn off the brain in that sense. But if you then start
saying to yourself, "What a pretty song! I wish it would sing
more; maybe it will help my meditation", then you have
gone out of meditation into discussion in your own mind.

The original Japanese terms with regard to the use of the
mind say that natural thought will do no harm to you, deliberate thought will. That is what I was trying to explain about
hearing the bird sing: that is a natural thought that goes
across the mind, because the mind is like a computer and it
gives you a read-out. But if you start discussing a natural
thought, then your train of thought will have started and you
will not have true meditation. You will have a discussion in
your head, and you will be back in the opposites, having a
discussion. So natural thought is perfectly all right. If you're
sitting in this room, you're going to see the spots on the carpet. Yes, there's a spot on the carpet. You can then decide,
"Well, so there's a spot on the carpet" and go on sitting, or
you can say, "Oh dear, I must withdraw the hem of my garment", and immediately you've stopped meditating again.
Anything can get at you.

And it is these discussions in our heads which are one of
the things which separates us most effectively from the
Unborn. A Christian priest whom I was talking with once
asked me, "How do I have conversations with God? I have
heard that Zen monks have conversations with the Eternal."
He talked non-stop for an hour and a half, all about the same
thing, and finally I said to him, when he paused for a breath
because he needed to take some water, "Well, why don't you

shut up and give Him a chance to get a word in edgewise?"
You have to give the Eternal a chance to "reply". And the
only way that can frequently be done is by silent prayer or
silent meditation. Properly done prayer and properly done
meditation are identically the same thing. We are so afraid of
words: "Oh, if people meditate they are into the occult, but
if they pray they are into religion." There isn't a difference,
for crying out loud! If it's done right, it's identically the same
thing. So, if you want to find the Eternal, sit down, be still,
and above all, let the Eternal have a chance!

> *Scripture:* "Just sitting, with no deliberate thought, is
> the important aspect of serene reflection meditation.
> This type of meditation is not something that is done
> in stages; it is simply the lawful gateway to carefree
> peace."

> *Monk's comment:* "There is no introductory practice
> that you learn in the beginning and then, when you
> get good at that, there is a secret practice you learn
> later on: it's all right there in front of you, right in the
> beginning."

This is why I got these meditation booklets done. I
decided when people first come to us, put it all up front. Let's
not have secrets.

> *Scripture:* "To train and enlighten ourselves is to
> become thoroughly wise; the koan (our spiritual
> problem that arises) appears naturally in daily life."

> *Monk's comment:* "And also in daily life arises the
> opportunity to deal with it through everyday training."

Scripture: "If you become thus utterly free you will be as the water wherein the dragon dwells or as the mountain whereon the tiger roams."

Monk's comment: "Now, a lot of people misunderstand that because they think, 'If I meditate, it will turn me into something'—whether that 'something' is good or bad. The thing that they miss, which is made clear in this passage, is that we become as the water wherein the dragon dwells: we become transparent. Or we become as the mountain whereon the tiger roams. The dragon and the tiger are the oriental symbols of the Eternal and we, if we meditate properly and practice, become the vehicle of That. But we are not the Eternal."

And, there is nothing in us that is not *of* It.

Monk's comment: "And that is seen when we practice and become still, so we become as the water: clear and transparent as the water. We become as still, solid, and quiet as the mountain, and then the tiger roams and the dragon comes forth."

You've often seen, I'm sure, these bamboo pictures (they sell them in Chinatown for a couple of bucks) with a dragon coming down, and there's a tiger walking down a mountain. That's what they are referring to: they are religious scrolls, actually.

Scripture: "Understand clearly that the Truth appears naturally and then your mind will be free from doubts and vacillation."

Monk's comment: "Avoid the tendency that I have always had: 'Is anything happening yet? I've been sitting here for, you know, for several minutes, several hours, several days, several years . . .'"

Are we having fun yet?

Monk's comment: ". . . 'several hours, several days, several years: is it—is it going to happen now?!?' It doesn't happen when you wait and expect things like that; it happens naturally."

It happens when all conditions ripen.

Scripture: "When you wish to arise from meditation, sway the body gently from side to side and arise quietly; the body must make no violent movement; I myself have seen that the ability to die whilst sitting and standing, which transcends both peasant and sage, is obtained through the power of serene reflection meditation."

Monk's comment: "The whole purpose of meditation and religious practice is to help us to realize and understand that we can live and die without fear, because we are one with the Eternal. Even though everything falls apart, and what we call 'ourselves' dies, there *is* an Unborn, Undying, Uncreated, Unformed, Unchanging."

That is one of the main things: that you can go into the Eternal, the Pure Love, the Immaculacy, and know It's there, and when the moment of death comes, there is no fear. There's a lovely old tale of how you teach children about death. They come under what are called the "Big Frog Stories".* You take the children out and sit them around a pond, preferably with a big frog in it. In the story, one small fish asks the big frog, "What happened to the lovely bug that was sitting in the pond, at the bottom of the pond with me? It's now all split out and empty and done for, and there's nothing: the bug's gone." And Big Frog says, "Well, look up there: there's a lovely dragonfly flying over the top of the pond. The big bug has split open and the dragonfly has floated up through the water and has become a dragonfly." And that's the way you teach children about death, especially children who may be going to die soon. Big Frog Stories are very interesting, but I've only got one volume of them (I can immediately hear people asking, "Where do we get the rest?"). My friend died before he did more of them. No, wait a moment . . . he did three, but I've only got one.

> *Scripture:* "It is no more possible to understand natural activity with the judgmental mind than it is possible to understand the signs of enlightenment; nor is it possible to understand training and enlightenment by supernatural means; such understanding is outside the realm of speech and vision, such Truth is beyond personal opinions. Do not discuss the wise and the ignorant, there is only one thing—to train hard for this is true enlightenment."

> *Monk's comment:* "If we go back to the analogy of swimming, you don't know what it is to swim until you swim, and you don't know what it is to become

---

* See E. K. Shinkaku Hunt, "The City of Mud Bugs" in *Buddhist Stories for Children* (Honolulu, Hawaii: Takiko Ichinose, 1959), pp. 14–17.

Buddha until you become Buddha. You can't analyze it from another position: it is something you have to *do*. And once you endeavor to commence in meditation and training, then you'll understand what this is talking about from the inside, not from the outside. The Truth appears naturally."

Dogen says if you want to try and understand it, trail your hand in the water of a river and then try to grab out a handful. There's nothing there, but you know your hand's in the river.

Scripture: "Training and enlightenment are naturally undefiled; to live in this way is the same as to live an ordinary daily life."

Monk's comment: "For someone who really practices this to the best of their ability, they live a life of purity. And that purity is the same thing as living in the world, and it is why Buddhism has always used the symbol of the lotus blossom that sits on top of really grubby, dirty, filthy water, with its roots in the mud, and you have this beautiful blossom. The place where the roots live is the muck. If you take the roots . . ."

Take a look outside at San Francisco! (laughter)

Monk's comment: ". . . if you take the roots outside the muck, the lotus blossom dies, because its roots are in the muck. So, what one does in daily life is learn how to make the greatest use of the muck."

And thus convert it into the magnificent blossom. As the daily scriptures say, "The lotus blossom is not wetted by the water that surrounds it."

Scripture: "The Buddha Seal has been preserved by both the Buddhas in the present world and by those in the world of the Indian and Chinese Ancestors, they are thus always spreading the Truth—all activity is permeated with pure meditation."

Monk's comment: "In the way that Rev. Master was saying earlier: no matter what you do, you can turn anything you do in daily life into meditation."

And into an act of Buddhism, a Buddhist act, if you keep to the precepts, which is what we are going to be talking about tomorrow.

Monk's comment: "There is a very quick story that Rev. Master told me about an opera that people don't see very much nowadays, called 'The Juggler of Notre Dame', about a man who joins a religious order. He goes into this order, in which there are scholars and poets and very educated and accomplished people, and for some reason, this fellow has just been a juggler all his life. He becomes more and more distressed, because he seemingly has nothing that he can do for his religious order so as to serve God. Everybody's looking down saying, 'Oh, you know, the juggler. . . .' And so one day, he goes into the Chapel of the Blessed Virgin Mary in his juggler's costume and juggles in front of the statue."

Does the finest act of juggling he knows how.

Monk's comment: "And when the monks come in, someone sees him and they're horrified, and they call the monks together, and the monks go running down to see what this fellow's doing down in the Chapel."

They are going to see if he's done sacrilege.

> *Monk's comment:* "They find that he has died, and the statue has bent down and is holding him. Which just goes to show that we may not think much of what we do, or the world may not think much of what we do. . . ."

It doesn't really matter, if we do it right.

> *Monk's comment:* ". . . if we do it with real heart, with pure and loving heart."

> *Scripture:* "It is futile to travel to other dusty countries thus forsaking your own seat; if your first step is false, you will immediately stumble. Already you are in possession of the vital attributes of a human being—do not waste time with this and that—you can possess the authority of Buddha."

> *Monk's comment:* "Just the way you are: all you have to do is train."

> *Scripture:* "Of what use is it to merely enjoy this fleeting world? This body is as transient as dew on the grass, life passes as swiftly as a flash of lightning, quickly the body passes away, in a moment life is gone. O sincere trainees, do not doubt the true dragon, do not spend so much time in rubbing only a part of the elephant."

The elephant is the saint in Buddhism, and there's always the bit of us that wants to be holy, and we polish that bit, you know. It's like polishing your brass halo. Don't just rub a bit of the elephant.

> *Scripture:* "Look inwards and advance directly along the road that leads to the Mind."

> *Monk's comment:* "Look into yourself."

> *Scripture:* "Respect those who have reached the goal of goalessness, become one with the wisdom of the Buddhas, Transmit the wisdom of the Ancestors. If you do these things for some time you will become as herein described and then the Treasure House will open naturally and you will enjoy it fully."

> *Monk's comment:* "In short, it works!"

Oh, I know it works! So, may I suggest that we take a very short rest, and then, while that's going on, we'll get the room ready for meditation. Now, those of you who want to sit on the floor, of course, can; but there's absolutely nothing wrong with sitting in a chair. Remember, what matters is that you sit. If you worry about: "Can I twist myself up like a pretzel?" you'll never find the Eternal. I have seen too many people get water on the knee from trying to do something that someone has said "must be done this way". If that were so, then a tremendous number of people who found the Eternal couldn't possibly have done it. I've known of a couple who found It sitting on the toilet!

So, you don't necessarily have to sit physically in front of a wall to do this: what you really have to do is make your mind sit, to put it still. I have often told people who say they

Rev. Master Jiyu with her hands in the gassho.

haven't time to meditate each morning, because they have to get to work and the like, "That's fine, sit on the bus, or on the commuter train, or whatever method you're using of traveling, as if your hands were in the gassho.*

Put the two halves of your brain together, still, in the mind of stillness, and just leave them there for five minutes, or two minutes, or fifty seconds. I don't care how long: just

---

* The gassho is the hand position of reverence and greeting in Buddhism. The two hands are placed with palms together, fingers pointing upward, in front of the chest. It symbolizes, among other things, the unity of the opposites.

make the effort of doing it." Every one of us, every hour of the day, has a few minutes when we can just stop still and hear the silence within ourself. And it is in those silent still-nesses that you will teach the mind to sit. You need formal meditation ("sitting"), don't misunderstand me: I am not saying you should not sit in meditation—you should. I'm talking now about the person who says, "I haven't got the time to." All right, make your mind sit. And when you have the time, physically sit.

QUESTIONS

So, how many of you have never tried meditating before?—Quite a few. Well, I'm ready and open for questions.

Question: "Do all Buddhists meditate in the same way?"

All meditation has the same end in view; let's get that straight from the beginning. What the different schools of Buddhism do is differ as to how the meditation is done. In Rinzai Zen, for example, everyone sits facing each other. In Soto Zen, everyone sits facing a wall. Some people believe that you should sit outdoors only, some that you sit indoors only. There are problems, of course, when there's rain if you're supposed to sit outdoors only. I can't give you speci-fically the differences between Vipassana and Soto Zen, because I really and truly don't know them. But I do know enough about all schools of Buddhism to know that the end result is the same, and the real difference is really where or how you sit and the exact position you sit in.

There's the Burmese method of sitting in meditation, which is one foot in front of the other. There's the half-lotus, which is something like this [monk demonstrates] which other schools adopt. There's the full-lotus, which they say you can't do without. Then, of course, there were the Egyptians, who weren't Buddhist but seem to have done it extraordinarily well sitting on a chair with their hands like this [demonstration]. The one big thing that is identical in all of them is that the spine must be as natural as possible. Remember: what is described in the *Rules for Meditation* in these booklets is the ideal, but no two people are ever totally alike, and most of us do not have the world's prize figure or the ideal body. You do the very best you can with what you have. That's the best answer I can give you, unless one of these two monks has read more up on Vipassana than I have. My apologies for not being able to give you a fuller answer.

> *Question:* "I have a problem keeping my eyes open looking at the wall. I have done zazen with them closed; is that okay?"

The danger of keeping your eyes closed, apart from the very obvious one that if you're slightly tired you can nod off, is, of course, that you can start imagining things if your eyes are closed. Now, visions do occur both during meditation and in ordinary life. They will not do you any harm at all, so long as you don't start thinking, "Oh good: the Buddha appeared to me, I must be holy", something along those lines. I have had a lot of visions; so have other Buddhist priests and monks in the Far East down the centuries.* They can be extremely valuable; they can be very important. But however important

---

* For Rev. Master Jiyu's discussion of some of her own visions, see Rev. Master P.T.N.H. Jiyu-Kennett, M.O.B.C., *How to Grow a Lotus Blossom or How a Zen Buddhist Prepares for Death*, 2nd ed. rev. (Mt. Shasta,

they are, if you get stuck with them and keep trying to bring them back, then they become totally useless.

One of the things Soto Zen found out (and you must remember that Soto Zen is the oldest of the three Zen schools: both Rinzai and Obaku came out of it) is that you can invite hallucination with the eyes closed. I'm not saying people do it for that reason, but you can invite it. One of the reasons they use the kyosaku so much in Rinzai is to prevent people doing that, because the eyes frequently are closed. So, if you can find a very comfortable place where they can rest so that they are not fully open, they are just drooping a little, after a bit of practice it works. And it does sort of keep you . . . forgive me, I've got hiccups . . . it does keep you sort of focused in your one place. I know that there are people who get very upset if you allow the eyes to move, but there are some people who, if they don't allow their eyes to do natural movement (I'm not talking about deliberate movement now, because deliberate movement is a different thing: but the eyes do move slightly all the time), and if they force them to focus onto one spot, can start making knots in the wood, for example, enlarge hugely, or things like this. So you must allow a bit of natural movement. It's the naturalness that matters: you must allow for the naturalness. And if you do that, then gradually, with a bit of time, that tendency will go away. If you've been doing it with the eyes closed, it can possibly mean that you will have to take a little extra time, a little extra care, to get used to it with them open. There are practical reasons for all of these things in meditation.

So, find a place where the eyes are comfortable; find a place where the head is comfortable; find a place where the

California: Shasta Abbey Press, 1993). For examples of visions in the Soto Zen tradition see the references cited in the footnote on p. xiv.

arms are comfortable, and a place where the feet are comfortable, and the spine. Then you can go so fast, if you do it on an individual basis and not on a "because I did it this way everybody else does it this way" basis. You'll find the Unborn a good five to ten years earlier: I know, I've seen it happen. But only if people are treated as individuals. If you go around having a sort of militaristic system where everybody is flogged unless they're sitting like ramrods, what you'll get is a bunch of ramrods, not a bunch of people finding the Cosmic Buddha or the Unborn. The other way doesn't look so neat and tidy; but then, we aren't there to look neat and tidy. It was the Chinese monks who pointed this one out to me, because I visited them, again, after I'd been in Sojiji for a number of years. I was visiting a temple in Hong Kong where they'd actually got tan* instead of chairs, because that is the other way they do it, and they were so untidy I was horrified. I said, "How can they meditate?!?" And they looked at me and said, "What have they been teaching you?!?" It was they who pointed this out to me, and the difference in their "attainment" (if that's the right word to use in Buddhism, which it isn't) was so great it was unbelievable. And if they needed to move during meditation, they moved. And they sat in the way that made each one comfortable and free of weight and tension. And I decided, "Well, when I go back to Japan, I will continue to do it the Japanese way, but if I ever have my own temple, I know the way I'm going to go." And that's exactly what I've done. And I have found that it has given, on the whole, far more people an opportunity to find the Unborn than otherwise would have done. So, yes, be as "smart" as you

---

* The tan is a traditional raised platform, covered with mats (or, in our case, carpeting) on which one sits for meditation, formal meals, and some ceremonies in Zen temples.

Monks sitting in meditation on their tans.

can, be as alert as you can, but don't try to be different, physically, from the real you. Therefore, the most important thing
if you want to meditate is not how you put your feet or how
you do this or how you do that, because these various physical things can be corrected and they are to stop you having
stresses and strains when you are actually sitting. The main
thing is what you do with your mind. And that is the most
important thing I can tell you at this stage. Yes, go ahead. . . .

> *Question:* "Sometimes what seem like important
> insights come during meditation, but then it
> becomes difficult to ascertain whether I have moved
> into the realm of thinking."

I did a little trick with myself on that. I don't go into the
insights during the meditation: I have a sort of mental "pad"
onto which I "write" them, and then go back to meditating.

When the meditation is over, I "look" at this. You don't deny the mind, but now I'm doing this (i.e., just sitting). Frequently, you'll find the thought has cooked itself a lot better by the end of the meditation. And that also, if it won't go away, is when you decide to count breaths for a couple of occasions. If it's any comfort, the most experienced meditator has what I call "spear thoughts" thrusting up from underneath now and then. It doesn't happen too often, but they do take place, and I have this sort of mental "pad" that I keep notes on, then let the thought go.

> *Question:* "Sometimes while I'm meditating, I will sort of find myself 'coming back', but I don't know where I'm coming back from."

I wouldn't worry about that.

> *Question:* "I don't remember thoughts, and I don't remember actually being in meditation, and it actually feels at times as though I've either been meditating for a very long time or no time at all."

What you are talking about is extremely common. Now, the thing is this: you never know when you're meditating right. You only know when you're doing it wrong. So frequently, if you're doing it right, a whole day's meditation feels like you've been at it, maybe, ten minutes. And you then think, "My God, I was at it an awfully long time." If you're doing it right, you don't know. It's amazing how long you could have been sitting for. That is actually one of the reasons it is good to have a timing device (often a stick of incense will do; you don't necessarily need a watch), because you should never take it further than forty-five minutes without getting up for a bit. Even the experts don't sit for longer than that, because you can hurt yourself. If the great Zen masters say don't sit for longer than forty-five minutes without taking a walk, then that should be good enough for everybody else who does Zen meditation. When I first went to the East, I badly wanted to sit for hours and hours. And my master got very angry with me because he said not only was I trying to pretend to be more holy than the holiest of monks, I was being downright stupid. I didn't realize quite how stupid I was until, some years later, an American friend of mine took no notice of his master, who had warned him of this, and ended up with "water on the knee" in both knees, which meant he could never again sit except in a chair. If you force yourself, it's no good. Find a way of sitting that is comfortable and erect, as we've mentioned before, and then just push yourself gently to do a little more each day: only one minute more. If you can do six minutes comfortably, then do seven. When you can do seven minutes comfortably, do eight. And so on up to somewhere between thirty and forty-five minutes.

> *Question:* "What do you do if you find yourself drift-ing off while you are *not* meditating, while you are going about your business, and you find yourself in a state where you are not quite sure what you've been doing when you 'wake up'?"

That really should not be recommended. I'm not quite sure how one gets into that, because I personally have never had that as a problem, but I have known people who have done it. One of the ways they've dealt with it in the East is giv-ing the person the job of bell ringer, or something similar, so that they've got to ring the bell in the tower every ten minutes or every half an hour, and gradually their mind gets trained out of doing it. But you most certainly didn't put them in the kitchen where they were likely to chop their thumb off or something of that sort. You gave them a reasonably harmless job where, above all, they couldn't trip over anything, because people in this state tend to fall down steps or put their hands on hot stoves, this sort of thing. Almost always the bell ringing section was made up of people who had this problem: it just kept them safe and out of danger. So do anything of that sort you can think of, anything that you can do that simply. It's the best advice I can give you. But do everything you can to devise a means to prevent it happening, and when you find that it has happened, bring your mind back to what you are doing. To lose track of time in meditation is fine, as I said, to "go off" and only have it take a minute—so long as you are actually meditating and not daydreaming. It's also fine to "go off" when you're watching lousy TV, but that's another story. (laughter) But I don't recommend it when you're going about daily work, especially if you're doing something like driving a car. I knew somebody once who wanted to meditate when he was driving his car, and what I told him to do was what I also told people who didn't have much time to do formal meditation, and that was to make the gassho every time he was sitting at a red light. Doing that, he had to move and to bring his brain back "into gear" (he was always missing the green lights); it worked. He did a lot of driving. Anything that will work, but try not to let that happen.

Question: "How long did we meditate for just now?"

What is it? Thirty-five minutes? No, just under a half hour. How long did it feel?

Questioner: "I couldn't tell, but I sure feel good."

But you see, that's as it should be if you do it right: you should get up so totally refreshed, with all the organs relaxed and happy, that you are eager to do it again. But if you're forced, this is again the problem of asceticism. There is asceticism of body: "Thou shalt sit pretzel-wise, like a ramrod." There is asceticism of body where the eye is unable to move. And then there's asceticism of mind. The asceticism of mind is that which I talked about earlier, which says, "If I don't do it in such-and-such a position, then it won't be real meditation." You have to get rid of all that stuff and find that exact right way for you. One of the problems of doing it, and learning it, in a big temple like Sojiji where I was, is that it has traditions. You know, like you go to a very famous boarding school or to West Point or something: it has traditions. And one of these traditions was that if you hadn't been flogged a hundred times in the first year you were there, there was something wrong with you. If you hadn't sat like an absolute ramrod, there was something wrong with you. Koho Zenji, my master, who was the abbot, kept trying to get them out of the traditions. The more he tried, the more they dug themselves in. As he pointed out, all it was doing was producing people who went back acting like supermen ("Look what I went through for five years!"), but who weren't really good at teaching meditation. When the Head Office of the Soto Zen Church sent over a couple of people the year before last (they sent a couple of people over because I hold a mandate from them and they came over to see how people were doing), one of the things that was really fascinating was they were saying, "The young Japanese can no longer do this. How are you dealing with the fact that they can't sit like ramrods any longer?" And they were overjoyed to see what we'd done: we'd cut holes in the sitting tan so that you could move pieces about, you know, like a checker board. If you had to sit with your feet down, you took out the front bit (if you were facing each other for meals or a ceremony) and sat on the back bit. If you were facing the wall and couldn't twist yourself up, you took out the front bit, put the second bit where the first had been, and sat on that with your legs down. They thought this was a brilliant idea, because the new generations just won't do it, and as the old monks die off, they are having to find another means of doing it. Which, I believe, is going to make for far, far finer priests than the old system did, because people are not being forced into an asceticism which the body frequently just can't handle.

I have long legs: what am I going to do—put one foot up around one ear? We are not built for sitting like pretzels. Some of us can do that, especially ballet dancers and really first-rate athletes can do it, but even some of them can't do it for too long. Once they hit around forty, it begins to be difficult. That means that we have to find the right way for us. And it's interesting that as the Japanese get taller (and the young do seem to be doing that), they are having exactly the same problems that we've had. So remember, what matters is to sit naturally for you: alertly but naturally. And don't have weight anywhere: heads can be awfully heavy if you put them in the wrong places. So that is why we have this lovely tan in our two monasteries, Shasta and Throssel, where we can move bits, and it works. Nobody's excluded from the meditation hall because they have to sit on a chair and there's no room for chairs; you just remove a piece of tan.

Question: "Any tips on nodding off?"

Yes, one very important one is: if you're really tired, don't try to meditate. That's one of the other reasons why I was saying, "Don't think the Eternal is going to look down on you, or you're doomed, you're going to hell or anything of the sort, if you miss meditation." If you are really, really tired, don't do it. Because it's useless: you'll swear quietly to yourself because you've "got" to do it, and you'll nod off anyway. That's the first one. The second is never do it in a room that's too hot. For most people, the ideal temperature (and all countries and all schools of Buddhism agree on this) is between 60 and 65 degrees. Never meditate in bright sunlight or complete darkness. Have a nice room that you prefer; if it's very bright, hang a curtain in front of the window or the door that will darken it somewhat or take away the incredible brightness. If it's very dark, put on some candles or something other than the sort of electricity that they have in this hall, which can make the room very, very hot. You want to keep it as normal as possible. One candle, you know, on a small shelf or an altar, or one small light bulb if you don't want to use candles, will do just fine to give the necessary amount of brightness if the room is slightly dark. You should also be sure that you're wearing clean clothes: oddly enough, that has a great effect on meditation, on whether or not you go to sleep. Don't ask me why, it just does. Incense, or perfumed flowers,* or both, are excellent. A small statue is nice in there. You don't want a lot of furniture. We'll talk more about this later, about setting up a personal altar. Then just know that this is your very private place: you generally should not let someone else sit on your cushion or your place.

---

* Generally, Rev. Master Jiyu recommended artificial flowers or a live flowering plant rather than cut flowers, as they do not require the unnecessary taking of a plant's life.

Monk's comment: "Also, if you find yourself falling asleep every time you meditate, you might have to come to a meditation instructor and have your posture checked, because if you're leaning in any particular direction too much, it can cause that problem."

And there also may be a psychological problem in that something in you doesn't terribly much want to do this. That's the other problem, and you need to look and see if perhaps you're feeling guilty because this is not a practice that was done in a church or in a synagogue or something when you were young—which is why it's so important to know that meditation is pure prayer. There are all sorts of little guilts that can pop up. "I should be getting breakfast ready"; that's a favorite. Or, "I should be preparing supper", or "The dog hasn't been fed." They are all little guilts that can make you nod off for some strange reason. And next we are going to show how to do walking meditation, which, if nothing else works, this will stop you going to sleep.

Monk's comment: "If you still feel like you're asleep during *that*, you should go to bed."

Yes, if it doesn't work, I'd just go to bed. Now, what you do is that you get up and take a slow walk. Again, make sure your spine and head aren't heavy: don't have your head poking forward or try to push it back; you'll damage yourself. You put your hands gently on your sternum, one over the other, again placing them where they and the neck and shoulders are loose. Some oriental monks believe one should be very tense. This comes out of a Rinzai Zen belief that the more you tense up, the quicker will be the release to enlightenment. Well, it may work for some people, but for the majority of people I met it didn't work at all: all it did is hurt them. So, whatever you do, make sure your arms are as loose and comfortable as your head, neck, and shoulders: weightless, and then walk. Walk slowly, but walk properly. As most people know, I believe, the correct way is to start on the heel, round the side of the foot to the ball of the toes, so you don't go flat-footed. Go very slowly, step by step, around the room until your legs are much more alive from the meditation, then walk somewhat faster. Keep this up for about ten minutes of a fifteen minute break, then, if need be, go to the restroom, and then sit down again.

It is very important you do not get so stiff that your legs do not function. That is the word of warning that we get from these Daruma dolls which I'm sure you've seen around. They can't be knocked over, but they also can't walk. The traditional story is that Bodhidharma sat looking at a wall for nine years, without getting up. That tale, of course, has some flaws in it, as I am sure you must realize, but that's what was officially said. If someone were to actually do that, they'd lose the use of their legs. Do not place yourself in that position; do not do harm to yourself.

> *Second monk's comment:* "Some schools of Buddhism use walking as their primary form of meditation; we use it as an alternate for sitting. If we are doing a lot of sitting meditation, we'll alternate every half-hour or forty-five minutes with walking meditation. The hand position, by the way, is to take your dominant hand (I'm a 'lefty', so I use my left hand), close it gently, and put it roughly at the base of the sternum, somewhere in the general area between the belly button and the base of the sternum."

You want your arms loose.

A lay minister doing walking meditation.

Second monk continues: "Put the non-dominant hand gently over the dominant hand, like so [demonstration]. Let your eyes cast themselves downward to a point on the floor that's convenient in terms of their natural focus. For me that's about eight feet or so ahead of myself—six or eight feet, something like that—and then slowly walk, one foot in front of the other. And now your mind: instead of being aware of just sitting, let your mind be aware of just walking. Now, since just walking is a more active thing than just sitting, that, in and of itself, will keep you awake. Also the fact of the physical movement will keep you awake. Different types of Buddhists do this at different paces, different speeds. Some are literally running."

That's Rinzai Zen.

> *Second monk:* "We tend to do it very slowly and deliberately: you raise one foot, you bring it forward, you put it down; and you do the same with the next one."

And you keep the mind in the state of "Don't think and don't try not to think."

> *Second monk:* "You're not saying to yourself, 'Now I am raising my left foot, now I am putting it forward, now I am putting it down, now I am raising my right foot, now I'm putting it forward, now I'm putting it down.' We don't do that. There are forms of meditation that do; that's fine. This one doesn't. You just walk, and let your mind be aware of what you are doing."

There are people who say you should coordinate your breathing with this. Koho Zenji and I both agree: you breathe when you need to breathe, and you walk at a slow speed.

> *Second monk continues:* "Now, if your mind wanders and you stop paying attention to what you're doing, . . . "

You wobble.

> *Second monk:* "You won't take long to figure it out, because you start to fall!"

And it really does wake you up!

> *Second monk:* "It really does. You can either walk in a nice, clockwise circle if you wish, or, if you're walking

along a straight path, when you get to the end of where you plan to walk to, you just very gently and slowly turn clockwise. Be aware of what you're doing, and go on back to where you came from."

There are a lot of people who say you've got to hold the arms up like this [demonstrates holding them stiffly at midsternum level]. You find where they are comfortable, which for most people is around the bottom of the sternum.

> *Second monk:* "If you're holding them up high, it looks great, but just do it. See, note what happens to these muscles here [demonstrates tension in shoulders], okay? And the muscles in the back: you're going to be sort of holding yourself up by your muscles, and it's going to get sore and tired."

I can remember junior monks marching around like that. Oh God, poor kids!

> *Second monk:* "If you start by putting it too low, again it pulls something in here [again points to shoulders], and it also sort of pulls you forward and causes a slouch. You don't want that, either. So it's somewhere in between: there's a middle way."

> *Question:* "Could you say something more about the role of visions in Buddhist practice?"

It happens: just go straight on with your meditation. And maybe, as it was pointed out to me, it will be "the important thing", who knows; in the meantime, let's continue. They never, when I was in the Far East, said that having a vision was a wrong thing; they never said it was a right thing; they merely said, "Well, it could be important, and let's go on with training." So there was no pushing away, no grabbing. It's what they said in the *Rules for Meditation*: don't push, and don't try to grab; just sit. Don't have deliberate thought, don't deliberately think, don't try not to think; just sit. And things happen. I've often likened it to sitting beside a stream or a river, or underneath a bridge over the top of which is going a freeway: everything is thundering back and forth, and you're just sitting there under the freeway. And it's all going on; that's all right, no problem. You can sit under the bridge and meditate peacefully, and the freeway goes crashing and banging on. Nothing's going to disturb your meditation unless you get up on the bridge and start thumbing a lift. Just sit there and meditate. So, have you got any more bits?

> *Question:* "What is the difference between meditation and self-hypnosis?"

Well, self-hypnosis and trances are the same thing. You should be aware of sounds, smells, sights. It's the reason why one doesn't close one's eyes completely: you should be aware of these things. When someone has a genuine vision, in Buddhism, it is always, as it were, "superimposed" on very sensible, normal things that are around one. One can see, for example, the windows or the doors or walls in a room, and this is superimposed over it; so, reality is never lost sight of. The danger of going into hypnosis or trance is that the reality of one's surroundings can be lost sight of. And, if you find that you still go into trances despite having your eyes open, the way to prevent that from happening is to do it by the "beeper" system. Set a soft, gentle "beeper", like on a digital watch or timer, for every ten minutes of your sitting or every five minutes of your sitting. When it goes off, gassho (so that you make an actual movement), and then go back to sitting. And sooner or later your mind will get very used to not getting into that trance state, and you can then eliminate the "beeper". It'll work; I've seen it happen. But don't try an alarm clock: those things shriek your head off, and they will destroy the atmosphere for you completely. Those wrist alarms are very good, although some of them are a little too "burr-y". You want a nice, soft, sort of "beep beep" noise.

> *Question:* "Is it safer to sit in a chair? I mean, those cross-legged positions look so unnatural."

I would say it's safer, but there is one other thing I would tell you to do if you sit cross-legged, which will help: do half the period with one leg on top and the other half with the other leg on top, or sit one period one way and the next period the other. Never sit with one leg longer in one position than in the other position. You tend to cause the spine to pull out a bit. And I had a lot of problems with that one: I was going to a chiropractor every second day for a year to get that back to normal. And if I don't keep my mind "in gear" when I walk, to this day my right foot will start splaying slightly and I can pull the whole thing out again. So do not favor one over the other; you don't want to pull anything out. Also make sure that you're not sitting flat on the floor; make sure you've got a cushion underneath you that is comfortable and high enough and stuffed well enough for your particular weight. This is another problem that one of the experts on zazen pointed out to me as being a big problem over in the East. People tend to think you've all got to have the same size cushion. You've not: you have to find where the right height of the cushion is for keeping your spine correct, with your feet and head in a comfortable position. Again, there is no tension down the neck or weight on the spine. And for some people a bigger cushion, both physically bigger and stuffed tighter, is necessary. Oddly enough, for larger people a smaller one frequently is more effective; I've never quite known why. But it depends on the individual. Find out what is right for you, and experiment with your cushion.

> *Monk's comment:* "On the advisability of changing your posture: for the sake of your back, it is equally true in the "Burmese" (or "one foot in front of the other") position, as in the cross-legged ones, because the same thing holds true. The foot that is forward most is stretched, is extended. It's as if you were standing with one foot in front of the other: your hip is extended downward and that is what causes your back to go out. One hip will be lower than the other. So, for myself, it works fine just to sit with the other foot upper-most and forward-most in the next sitting. It doesn't feel necessary for me at this point to have to switch feet in the middle of the sitting, but if it's right for you to do that, it's very good to do."

Whatever you do, you must compensate with each foot or the back will go out; that's a guarantee. And chiropractors not only cost a lot of money, they hurt! (laughter) There's not much point in it. So, it's a very simple thing to deal with.

> *Question:* "I'm quite stiff, but I'd like to try meditating in some way other than a chair; are there any exercises that could help me do that?"

I have never used any exercises specifically for that purpose. Perhaps one of these monks could give you more information on that; I started rather late in life. But one thing I personally do, which I found keeps me in reasonable general condition, considering my age—I'm nearly 60—is I do a bunch of isometrics, the pitting of one muscle against another, which I can do sitting on a chair or sitting around the fire. And that tends to limber up the spine. But I don't walk as well as I'd like to, except on the flat. That is something that I've had as a legacy from the East ever since I came to this country. So helping people with legs is something I'm not so good at. Yes, go ahead.

> *Monk's comment:* "I think, in general, the one thing I've found is that there is so much variability in what you need that it is very difficult in a class like this to give general descriptions. I would, however, say that this is a general rule: that if you did some simple stretching (I am fond of the very basic Hatha yoga stretching exercises), some of the stretches for the back muscles and the legs, some that limber up the back, that will be likely to help. But everyone should just take it very easily and do what's right for themselves. I think that those exercises that stretch the muscles are preferable to those that exert the muscles. I think that the Hatha yoga approach of gentle stretching is preferable to the calisthenic approach of hurtling one half of the body against the other, like touching your toes, where you throw the upper body down at the floor."

Where, for me, my isometrics works best of all; so it's different for each person. There are a bunch of people in Shasta who do the Canadian Air Force calisthenics stuff, and they do very well on it. That's something I never get into with any of them: It's "the truth, the whole truth, and anything else that works" as far as I'm concerned on that one.

They know their individual body best. But I do agree that anything that stretches muscles is preferable. I have really found that isometrics work wonders on my spine and neck and other places, but that's probably because of my age. I'm hardly the sort that could do running in place for twenty minutes, as I occasionally hear "crunch, crunch, crunch" coming out of upstairs rooms. I'm not quite the age that can do that any longer. One of the things that helped me in the East was that when I was young I used to do a tremendous amount of dancing, and if I hadn't done that, I'm not at all sure what would have happened. I also did a fair amount of fencing when I was young and that helped too. But neither of those would I get up to now, other than an occasional jig around my room when nobody is about. (laughter) So that's the situation. Next question please?

> *Question:* "Regarding meditating in a chair, I read that you should sit on the edge of your chair; is that right?"

Well, you don't want to sit back in it, but if you sit too much on the edge, then you will find that the edge of the chair will cut into the thighs and start making circulation difficult. You want to find a comfortable place on the chair where nothing is going to cut into you but definitely not sitting back against the back of it. That's the point, and everybody is going to be different on that. There's no way you're going to be able to line them up in a straight line and be able to go around with a yardstick, which is what they do in the East, or what they did in Japan.

> *Question:* "Since I've been meditating it seems to me that I've become more aware not only of things in the present, but also of my own past; is that usual?

Sometimes it is so strong that tears come up while I am sitting."

Meditation does break down the barriers that we have set up to what has happened in the past. Meditation dissolves what we have hidden things in, the things referred to in the old statement of "Time will bury everything if you sit back and give him a chance to use his shovel." One of the things you definitely do, when you meditate, is you start unburying things that you have buried, which is one of the reasons that some psychologists feel that it is useful for people who've got stuff stuck. And if you are having tears coming up, you are likely to have memories come up. And if you look at them, now, in this state, you can see why certain things happened and you can start realizing that they no longer need to control you. So many people live in the past, with the hope of the future. They don't live in the now, because the now is so painful. And it frequently happens that people who have difficulty with living in the now have a lot of stuff buried— not necessarily, but they sometimes do. And this stuff comes up because you are, so to speak, unfreezing things within yourself. That will cause that to happen; don't worry about it. When you actually have a full kensho much worse things than that will happen! (laughter) I always warn people to carry a dime with them, if they are meditating, just to be able to call somebody if something should happen. If you remember reading many of the old books on Zen, you will remember that it is said quite clearly when somebody has a full kensho sometimes they laugh, they cry, they roll on the ground, they kick like babies, they scream like children. Just imagine what would happen if one of these monks here suddenly had one and started doing that in the grocery store. I can tell you roughly what at least someone would do, and that is to go out and call an ambulance to take them up to that place on Parnassus Street (Langley Porter Psychiatric Hospital). (laughter) And if you are in meditation, and you've been doing it really seriously, this sort of thing is likely to happen at some time or other. Now, nothing is going wrong with you, and you are not crazy nor are you going crazy. What has happened is that you've undone all these watertight doors that you've fastened up inside yourself, and all this pent-up emotion and stuff are coming out of you. It's going to go away in a very short time, but try explaining that to an ambulance man when you're kicking with your clothes flying in the air. It does happen. So always keep a dime with you so you can call somebody who can get you out, if you're traveling around. You do not want to be placed in such a situation. If you are meditating that well, and things are already beginning to loosen up, I strongly recommend you have a dime with you. You'll love it when it's over; it's worth it, but do take precaution.

> *Question:* "At what point would you recommend that someone check in with people; I mean, how strange do you let it become before you really need to be getting some advice?" (laughter)

Always know someone—a trained meditation teacher—you can call on the phone. It's not necessarily advisable to have someone sitting with you, though most people find that helpful. But some people find this such a personal thing that they really have difficulty sitting with other people. But always you should have someone you can call. At what point should you do it? Our friend here mentioned that tears come up, and when that starts you need to have someone to take advice from—or when you have a lot of laughter come up, or a lot of shaking, or a lot of twitching. Twitching especially: twitching can mean that you're getting fairly deep in. And there are a lot of very funny twitches that can come out of someone. If you suddenly have the sort of reflex action that somebody gets when a doctor bangs his knee with a hammer, without any reason, that's when you need to be able to call somebody. Not because it's going to do you any harm: it merely means that the doors are beginning to dissolve and you might need some advice. You're not going to need to go anywhere, or get a doctor or anything; there's nothing wrong with you in that sense. You're just getting rid of all the tensions. One of the things meditation does, by the way, is to reduce high blood pressure, because those tensions are what is causing tension in the blood. So that's one thing that happens.

Another time to get some help is when you're slowing down. If someone tells you that you seem to be getting slower, or if you personally feel that you're getting slower, then that is the time to call, too. This meditation is not to make you sick: it is to make you completely and absolutely well in body and mind. If you find you are getting slower, if you find you are getting less alert, less intelligent, you had better ring up, or go and see, someone who knows about meditation, because you are doing something wrong. What it should do is make you a good 50 percent or 75 percent more alert than you are right now. If it is damaging that side of you, then somewhere along the line you are either sitting incorrectly or using the mind incorrectly. You should not be going around like a zombie or a "drowsy cow", as some people were once likened to in England. That is not the purpose of meditation. The finding of the Unborn will make you alive, alert, and very dynamic. But remember, that's not the purpose you go looking for It. You go looking for It because that is the purpose of life and death. So remember, if you find anything of that sort happening, ring up whoever it is you regard as your teacher and find out what it is that you are doing wrong.

> *Monk's comment:* "One comment on this general area. One thing you might consider avoiding is, when something slightly unusual does happen, the mind will naturally tend to say, 'Oh boy, something is happening, here we go!' And it's the natural tendency of the mind to do that, but understand that as soon as you do that, what you've done is created a duality."

You've closed it down again.

> *Monk continues:* "You can't avoid that happening, but understand that when it does happen, it totally puts the brakes on the process. So try to simply understand that sometimes unusual things happen, sometimes they don't. They may happen for years, they may happen only once or twice, before an opening of sorts."

I've had people sit and have one particular twitch go on for five years. And, remember one other thing: don't start meditating unless you're willing to go the whole way. Because, if you start off, and do a bit, and then stop, the process may not necessarily stop. And, for example, you may be out one day and suddenly you'll twitch violently for no apparent reason. A lot of people go to doctors to find out the causes of these twitches, and then they're told they have something for which there is no apparent cause or reason. And the poor person goes away wondering if they've got some special strange disease. Whenever I hear of that, what goes through my mind is, "I wonder when they meditated properly?" because sometime or other he or she allowed the release mechanism to start. And after a certain amount of time, you can't stop it. So, if you don't want to go the whole way, you shouldn't start.

> *Question:* "Are you saying that these things come to you during meditation, realization of your . . . of maybe something that you've done and are sorry for, for example?"

It usually comes to you when you're not expecting it. It can come in meditation; it can come while you're lying in bed, when you're sitting relaxing. I have known somebody drop a pan full of fried chicken in the process of putting it on a stove when they suddenly truly saw what they were doing in eating their fellow beings. It can come at any time. Usually there is no violent or dangerous reaction: I've only ever known this one person who had the accident out of hundreds and hundreds of people who've had it happen. But I can't say that it will never happen that there won't be an accident at the time, because I know of the one with the pan of chicken. I'm not going to pretend it can't be that way.

> *Question:* "If we sit down to meditate, do we have that intent in our mind: that I am praying for the purpose of meeting the Unborn?"

That's the only purpose you should be meditating for.

> *Question continues:* "But do I actually hold that thought consciously in mind?"

No, just sit. If you hold that in your mind, then you won't find It. You just sit there, still. And just the process of being still will cause it to happen. You see, what you've got to understand is that all this past stuff that you've buried is, as it were, clouds that hide the sun. As you sit in meditation, if we use the analogy of the Unborn being the sun, you are sitting there under a bunch of clouds. As the clouds clear, so It appears, naturally.

And you will have all this stuff to go through, stuff to come up and to deal with. Some of it you can't deal with because it's so old it's impossible. Some of the stuff way back from my childhood . . . half the people are dead anyway. The best thing then is to wish it hadn't happened, and to make sure it doesn't happen again: it's that simple. There's nothing more you can do. But you do what you can; it's the intent that matters more than anything else. What you're really doing is clearing away the clouds that hide the reality so that you can find What was always there. But you don't sit there thinking about that; you do what must be done because it must be done.

Buddhism contends, and I believe and have proved for myself, that there is nothing hiding the Eternal from us other than ourselves. We have hidden It from ourselves, and we go on hiding It from ourselves by using external means to cover up what we do and to keep ourselves interested, distracted, because it would be too painful for some of us (or so we think) to take a look at what is inside. But one has to remember, the Eternal will never allow anything in this process of clearing things up (or we won't allow it, whichever way you like to look at it) that will actually do us complete, deadly harm. You will never have anything come up that you cannot really deal with. However unpleasant it may seem, we can deal with it; it won't come up unless we are ready to deal with it.

Question: "A number of friends I know who have meditated in the past ended up discontinuing after six months to a year. It seems like it's a fairly common experience. I had the same experience myself, and I'm not sure what sort of resistance people come up against after they've been doing it for awhile, but for me it seemed as though I got to a point where it became uncomfortable dealing with the . . . the 'nothingness', in a way. I'm wondering what your experience with people has been about that?"

Now, that's why I started these lectures the way I did. If you tell somebody it's just nothingness, after a bit they're going to sit there and say, "So what?" But, you see, if you're over in the East and you really understand the language, they explain to you what the "nothingness" is, and, as I've said, it's the fullest nothingness you ever bumped into. You know what you've gone there for, and therefore that doesn't set in.

There's another thing that sometimes happens to people, which may be what you're referring to here, and that is when someone first starts to meditate, it's frequently quite interesting: it's new, and also things happen, okay? But after awhile the newness wears off, and then the hard work begins, and if people have no notion of why they're doing this in the first place, then, when "interesting things" stop happening, they're at a loss. They think they're doing it wrong or there's no point; it "isn't working". But it is normal to have long periods where nothing "interesting" happens. It's somewhat like digestion: you can't always be eating dessert; you need to eat mostly good, plain food and then take awhile to digest it.

So there is no reason to despair: remember, "Anybody who comes to meditation", said my master, "runs the risk of being grabbed by the Cosmic Buddha." And this is not a popular thing to say, at least in the West. I'll tell you another story about this. I can remember him telling this to a couple of British professors who turned up with all these lovely theories in their heads, and they said, "Oh, this is not a Zen master! He's talking about gods!" And they went back to London and they wrote some dreadful things about him, and he wrote them a letter back saying, "Thank you very much for your article. It's nice to know that the professors at London University know more about Zen masters than the Archbishop of Tokyo." And they didn't even see what he'd said, but it was a good point. It comes out of this misunderstanding that took place way back in the 1880s, 1890s. We're still reaping the consequences of that, and one of the things I'm trying to do is to stop that. There are people even today who look at me and say, "But, you're wrong!" And, you know, I don't care whether they say I'm wrong or not; it doesn't worry me.

Right: friends, you have seen this morning something of how meditation is done. I'm sure, because we went through the meditation instructions somewhat quickly, that there will be a lot of other questions you will want to ask, and some of those questions you may not want to ask in public. This afternoon, if there are any questions you would like to ask in private, please see one of my two assistants for that purpose. And, of course, there will be another question and answer period.

3.

How to Live the Life of Buddha

This afternoon you will see what sort of a lifestyle comes out of this kind of training by means of seeing what the Buddha did after His enlightenment. Everybody is so busy talking about how wonderful it was and what He went through to get to His enlightenment; almost nobody talks about what He got up to afterwards. In other words, when you have found the Eternal, how do you show to the world what you have found? How do you express it? What does an enlightened person do? I was told once, by the way, when I was speaking at the Hilton in San Francisco, that "Enlightened people always burn incense." They then went around and proceeded to place bunches of incense out on the carpet and light them, and they got very upset when I informed them that enlightened people did not burn down the San Francisco Hilton! (laughter) Studying and following a way of life based on enlightened action, even though we do it imperfectly, is the other foundation of Zen, alongside meditation. The latter brings us to the Truth from the inside out, the former brings us to the Truth from the outside in: they complement and nourish one another. Both are necessary.

REALIZING THAT ACTIONS HAVE CONSEQUENCES:
THE LAW OF KARMA

Now I'm going to ask one of my assistants here to read the next portion of the *Shushogi*, so that I can go through it in depth. This particular scripture, by the way, was not written as one complete scripture. Around the 1880s or '90s, the Soto Church in Japan took parts of the *Shobogenzo*,* the main collection of Dogen Zenji's works, and put them together to make one scripture that would include the most important parts of the *Shobogenzo* for ordinary people like you and me. So if you look through the *Shobogenzo*, you will not find this scripture, but you will find paragraphs of it in various other chapters. I just wanted you to know the sources because I know that some people sometimes go back, hunt for the *Shushogi*, and say, "Where is it?" Well, it was put together. Remember what I've said of the sort of person who comes to study this: good, ordinary people. By "good" I don't mean "do-gooders", but people who are sincere, who really want to find something with which they can do something with their lives, and help others.

> *Scripture:* "Avoid the company of those who are deluded and ignorant with regard to the Truth of karmic consequence, the three states of existence and good and evil. It is obvious that the law of cause and effect is not answerable to my personal will for, without fail, evil is vanquished and good prevails; if it were

---

* Several complete and partial English translations of this work are available, including those by Nishiyama et al., Nishijima and Cross, Rev. Master Jiyu-Kennett, and Rev. Hubert Nearman.

not so, Buddhism would never have appeared and Bodhidharma would never have come from the West."

Avoid the company of those who do not understand karmic consequence. Those who do not understand karmic consequence are those who do not know that Buddhism has precepts, or who think that because they had an enlightenment experience, a glimpse of the Eternal, they are free of karma. Karma is an inexorable law: if you do wrong—if you harm other beings—there will be consequences. If you steal, there are consequences. I shall be going into this in great detail with you in a few minutes in this lecture. If you kill, there are consequences. Just because you have had an enlightenment experience does not free you from those consequences. Unfortunately, in this country, and in England too (as a result of many really good Oriental teachers who could not speak the English language terribly well), a grave misunderstanding has occurred. I have heard them tell people, "You are totally free once you find the Eternal." They are right! And God help you if you take that too far. You *can* do anything you wish, you *are* totally free once you know the Eternal, and even before you know the Eternal, *if you are willing to take the consequences of what you do.* The fact that you know the Eternal does not free you to do as you like, because then you have misunderstood the thing totally. And what you have done is gone straight into sorcery: "Do what thou wilt shall be the whole of the Law."* There are precepts in Buddhism, just as there are commandments in Christianity

---

* This phrase was attributed to Aleister Crowley as being the essence of the teachings of his modern Western sorcery.

and Judaism. The only difference between the two is that a commandment says, "Thou shalt not . . ." and a precept says, "I'll do everything to teach myself not to do. . . ." In one case you are doing it with yourself, in another case somebody is telling you not to do it. It doesn't really matter which way 'round you want to think of it; the main thing to realize is that you can't do it! That's the point at issue.

One of the things that has brought a lot of people, especially Westerners who teach Zen, into disrepute is the fact that they think that because they have had an enlightenment experience they are totally free of karma, and they are not. I can remember meeting a couple in Japan who were convinced that anybody who studied the precepts was just plain silly: what you had to do was get beyond the opposites, and then you were totally free. The only time I saw my master, Koho Zenji, shudder was when I told him this. And he said, "I fear for Zen if this is so." So please remember, if you meet a teacher who says he or she can do as they like, without karmic consequence, without "comeuppance" if you like that term better, watch out! That's a very dangerous person.

That is what this paragraph is talking about. We are not talking of anarchy and all that sort of stuff, we are talking of responsibility. Buddhism teaches responsibility: you are responsible for you; you are responsible for everything you do; there is nobody who is going to take the fall for you. There is no savior in Buddhism. You have to be an adult, you have to be responsible. I was asked on one occasion, "What do you think is the second most important thing people get out of meditation, seeing that finding the Eternal is the first?" I said, "Learning to be responsible, totally responsible, adults." This, above all, is the second thing you will get out of this, because when you find what the real consequence of breaking the precepts (or the commandments, for that matter) is, you discover that the person you have hurt is you. A person who steals, steals their own peace of mind. A lot of people do not realize this; they steal from themselves. I'll go into that a bit further on. Would you read the next one? This is all connected together.

> *Scripture:* "There are three periods into which the karmic consequences of good and evil fall; one is the consequence experienced in this present world, the second is consequence experienced in the next world and the third consequence experienced in a world after the next one; one must understand this very clearly before undertaking any training in the way of the Buddhas and Ancestors, otherwise mistakes will be made by many and they will fall into heresy; in addition to this their lives will become evil and their suffering will be prolonged."

"Why does so-and-so get away with something and nothing happens to him?" Give it time. This isn't the only time 'round. There will be consequences. And another point to watch with regard to this responsibility is this: supposing something is set up by a person and he or she dies before the consequences hit. Some poor being in the next generation or the generation after that will take the consequences of this. The best example I can think of this is World War II: what England and France did to Germany in Versailles in 1918 was so absolutely insulting that it guaranteed that someone like Hitler would come forth. And my generation reaped World War II. Be very careful what you set up, what you do: your actions this time around may not hit you, but there are other people to be concerned about. You have to take the responsibility of being sensible and not vindictive, for it will come back on a nation, or a family, or even fall on individual people, who have really nothing to do with it except that they inherited the karma. I blame the country of my birth very heavily for what happened. Germany was reduced to total poverty. Somebody, a crackpot admittedly, turns up and says, "You don't have to feel that way", and the consequences are already in action. When you understand responsibility, understand it thoroughly. And, as they said, evil will arise. Be very careful what you do. Study each of these paragraphs with great care. Dogen was absolutely brilliant; he saw these things very, very clearly. If you would emulate him, or the Buddha, remember these were just ordinary men who took the trouble to go looking for the real answers to life; since they were ordinary men, you can do this too. The Ancestors were ordinary men and women (there were plenty of women who've done this; don't think that, when I use the word "men", I am leaving women out of it). Think carefully what responsibility means: know that your every action will have a consequence. The fact that there will be karma does not mean you must not act, because there will be consequences of that as well. You can't live that way, as the next paragraph's going to tell you.

This brings me to: "Is there a soul that reincarnates?" And the answer is no. There is not a separate soul in Buddhism. To get to become one with the Unborn and the Undying is to become one and not many. That is why I use the terminology "becoming one with the Unborn". To use a simile I have used many times, in this room some of the lights are on, some are off. Whether they are on or off, there is just the same amount of electricity. If you think of the electric current as the Unborn and the Undying, then sometimes "we're" plugged into it and sometimes "we" don't seem to be. Sometimes "we" are alive, and sometimes "we" are dead, but still there is the same amount of the Unborn. If you understand it from that angle, then what I am speaking of is not going to be frightening. Once a person really takes his training, or her training, in their hands to do something about it, such things as separate souls or separate individual existence after death lose their importance.

And once one finds the Unborn, the immensity of the thing is so great, so vast, that, as an individual, one's own insignificance becomes overwhelming. It is overwhelming to such an extent that there is no point whatsoever in thinking, "Could there possibly be a separate soul?" Now, after all, look at what it is you're trying to do: to become one with the Unborn. Why would you want to become *two* with the Unborn? Are you asking to become God, or to become one with God? The Buddhists say, "I am not the Unborn, and there is nothing in me that is not of the Unborn." Or, as a Christian would put it, "I am not God and there is nothing in me that is not of God."

To separate oneself off, in Buddhism, is to wish to have a separate soul. This is the difference, then, between rebirth and reincarnation: to be reborn, out of the Unborn and Undying, is one thing. To be reincarnated as a separate entity is quite another. Therefore, when the Buddha taught that karmic consequence is inevitable, whether in this life or a subsequent one, do not take this to mean that there is a "you" that will reincarnate down the ages. People are neither born differently, nor born not differently, from someone who has died: ultimately, there is just the Unborn and Undying. As to karma, think of it as a mound of karma, which, as we are born, people pick up lumps of and deal with; and when they've cleaned 'em up, they are back with the Unborn again (which they actually never left, but couldn't see because of the clouds in the Clear Sky). And as to the physical body, at death it will be eaten by worms and the like, and thus it will be "recycled". There never has been a separate individual soul nor a separate individual body which we can call our own. Always and in all respects "we" are part of the never-ending flow of the Eternal.

I used to keep what I call a "wiggle-woggle lamp", which was one of those lava lamps. Have you ever seen them? You know, there's this huge glob of stuff, and it "bloops" up, and sometimes it's separate and it falls down, and it keeps massing around, and you never get two bloops quite the same. Very valuable for teaching how the Unborn works: we "bloop" here and "bloop" there, and we're never quite the same person. Therefore, anyone who really takes the trouble to try and do something about the mountain of karma that he or she happens to be carrying is literally saying to the Unborn: "I want to do Your work. I want to help clean up this mass of karma." And that is what they are doing. And when that is cleaned up, there is the pleasure of being one with the Unborn and the Uncreated for the rest of this lifetime.

What happens when you go back to the Unborn at death? I don't know. I hope I don't have to come back again. But if I'm required to "bloop" again, then I will. And I'll pick up some more and deal with it. The point is to clean it up and to get back There as soon as possible so that you can help others to do the same thing. The details of what happens after you're dead are not of importance.

> *Scripture:* "None of us have more than one body during this lifetime, therefore it is indeed tragic to lead a life of evil as a result of heresy for it is impossible to escape from karmic consequence if we do evil on the assumption that, by not recognizing an act as evil, no bad karma can accrue to us."

"I won't do anything; then nothing can accrue to me."
Meanwhile, over the road, the blinds and the shades are up
and there's somebody strangling his wife. That is not Buddhist action! "Oh dear, I'll get involved; I don't want to get
involved." You have to get involved; otherwise something
much worse can happen: somebody can die. There is no
escaping karma. And it doesn't just have to be bad: karma is
good and bad, and there is doing the right thing as well as
doing the wrong one. If you do what you do because you
truly believe that this is the right thing to do, yes, there may
be bad consequences, but you've still done the right thing.
You must know this. Just as much as you must know that if
a master does something that is contrary to the precepts
(and there is the famous story of the master who beat the
deer, and all his monks were horrified), then you have to do
what the monks did: quite seriously and respectfully ask him
why. His answer was that there are too many hunters: if the
deer trust men—that they will feed them as the monks had
been doing—then they will come down and they will be
killed. They have to naturally distrust men, because men
frequently want to kill them. But the master took the consequences of the act. I often suspect that several of his
monks walked out in disgust. It was a cruel action; it was
contrary to the precepts. Sometimes one has to do something that is contrary to the precepts, and, as I have pointed
out to my monks whenever I do that, don't go off in a huff
and a huddle and sort of talk about me behind my back,
come and ask me why I did it. And I will give you an
answer, because I am trying to live the best way I know how
within the situation, a situation that cannot necessarily
always be ideal, even in a monastery.

So remember, that because you do not recognize an act
as evil, because you wish to just sit in your meditation and

do nothing, doesn't excuse you from the consequences. In fact, it means that you have robbed yourself of your own responsibility and your own peace of mind, because you know it's wrong. How many of these TV things have you seen where people haven't come forward because of nervousness, and they have gone through hell for a few nights and finally come forward to say something? They could have saved themselves the hell of a few nights. And, yes, perhaps the consequences will be serious for them, but I would prefer to risk that than not. So keep this in mind: because you do not recognize an act as evil, does not get you off the hook. This principle applies, by the way, not only to inaction where action is called for, but also to deliberate ignorance—to not looking at the consequences of what one does—in the belief that if one is not aware of the harm one is doing, there is no responsibility for it. It does not work that way. Wonderful practice, magnificent meditation. I suppose you could say, "Practice what you preach", but that's not really it. When you meditate, you must live up to that meditation, and you must live up to what that meditation implies: true faith and genuinely true responsibility. This is for adults, as I have said; it is not for spiritual children.

> *Scripture:* "Freedom is gained by the recognition of our past evil acts and contrition therefor. Because of their limitless compassion the Buddhas and Ancestors have flung wide the gates of compassion to both gods and men and, although karmic consequence for evil acts is inevitable at some time during the three periods, contrition makes it easier to bear by bringing freedom and immaculacy: as this is so, let us be utterly contrite before the Buddhas."

Yes. What we are speaking of here is what I was talking about to our friend about all the stuff that comes up when meditation starts to break down the walls we have built against seeing who we really are: as it comes up, deal with it, allow it to go, and above all, sit up straight and face yourself and say, "Yes, I did this; I am going to do something about it." And get on and do it, if it is possible. And if you need help in doing it, get some people to help you. These things have to be dealt with. The beauty of meditation is that it will assist you in doing it, and, as the scripture says, you will gain freedom and immaculacy. There is a difference between immaculacy and emptiness. Bodhidharma, the great master who brought Zen from India to China, wrote a very fine treatise on this. He points out that "emptiness" is a word you can use because it stops you grabbing on to something, but It is something much more than emptiness: It is an Immaculacy of Emptiness, the Eternal. You can't say It's something, you can't say It's nothing; you've got to get beyond this and experience It. Immaculacy means freedom to be one with the Eternal, having cleansed yourself of the karma, and, while you live, taking the consequences of that karma.

Again, this particular scripture, the *Shushogi*, tells you first the purpose for meditation and then tells what will happen in meditation as each thing comes up. And the first thing that comes up, after you've realized you must have faith in the Eternal, is all the junk that's got in the way that you need to clean off so that you can really see the Eternal. After all, if you will "make clouds in a clear sky", as one of the great Zen sayings said, don't blame me if you can't see the blue above it. Many people make clouds in a clear sky. All you have to do is watch the soap operas that are on TV of an afternoon to know that! Soap operas thrive on clouds in a clear sky: it's their main stock in trade; it's why they're soap operas. Therefore, get this stuff out of the way: let the old baggage come up, let it be looked at, let it be dealt with, get rid of it, and be free!

> *Scripture:* "Contrition before the Buddhas brings purification and salvation, true conviction and earnest endeavour: once aroused, true conviction changes all beings, in addition to ourselves, with benefits extending to everything including that which is animate and inanimate."

Because you have respect for all life, all things. Contrition comes out of recognition within oneself of the full reality of what one has done. The word "confession", yes it's right, too: you confess to yourself what you've done, but you also take a look at yourself and realize that you need to clean things up. Understand clearly what this is talking about. It is not saying you must go along to the police and tell them everything you did, although that may in some cases be necessary. But you need to look at what it is.

Now, the big problem that comes about here is that the word "confession" implies guilt to many of us, but it is not guilt that makes us deal with the things; it is simply the fact that we're now taking time to have a really good look at them. We're not driven to saying we're sorry because of the danger of punishment, or of being found out: we're driven to saying we're sorry because we do not want to repeat that which we now find we are carrying around within ourselves and which we have not actually, properly dealt with. So the words "confession" or "contrition" imply taking a good look at what's inside, and really trying to do something about it, and making sure it doesn't happen again; in other words, it is simply doing the best you can. Although this is the implication, it is not confession in the sense of confessing to guilt. Now, there may be some guilt in it, especially for those who have come out of other religious traditions, but a true act of contrition, called sange in Japanese, is having a full look at what is in there and saying, "Oh dear! Did I really do that? Was I really that stupid?" and taking a look at how and why, and making sure that it doesn't happen again.

Therefore, in this chapter, when speaking of this, Dogen says, "It is important to sit up straight in the presence of the Buddhas and Patriarchs." So you take refuge in the Sangha, in all of the people who know the Eternal, and you have a look at what is within yourself, because now you can see it without all the external distractions. You have a good look at it and say, "Right, how did those Buddhas of the past (for a Buddha is what you are to become, once you become one with the Unborn), how did those people in the past, deal with this?" Well, they had a good look at themselves, and they cleaned up as much of what they had done as they felt they could really do something about. Maybe that's just writing letters to somebody saying you're sorry for some way you hurt them. It can be a number of different things; or maybe you have to do some act to help someone whom you have injured or hurt. All these things have to be taken care of to the extent that is possible and wise. Once you have done all of this, you'll have done what the Buddhas and Ancestors have done in the past, and you'll have sat up straight in the presence of the Buddhas and Ancestors. You've not pretended you didn't do it, but you did not deal with these issues out of guilt. You dealt with them because they had never been dealt with. You were carrying them around with you. And, oddly enough, all such acts, whether they are just unkind words or whether they are actually acts of violence, will cause various tensions throughout the body. As you meditate, so these things come up, and the tensions fly off as you deal with them. We all do take the consequences of our actions at all times, but not as the average person thinks we take them: we carry them around within us automatically.

Now, I said that all this can be looked at in another way as just doing the best you can. Just doing the very best you can changes all things, and that is really all you are asked to do, but have you ever thought what a huge thing "to do the very best you can" is? It's colossal! I can remember being in the Far East and complaining bitterly to my master, the Archbishop of Tokyo, whose secretary I was at the time, that I couldn't begin to do what he wanted me to do because of all the difficulties that people were throwing in the way, and he kept saying to me, "All I ask is that you do the very best you can." And one day I realized what he was saying to me, which was, "Do the *very best* you can." When I heard the words he was actually saying, which was do the *best* you can, then it worked, and within about two months I discovered I'd got about four hundred people in his Foreign Section, which made him very happy. But I had to find out for myself what it was he was asking me to do. Above all, I had to discover what it was *I* was trying to do, and I wasn't trying to do what he was saying for those first two months; I was doing something rather different. So remember, you are required to do the *best* you can. That this does, or does not, have the desired consequences is fine. That this is not what you would necessarily like to do is fine. According to the Buddhas we should always be "disturbed by the Truth". To be disturbed by It means we should always be not completely satisfied with our own training. Any time somebody comes to me and says, "I don't think I'm doing as good as I could", something inside me rejoices. Any time somebody comes to me and says, "So do I need to ask any more questions? I think I've got it now", I am in terror, because we're about to have somebody go out and polish their halo and sit on a throne. It's important to know that "they travel fastest who are not there", as Dogen put it.

Therefore, do not be worried if you occasionally break the precepts; sometimes the world will force you to. Without meaning to, you will find yourself doing things you don't want to do. Put on one of its lowest levels, I came up from Santa Barbara recently with somebody who was breaking the speed limit all the way. If he hadn't, it would probably have killed a whole lot of people on the freeway because everyone else was going even faster. It was unfortunate; one does the best one can, and still it is necessary to wish one was not breaking the law, and yet one must do the best one can. But you understand what I am saying: do not get caught up in rules and regulations so that they make it impossible for you to move, and also recognize that if you break them there will be a consequence, and don't be afraid of it. This is not a religion for spiritual children; it is a religion for spiritual adults. There is a big difference.

> *Scripture:* "Here is the way in which to make an act of perfect contrition. 'May all the Buddhas and Ancestors, who have become enlightened, have compassion upon us, free us from the obstacle of suffering which we have inherited from our past existence and lead us in such a way that we may share the merit that fills the universe for they, in the past, were as we are now, and we will be as they in the future. All the evil committed by me is caused by beginningless greed, hate and delusion: all the evil is

committed by my body, in my speech and in my thoughts: I now confess everything wholeheartedly.' By this act of recognition of our past behavior, and our contrition therefor, we open the way for the Buddhas and Ancestors to help us naturally. Bearing this in mind, we should sit up straight in the presence of the Buddha and repeat the above act of contrition, thereby cutting the roots of our evil doing."

Someone asked me yesterday, "How did you deal with this stuff when it came up for you?" This is the way I deal with it. There is the act of contrition, confession, or "the way to deal with it", whichever you prefer. The beauty of this particular thing is it says, "They were (these Buddhas and Ancestors) as we are now, and we will be as they in the future." Nothing can come between you and your own Buddha Nature. Do not allow anyone to put upon you the fact, in their mind, that you can't make it. *Every single living thing can make it!* And anyone who tells you that you can't does not know anything about genuine religion! Sit up straight, face what you've done, face the karma that you have inherited which you need to clean up, accept and embrace it, send it to the Eternal, and be done with it. And know that, yes, if after this you do anything really horrendous, you will have to sit up straight again. But if you have done this truly once, the chances of your doing anything big, I would say, are infinitesimally small. You won't understand this if you do not understand the importance of responsibility: the importance of not making karma that others will suffer from. As we go into this next section, you'll understand a lot more about that. This lecture is a bit long, by the way. My apologies, but there is no way I can stop that.

PRECEPTS: THE EVERYDAY ACTS OF BUDDHAS

> Scripture: "Receiving the Precepts. After recognizing our evil acts and being contrite therefor, we should make an act of deep respect to the Three Treasures of Buddha, Dharma and Sangha for they deserve our offerings and respect in whatever life we may be wandering. The Buddhas and Ancestors transmitted respect for the Buddha, Dharma and Sangha from India to China."

I think there's a bit in the Bible somewhere which says that a man cleans up his house and comes back (all the demons are out of it), and he comes back and it's empty and clean, and "Oh, it's boring: there's nothing in here." So he goes out and gets a few more demons to bring in, because there's nothing there. The instant you have done this act of contrition we're talking about here, you must take immediate refuge in the Buddha, Dharma, and Sangha. Otherwise you will be casting about for something to take the place of all this stuff. Now, you've just got rid of it; who wants to scrub the house twice? Dogen makes it very clear: you've got to get the Buddha in there immediately. Faith, study, trust: they must take the place of the karmic baggage. You must get that in at once.

> *Scripture:* "If they who are unfortunate and lacking in virtue are unable to hear of these Three Treasures, how is it possible for them to take refuge therein? One must not go for refuge to mountain spirits and ghosts, nor must one worship in places of heresy, for such things are contrary to the Truth: one must, instead, take refuge quickly in the Buddha, Dharma and Sangha for therein is to be found utter enlightenment as well as freedom from suffering."

The main heresy of which they are speaking is teachers who say that if you find enlightenment (they usually don't say "the Eternal" because that smacks too much of the word "God"), you are totally free to do whatsoever you wish. This is why, when I teach Zen, the most important thing first of all is for me to speak of the Eternal, and the second thing to speak of faith, study and trust, and the third thing, responsibility. You need to talk about these things before somebody's got so involved in meditation that the baggage they've had is starting to come up and they're getting terrified out of their wits as to what happens. We had a lady come to Shasta on one occasion for a retreat, which is a meditation weekend. She was Christian, and she had never meditated before; she learned very fast, and that day a whole bunch of past life stuff popped out. She was terrified, because with her Christian background this could only be a bunch of demons, and what was this stuff that was coming up? Before anyone sits down to meditate (which is why I spoke to you the way I did yesterday), you must know that everything hidden will come up and that it's normal, and not be scared of it. And that it doesn't alter, it doesn't damage, your belief in God or anything else: you just must do something about realizing it takes place, not get worried about it, and be willing to look at it honestly and make some changes in your life. Okay?

> *Scripture:* "A pure heart is necessary if one would take refuge in the Three Treasures. At any time, whether during the Buddha's lifetime or after His demise, we should repeat the following with bowed heads, making gassho: 'I take refuge in the Buddha, I take refuge in the Dharma, I take refuge in the Sangha.' We take refuge in the Buddha since He is our True Teacher;

we take refuge in the Dharma since it is the medicine for all suffering; we take refuge in the Sangha since its members are wise and compassionate."

And the Sangha includes the laity.

Scripture: "If we would follow the Buddhist teachings, we must honor the Three Treasures; this foundation is absolutely essential before receiving the Precepts."

Yes, there has to be faith. You have to know that what you study, the Dharma (which comes forth from the Dharma Cloud, the cloud that hides the Eternal from our sight, as we say), is the medicine for all our ills. Remember: the "Buddha That Was to Come" was the "Doctor Buddha" who had cleaned up all His ills. We have to know that we can clean up all our ills, and we have to know that there are wise and good people who can help us. So, the taking of the Three Refuges is essential: it is the only thing that is really a formalized "prayer", if you like, in every school of Buddhism. After that, they all have differing bits and pieces, but this one is common to every single school.

Scripture: "The merit of the Three Treasures bears fruit whenever a trainee and the Buddha are one; whoever experiences this communion will invariably take refuge in the Three Treasures, irrespective of whether he is a god, a demon or an animal."

Now what they're talking of there is that whenever the trainee and the Buddha are one, whenever a trainee finds the Eternal, that refuge is immediately cemented.

Scripture: "As one goes from one stage of existence to another, the above-mentioned merit increases, leading eventually to the most perfect enlightenment: the Buddha Himself gave certification to the great merit of the Three Treasures because of their extreme value and unbelievable profundity—it is essential that all living things shall take refuge therein."

Now, the Three Refuges—taking refuge in Buddha, Dharma, and Sangha—are also called the First Three Precepts. Then come the Three Pure Precepts: cease from evil, do only good, and do good for others. Now these are not as obvious as they seem on the surface. Cease from evil: everyone can understand the words of that, but not everyone knows what "evil" is. Ceasing from evil is a collective precept about refraining from harming other beings that comes about as a result of having "evil" analyzed out into the Ten Precepts, which we will come to later. If you like, these Ten Precepts telescope into "ceasing from evil". Don't kill, don't steal, don't covet, etc.: these are what bring about "evil". You have to look at that. So, ceasing from evil, doing only good, and doing good for others are the Three Pure Precepts.

One has to also know what "doing only good" is, because "doing only good" for some is one thing and "doing only good" for others is another thing. Again, you have to take the Ten Precepts and telescope them into that. You then have to take the last one, which is "do good for others", and that is much more complicated, because what it really means is don't set up some karmic thing or other that will cause others to do wrong, just because you think it's good. The example I gave of what was done at the end of World War I is an exact example of that. That is going to bring about horrendous horror. You mustn't set up a chain of causation that will influence others to cause great harm. So you have to fit all the Ten Precepts into that one as well.

So if you start with the Three (cease from evil, do only good, and do good for others), you can literally turn—telescope—them upwards into the Three Refuges and downwards into the Ten Precepts. Because if you don't have faith in the Buddha, you're never going to be able to do this; if you don't have places where you can find out what "good" is and what "bad" is, and what "evil" is and all the rest of it, which is the Dharma, you won't have a rule of thumb to go by; and if you just think you are always right and never go and ask anybody, which is to take refuge in the Sangha, you will never get beyond your own opinions about all this. So, the Ten Precepts telescope up into the Three Pure ones, and they, in turn, telescope into the Three Refuges.

> *Scripture:* "The Three Pure, Collective Precepts must be accepted after the Three Treasures; these are:– Cease from Evil, Do Only Good, Do Good for Others. The following ten Precepts should be accepted next:– 1. Do not kill, 2. Do not steal, 3. Do not covet, 4. Do not say that which is untrue, 5. Do not sell the wine of delusion, 6. Do not speak against others, 7. Do not be proud of yourself and devalue others, 8. Do not be mean in giving either Dharma or wealth, 9. Do not be angry, 10. Do not debase the Three Treasures."

Now, the *Kyojukaimon** at the back of the booklet will speak of these in great depth. But the thing that each one

---

* Great Master Dogen, *Kyojukaimon: Giving and Receiving the Teaching of the Precepts* in *An Introduction to the Tradition of Serene Reflection*

telescopes into is very interesting. If you steal, in the end you realize that you stole from yourself. If you kill, you realize that you made yourself less than human. If you covet, you realize you have stolen your own peace of mind, because you are never contented. If you go against any of these precepts, the person who you harm, besides others, is yourself. Why do you make clouds in a clear sky? Do not make clouds in a clear sky. When you realize that all of this is "soap opera" that you have created in what was a very, very clear sky, you can start to see how to deal with these things. The First Noble Truth of Buddhism is that suffering exists: "there is birth and death", "how do I escape from it", "I am so frightened", etc. Suffering exists: pain, grief, illness, misery, family problems—they are all suffering. How do you deal with this, then? Suffering occurs because of a not understanding of the precepts, a non-keeping of the precepts. You take a look at yourself thoroughly as the stuff comes up in meditation, and you deal with it. The end of suffering comes when you find the Eternal and realize that the only way to live is by keeping the precepts. But you can't keep them in a nice, neat package, because they are always impinging on each other, so the aim has to be to do only good, to cease from evil, and to do good for others by not causing them to do evil.

Now, there are different forms of these precepts in Buddhism, which is something a lot of people misunderstand. For instance, the oldest form is, "I promise to undergo the rule of training to teach myself to refrain from. . . ." Think of the amount of qualifiers on that: there's a tremendous difference between that and "Thou shalt not". "I promise to

---

Meditation, 5th ed. rev. (Mt. Shasta, California: Shasta Abbey Press, 1997), pp. 32–36.

undergo the rule of training to teach myself to refrain from killing", or "... to refrain from stealing", or "... from talking against others". Another example of a different form occurs on the precept: don't sell the wine of delusion. Now, one form of this one is to refrain from abusing alcohol or drugs, and a lot of people think this is all it means. It isn't. It is also saying, "If you delude other people with your theories and your opinions, they will become 'drunk' on those theories and will not be able to use their own minds to see what is really going on." If you like, it is a precept against brainwashing. "Do not sell or spread the wine of delusion": a very important piece of Buddhist teaching.

Now, in applying these precepts, you bump into all sorts of complications. Would it be wiser to tell the truth in a certain circumstance and perhaps speak against someone? Would it be wiser not to tell the truth and not hurt them? What is the best way to go? The answer is: absolutely cease from evil; do everything with the best of intentions. That you may or may not make mistakes is another matter. All the Ten Precepts are subject to this very careful scrutiny: what am I doing; am I doing the right thing; am I doing the best thing?

Sometimes we have to break one precept in order not to do something much worse. Whether we break that precept or not, we are going to take the karmic consequences of what we do; we are going to grow some more karmic consequence. If we break one precept, we will take the consequences of breaking that precept, which may be a lot less than the consequences of not breaking it, because we would have then done something much worse. Once again: Buddhism is for spiritual adults; it is not for spiritual children. The Ten Precepts tell you what can cause karma; then you have to work out how to combine them properly so as to cause as little karma as possible. So, there is no such thing as irresponsibility in Buddhism. You have to be a terribly responsible person or you cannot be a true Buddhist. And you have to be willing to take the consequences of every action.

Furthermore, you have to "mix and match" your precepts so that they will telescope nicely into the Three Pure Precepts. When people say to me, "How do I behave? What do I do?" I say, "Well, you ask yourself three questions. First, are you ceasing from evil? If you get a 'yes' to that, you can go on and ask the second question: am I doing only good? If you get an answer that says 'yes' to that (and you ask these questions in the mind of meditation), go on to the next one: am I doing good for others? And if you get an answer that says 'yes' to that, then go ahead and do it. And you could still be wrong." It's important to know that you could still be wrong, because you might have got yourself in the way of it. So, because you always could be wrong, you then go and see a member of the Sangha. Whether that is a relative, a friend, or a priest, go and see someone who is outside of the situation and can perhaps help.

There is a saying in Zen, "When we find the source of the Yellow River, it is not pure." This means that however hard we try, nothing ever comes out quite as clean as we'd like it. (laughter) Keeping this in mind, remember that the person who gets hurt if you break the precepts is always you. If you go through the *Kyojukaimon* in detail, you will see how these things can harm you. It is you that gets hurt, along with a lot of other people. In other words, you've made a thunderstorm in a clear sky, which is an awful shame.

Now, how do you start putting these precepts into practice? Sometimes living by the precepts seems like such a daunting task that there's no point in even trying. Well, you

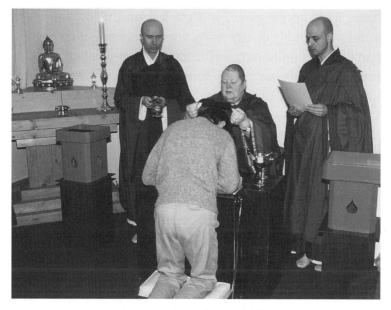

Accepting the Precepts at Jukai.

start by simply saying, "Okay, for today I am going to try to keep this precept, or that precept." I tell people, if they've never done it before, to pick one, and not pick the hardest, and see how well they can keep it for the day. I learned this from the Chinese; I really admire their practicality. There is a set of ceremonies called "Jukai" (the formal taking of the precepts) in all Buddhist countries, and only in China is it possible for you to take as many precepts during that time as you really feel you can keep. For example, a butcher would not take the precept against killing. A merchant usually does not take the precept against stealing, which I found faintly funny, and you will find prostitutes who will not take the one against sexual indulgence, and that is understood. So start by taking one you can keep and, having discovered the joys that come from keeping one, you work from the known to the unknown. And it is surprising what happens: several of the female monks who were in the monasteries had been former prostitutes who, having suddenly discovered the joy of keeping one or two, said, "I think I'll try to do a few more." Choose one you can go with; don't start the hardest way possible. Look at your character (only you can know your character thoroughly) and choose the one that is best for you, and that's the one you start with, and see how well you can keep it.

I used to love gossip at one time, and I can remember that I decided the one I was going to start with was talking about others, and I discovered that for three days I didn't say a word! (laughter) Which showed me how much wasted breath I'd been coming out with, and then I started thinking about how to talk to people and about what was truly useful conversation. So you start from the known and work to the unknown, and by keeping one precept you end up keeping the whole lot, and you end up knowing the Eternal, and that's really what you're out to do.

The fourth of the Four Noble Truths that the Buddha found was the Eightfold Path. Having got to the state where you've cleaned things up, you've dealt with the cause of suffering, now you come to the cessation of suffering, which is taking the precepts absolutely to the very best you can and being willing to always telescope them into each other and to go for help as needed (whether that be study, faith, or finding someone who can help you). When you've done that, then you can go on to what is called the Eightfold Path. That Path is the fruit of preceptual living: Right Thought, which leads to Right Speech, which leads to Right Action, which leads to Right Activity, and Effort and Determination and so on through the eight. Which comes back in the end to Right

Meditation, which is why you need to meditate night and morning even if it's only for a couple of seconds: it "puts your brain in gear" for what goes on elsewhere. If you put your brain in gear for only a few seconds or a few minutes, the day will be much, much better from every angle.

> *Scripture:* "All the Buddhas have received, and carefully preserved, the above Three Treasures, the Three Pure Collective Precepts, and the ten Precepts. If you accept these Precepts wholeheartedly the highest enlightenment will be yours and this is the undestroyable Buddhahood which was understood, is understood and will be understood in the past, present and future. Is it possible that any truly wise person would refuse the opportunity to attain to such heights? The Buddha has clearly pointed out to all living beings that, whenever these Precepts are Truly accepted, Buddhahood is reached, every person who accepts them becoming the True Child of Buddha."

On that note (which I don't need to explain at all because you are then one with the Eternal, at least until you break the precepts again, at which time you have to do something about it and then you are back), we will break for a few minutes. I told you this one was going to take a long time. [pause for rest break]

Now, can we have the next bit, please?

> *Scripture:* "Within these Precepts dwell the Buddhas, enfolding all things within their unparalleled wisdom: there is no distinction between subject and object for any who dwell herein. All things, earth, trees, wooden posts, bricks, stones, become Buddhas once this refuge

is taken. From these Precepts come forth such a wind
and fire that all are driven into enlightenment when
the flames are fanned by the Buddha's influence: this
is the merit of non-action and non-seeking; the awakening to True Wisdom."

This describes what happens at the time of finding the
Eternal: the realization that you are beyond the opposites;
there is no-thing that is outside of the Eternal, no-thing in
this world that is not part of the Eternal, no-thing in the universe that is not part of the Eternal. And the "wind and fire",
well, if you meditate properly, you'll find out about the
wind and the fire. It is after reaching this viewpoint that we
really commence true training. It is when you have reached
the realization that everything is doing the finest job it can of
being a Buddha that you are open enough and positive
enough to be able to do really good training. While you are
still nagging and grousing and griping about everything,
you are mostly just spinning your wheels. But it is when you
start looking positively and saying, "Well, if so-and-so knew
better, he'd be doing better, so he is showing his Buddhahood to the best of his ability at the moment" instead of
griping about how he is, it is when you start seeing that the
carpet is nice and warm for you to sit on rather than seeing
the spot that is on it, it is when you start seeing the good, the
Buddhahood, in things, that true training can commence in
earnest. It is the same with the precepts: while the precepts
are only rules that bind, not very much can be done, which
is the danger of the "Thou shalt not" idea; but once you have
got to the positive side, once you have given up fighting these
things and seen the Buddha within them, then true training
has well begun.

QUESTIONS

> *Question:* "I'm still not clear on why there is no self or soul, if the purpose of religion is for *me* to become one with the Unborn?"

That is the meaning of *Mu*: "nothingness". When the karma is cleaned up, the Unborn and "you" are one and the same thing, and you know there was no "thing" from the first. There is no "you" left, so how can any-thing go back to It? All you are is with It; you have found It. That is why the understanding of the character *Mu*, "nothingness", is so very, very difficult. Because you are stuck with a "nothingness" that's a . . . nothingness. Do you know what I'm saying? You're stuck with a something that's nothing, and "nothing" can be awfully big when you're stuck with it. But the point is not to get stuck with any-thing: neither a "something" nor a "nothing". So, what returns to the Unborn? Nothing. Once the karma is cleaned up, there *is* the Unborn and the Undying. I know it isn't simple; find That Place, you'll understand what I'm talking about. Anybody else? Yes. . . .

> *Audience comment:* "There's so much karma to clean up in this lifetime; so little time."

Don't worry.

> *Audience comment:* "But . . . the past—it's so huge!"

Oh, now that's very interesting. Hey, this man's got some good questions! That's very interesting indeed, because, you see, we judge ourselves by our own standards. Do not

think that the Unborn has our standards; It doesn't. That's
the first thing to remember. What we think was terribly bad
may not be of importance at all because what mattered most
was the intention. We tend to look only at the result. But the
Cosmic Buddha, the Unborn, looks at the intention. If the
intention was to do good then, yes, you're going to take
some of the consequences in this life of the action, but what
is going to come up at the time of death is: "Was the intention good, was the intention to do right, to cease from evil?
Was it an attempt to do good, or to do good for others?" And
that is where the thing matters most, not the result.

> *Question:* "What is the ultimate motivation behind
> the act of contrition? Why do people feel the need to
> clean these things up other than from guilt? I mean,
> I know we do feel that, and it's right somehow, but
> where does that come from?"

It is our longing to return to the Unborn, to the Undying. That is actually the motivation for everything, but you
don't realize that until you find It.

> *Question:* "Don't we also do it simply because we
> want to feel better?"

Yes, and when you see it that way, self takes an interesting turn. Now, "self" is what it sounds like: interested in
itself. And, when it realizes that it is hurting itself, it does an
about-face immediately and takes on a sort of intermediary
place between the non-egocentric self and the egocentric
self: "Well, if I do so-and-so, I'll help me a bit." And so it
has already started training itself, and it is sitting in the middle. This is a dangerous place to stay (you want to go on all

the way), but it does begin to see what it has been doing and takes a lot of care not to continue doing it, even if for primarily selfish reasons. So, what you are actually doing is genuinely cutting the roots of evil-doing, albeit for selfish reasons.

> *Question:* "In regard to the cleaning up of karma, it seems to me that sometimes, because of something we don't understand—some cloud in regards to one or two of the precepts—it can seem very confusing about whether we're breaking them, or how we're breaking them, or all of that."

You must not be afraid to break precepts, because that means you're afraid to make karma, and you can't stop making karma. One of the things that the Tibetans—at one of the Tibetan ceremonies (and one they do in Japan, too)—do is a ceremony to bless all the insects and microbes that you're going to murder in your breath and as you walk about. It recognizes that this is going to happen. The thing you must do is act from: "I take refuge in the Unborn, and I will do everything I can not to do harm." As I said this morning, when I come up against a really serious problem, the first thing I do is sit down in meditation and ask very seriously and very deeply, "Am I going to cease from evil if I do this act?" If I can get a "yes" to that, in the deepest part of me, then I sit down and ask, "Am I going to be doing good, and nothing more?" If I can get a "yes" to that, then I'll ask the next one, "Am I going to be doing good for others?" And if I get a "yes" to that, then I take refuge in the Sangha and know I can go ahead. But supposing I get a "no" to either of the two later ones yet I still have to act, then I have to say, "Okay, now I'm ceasing from evil and I've got to act: which one of these alternatives is going to do the least harm and collect up the least karma?" You mustn't be afraid of that.

> *Question:* "What did you mean then when you said once, 'Don't become like a centipede with wash-cloths', in regard to the constant looking and looking for more karma to clean up?"

You have to accept that you do make some karma. You can't mop up every tiny bit of it. You do the very best you can; the intention again is the main thing. Otherwise, you spend your entire life going around trying not to make karma and you never live at all. You're never really helpful, either. Yes, go ahead. . . .

> *Question:* "I think you may have just answered it—something like: you walk down the street of life and say, 'Look at all this dirt! It's going to take my entire life to clean it up: leaves, potholes. . . .'"

You clean up what you can. If you try to do it any other way, you're trying to become God. Don't try to become God; you can't. You start right where you are. I can remember they found a place for us to live over in England, which was—well, I've seen pigsties that looked a lot better—and I remember standing in the middle of this and calling for a broom. Somebody said, "Where do we start?" And I said, "Right here!" And I started in front of my feet: I mean, where else do you start under those circumstances? Right then and right there! Go ahead.

> *Monk's comment:* "I have a bit, a comment to two questions I was asked outside, and that has to do with

karma, which we were just talking about before. Karma is used by Buddhism as a natural law, but it is not the only natural law that Buddhism recognizes. There are five of them, in fact there are five whole sets of natural laws, and we aren't going to have time to go into all that because that's at least a weekend all of its own, but the point being, if what we've said makes sense to you, and you begin to think of things in terms of karma, don't go overboard to try to explain everything as a result of only karma."

There are four others.

Monk continues: "Amongst three others of those five are included things like all of the things which we Westerners would include in physics and chemistry, and biology, and psychology, and all that stuff. So don't take karma to the point of reducing everything to an explanation on a basis of karma."

Not all things are answerable to my personal will, is what he's saying.

Question: "Where does karma come from? I mean, is there a Supreme Being that might say, 'You're going to have to suffer this because you did something you shouldn't have done'?"

No: there's no Supreme Being that will do that. But there is a Greater You which will say, "Fine, you can do this; and there will be natural consequences, and you will have to deal with them. It's no skin off my nose." Karma is a natural law; it's got nothing to do with a Supreme Lawgiver.

Question: "What are the other four laws of the universe in Buddhism, aside from karma?"

You brought it up. . . . (laughter)

Monk: "I brought it up. Um, okay. . . ."

You've got twenty minutes.

Monk continues: "Oh, well, I've got twenty minutes and all she wants is for me to explain the laws governing the entire universe!" (laughter)

You won't get away with that one!

Monk: "They have different names depending on how you do it. The first one, as I think of it, is essentially the inorganic laws of the universe. In other words, physical laws, the laws pertaining to that part of the universe we Westerners chop up into chemistry, physics, and the other sciences that deal with inorganic qualities. The second one has to do with the laws of life, the life sciences, biology and that whole business. The third one is karma. The fourth one is put in two ways: one is that, in the end, the Truth will out; another way of saying it is that . . ."

Without fail, evil is vanquished and good prevails: that is this one of the four.

Monk continues: "Over a very long haul. Another way of saying it is that the Wheel of the Dharma is always turning, the Wheel of Truth. In other words, she's saying in a very big picture, over the very long haul, beings do tend towards the direction of enlightenment. Also packaged alongside these religious principles in this one, by the way, are what we would think of as the psycho-social sciences. And the fifth is that in each person's lifetime, there is an opportunity to understand the Truth. Always at least one opportunity: we all get at least one shot at it."

If any of you've got a copy of *The Book of Life*,* I've got them written out in that. I think I'd agree with you on everything except one, the fourth.

Monk: "Well, there are different ways of looking at it."

Yes, but surely not psychology![†] (laughter) But of course, as I said, that could just be me.

Monk: "Well, it's all just fancy biochemistry anyway."

Watch it!

Monk: "Well, it is!"

As you understand, we do not have "yes men" in this organization, nor should we.

---

* Roshi P.T.N.H. Jiyu-Kennett and Rev. Daizui MacPhillamy, *The Book of Life* (Mt. Shasta, California: Shasta Abbey Press, 1979), out of print.

† The monk concerned is one of several of Rev. Master Jiyu's disciples who were psychologists prior to ordination; she and they enjoyed kidding each other about the relationship of psychology to religion.

Monk: "A psychologist 'explains' religion, reducing religion by explaining it as psychology; and a biochemist comes along and reduces us, by 'explaining' it all as neuro-biochemistry."

Any Buddhist monastery that contains a line of "yes men" is in trouble. You must find things to be true for yourself. You have to have the three basics: Buddha, Dharma, and Sangha; we agree on that, and the precepts. Thereafter, the "baggage" we can discuss. Anybody else?

Question: "You were talking about there being one opportunity per lifetime, at least; is that typically at the moment of death?"

Monk: "Not necessarily."

It can be, but not always.

Monk: "There's often one then, but there's frequently one before then."

I have known that, roughly speaking, there is one (and these dates are very, very "ballpark-figurish", okay?) usually offered around the age of seven, another one usually not too long after puberty, a third anytime between about twenty-eight and forty-five, and then there may be one later on, but there's always one at the time just before death. "All are called; few answer."

Question: "A moment ago you mentioned evil being vanquished; what do you mean by 'evil'?"

Slightly saddened love. Would you like to take that one, because you and I had a big discussion on this recently?

> *Monk's comment:* "This is something that you find by tracing back a chain of karmic causation to its roots, its original source, whether that be in this lifetime or through a series. What you seem to find if you look carefully enough (and so far I've never found an exception to this) is that at its source, at the source of this whole sad chain of unfortunate or painful karma, there is not an act that can actually be called 'evil'. I don't really know what an evil act is any more."

There is no such thing as an evil act, really.

> *Monk continues:* "Instead, there's simply a purity and a love which somehow (and there are a lot of ways this can happen) was unable to be expressed completely or was unable to be understood, and therefore came out slightly twisted; it was unable to be expressed, perhaps was unable to be shared, and therefore became slightly saddened."

And next time around it became a little more twisted up or sad.

> *Monk continues:* "Or resigned. And, as a result of that, some action was done which created suffering instead of communicating the purity or love. And that suffering, if it wasn't understood or one wasn't able to get back to the original purity, then produced further suffering, which even further saddens or resigns or

twists the original pure intent. And this goes on until, in the end you can end up with a tendency or a behavior or a proclivity which appears to be absolutely depraved or absolutely evil or absolutely perverted. But, if that desire or proclivity or tendency or act or set of habitual actions is not rejected, is not turned away from, is not condemned as evil or perverted, but is accepted and treated with love and with respect, then you eventually can get back to the purity of intent that was there originally. And when you do that, that is the transformation and the transcending of what appeared to be evil and perverted. Thus, even what we think of as 'evil' is void, unstained, and pure."

And, again, it is so terribly important not to get guilt involved on the way, because as people usually understand it there may be guilt involved; as we understand our present-day morality, it may look as though there is guilt involved; but you've really got to keep guilt out of the way. You've got to get beyond that.

> *Question:* "The equality of women within your own Order, does that have its basis in Zen teachings?"

I'll speak to that a little later, because the next two sections we'll be doing of this thing this afternoon speaks of women, saying even a little girl of seven, if she has found the Eternal, is the mother of all Buddhas and a great Buddha. It's finding the Eternal that makes you a Buddha. It's got nothing to do with your sex, nor for that matter does it have anything whatsoever to do with one's sexual orientation; the Eternal is not involved in that. The precepts are not commandments, which is why this is such a wonderful teaching for all people.

First monk's comment: "The way the scripture that we talked about this morning is written, it can sound a little bit like a commandment. It is put in telegraphic style: "Do not kill." But remember, the full, ancient way is to say, "I vow to undertake the way of training that I may refrain from . . ."

To teach myself to refrain from . . . killing.

Monk continues: ". . . Or stealing, or whatever."

That's another thing: they don't say "stealing"; they say, "I vow to undergo the rule of training to teach myself not to take that which is not given." There's a lot of difference in "that which is not given" and "stealing". A lot of things aren't given. It's the next thing up from stealing.

I mentioned earlier that the precept about the wine of delusion needs a bit of explanation too. Recall that in the beginning, when you first give people the precepts, when you give them the list, they see it as "Don't get drunk". Well, when you've learned not to take drink and drugs, that precept would appear to fall away, but it turns into something else. Wine deludes the mind. And now that you've learned not to take that which deludes the mind, how about not deluding the mind? There are other ways of deluding the mind besides getting drunk. It's not just drink; it's not just drugs. How about keeping a nice, clear head? One of the wines of delusion is bigotry. Bigotry is a wonderful wine of delusion: makes one feel euphoriously gorgeous. Have you ever noticed anyone who is bigoted and how righteously happy he or she looked? When I was very young there was an organization in England called the "Lord's Day Observance Society", whose main occupation was making everybody miserable on Sunday. And whereas the young could have gone to the pictures, to the cinema, or they could have gone to a concert on the pier or something else, they had nothing to do except go up into the hills (and you imagine what they got up to!). But, because of the Lord's Day Observance Society, there could not be anything like a dance or a cinema open, or anything of this sort. One of the strangest things I ever saw was Abbott and Costello, two famous comedians, one of whom had to stand in the audience and one on the stage, because if they were both on the stage they couldn't be doing a "recitation"; a "recitation" was one person expounding on a topic, and you could have those on Sunday. We were going to have a hypnotist one Sunday in the local pavilion, and everybody turned up, and he'd invited the boss of the Lord's Day Observance Society to come up there, and everybody was yelling, "Put him to sleep! Please!" (laughter) This was in my youth—I was about fourteen or fifteen at the time—and he was saying how wonderful it was, and the fact that this place was free of sin made him want to dance and sing, and he started singing "Onward Christian Soldiers" or something, and, you know, he was euphoriously happy. He had drunk so deep of the wine of the delusion of self-righteousness that he was drunker than any skunk I've ever seen. That's what we're talking about with the wine of delusion. Take a look: it's easy enough to say, "Don't get drunk, don't take drugs", but let's see where this goes: there are far more wines than one.

You know, you can even make watching baseball or football into a wine of delusion, as many wives, "football wives", have found out. I remember telling this to one gentleman once, whose wife had come to me saying she was thinking of leaving her husband. "He just lives for football." I said, "How many six-packs does he drink on a Sunday?"

And she says, "Only one; it's the football!" And I said, "Yeah, it is; that's what he's drunk on." Understand that there are many, many more "drinks" than just wine. Anything you are so stuck with that it makes everybody else fed up with you means something is seriously wrong, and that's what that precept is about in its deeper meaning.

In the beginning it is definitely "Don't get drunk." And in the beginning, it's "Do not steal." Later it becomes "Don't take that which isn't given." And still later it becomes "Don't steal from yourself, don't steal your own peace of mind." There's a lot of stealing that people do not see as stealing. Getting late for work is however-many minutes stolen, if it's done deliberately. If it's accidental, that's another matter: you can't avoid accidents on the Bay Bridge. You follow what I'm saying? The wine of delusion has many, many meanings, as many a poor wife has found out. But then, of course, there is the delusion of the wife. I've known of the "delusion of the Tupperware party", which was held every week. Anything you turn into something that will take you over completely is a delusion. That doesn't mean to say you shouldn't go to a football match, a baseball match, or watch one, but don't be taken over by it. I was taken over by books for ages; I must have been a pain in the neck to my friends. Then one day, I discovered that life was "skittling by", and I'd better do something about it. So, remember there are many delusions.

4.

The Mind of the Bodhisattva

Scripture: "Awakening to the Mind of the Bodhisattva."

When meditation and preceptual living bear fruit, our entire outlook on life begins to change, and this is the arising of the mind of the Bodhisattva. What seemed to "matter" before no longer seems important; what comes to the forefront instead is the necessity to live by a few very simple things: charity, tenderness, benevolence, sympathy, and gratitude. The first four of these are what are known as "the signs of enlightenment": what to look for if you are really keeping the precepts. This is what you should see in someone who is really keeping the precepts and who has found the Eternal. The fifth, gratitude, is one of the special foundations of the Serene Reflection, or Soto Zen, way.

> *Scripture:* "When one awakens to True Wisdom it means that one is willing to save all living things before one has actually saved oneself: whether a being is a layman, priest, god, or man, enjoying pleasure or suffering pain, he should awaken this desire as quickly as possible. However humble a person may appear to be, if this desire has been awakened, he is already the

teacher of all mankind: a little girl of seven even may be the teacher of the four classes of Buddhists . . . "

That includes priests and lay people.

Scripture continues: ". . . and the mother of True Compassion to all living things. One of the greatest teachings of Buddhism is its insistence upon the complete equality of the sexes.

"However much one may drift in the six worlds and the four existences even they become the means for realizing the desire for Buddhahood once it has been awakened: however much time we may have wasted up to now, there is still time to awaken this desire."

Which means that in any one of the six worlds (whether animals, or ghosts, or humans, asuras, heavens, or hells) there is always a Buddha that can be seen in each one of them. If you see a picture of the six worlds, you will see a Buddha in each one of those six worlds. If you are truly looking, you can find the Eternal no matter how much you are suffering.

Scripture: "Although our own merit for Buddhahood may be full ripe, it is our bounden duty to use all this merit for the purpose of enlightening every living thing: at all times, there have been those who put their own Buddhahood second to the necessity of working for the good of all other living things. The Four Wisdoms, charity, tenderness, benevolence and sympathy, are the means we have of helping others and represent the Bodhisattva's aspirations."

Remember that if you wait until you are fully enlightened, you miss a tremendous number of opportunities to help people. You have to be careful that you don't think that you can't be of help until you personally have found the Eternal, because if you try to do that which the Eternal does, if you try to follow the precepts, just doing that itself will start to help. You need to keep that in mind.

CHARITY

Yesterday, I talked to you about the importance of having a look at what was inside of you and how that is made easier by not putting more in. I also explained to you something about the precepts. One needs to know if one is doing the right thing (if one's going in the right direction), and there are certain signs that will give you a clue as to whether you are in fact going in the right direction. These four are called the signs of enlightenment, but you have to be careful that you do not think of them in the normal usages of the four words. They are charity, tenderness, benevolence, and sympathy. Now, when you have an abrupt awakening, these four can hit so quickly that there seems, or would appear to be, a total change in personality. It is because of this abrupt change in personality that Soto Zen feels it is not terribly wise, it is not good, to shock your friends and relatives with a radical change overnight: they tend to get rather worried about it, especially in this day and age when psychologists and psychiatrists are in some respects the priests of the new religion. So, perhaps Soto is the safer method: the slow way. In fact, many Rinzaists nowadays feel that the slow way is probably much preferable.

These four signs—charity, tenderness, benevolence, and sympathy—are the signs that we are, in fact, using the precepts correctly, keeping them in the right way, which is, as I said yesterday, not necessarily in the letter but truly in the spirit: in the sense of ceasing utterly from evil, doing only good, and doing good for others. Dogen very carefully explains what is meant by these four, but you are really not going to know thoroughly what they mean until you have started to dig up some of the stuff from within yourself. Most people, I have found, find it extremely difficult to forgive themselves for a lot of things that they have done in the past. And even more find it extremely difficult to forgive parents or teachers or close relatives for what was done to them when they were children. And it is for this reason that they frequently have taken to distracting themselves with external things and have caused this stuff to be hidden. One of the monks had, when he was three, been tied up by a bunch of school friends of his at the nursery school and left in a garden. And at the age of well over thirty, when he found this out, he still wanted to wring their necks and finally could let it out and admit to himself that he had wanted to commit murder. But the horror of that thought had been so much that he had sat upon it for well over thirty years. To admit to himself that "Yeah, at three I would cheerfully have liked to murder the other kids", was quite a shock. So remember, you are going to dig up an awful lot of stuff that you're not going to like. And remember that it can't hurt you: it's only shadows from the past. It's a bunch of shadows, a bunch of just junk, that you're carrying around which is hiding your true situation, your True Home, which is the Undying. Do not allow stuff to get in your way that has been from far, far back and which really is just a bunch of shadows. Do not allow it to do damage. Now, Dogen continues:

> *Scripture:* "The Four Wisdoms, charity, tenderness, benevolence and sympathy, are the means we have of helping others and represent the Bodhisattva's aspirations. Charity (which is the first of the four) is the opposite of covetousness; we make offerings although we ourselves get nothing whatsoever."

Last Thursday I was giving a lecture here in San Francisco to a private meeting of some people. I was asked, "Should one expect gratitude from those one helps?" And my answer was, "Not only should one not expect it, one should be mightily surprised if one gets it." Because I have yet to find anyone who is truly grateful (other than an actual fellow Buddhist) for someone helping them and expecting nothing in return. It is regarded as being slightly, almost "wrong": you have got to be on the "me" side, otherwise what else have you got to hide, what are the obligations? It's a sad comment on our society that this is the way it is, but that is the way it is. It is extremely difficult to get it through the heads of the majority of people, and especially government officials, that you are not "on the make" if you are offering a service to other people. I can remember the state officials in Sacramento being absolutely amazed and disbelieving when I made it clear that the only charges we had in Shasta were for board/lodging. There had to be some catch: did we not let them go afterwards? Did we brainwash them and send them out to do various things afterwards? Were we anti-government? And I was actually sent off, I actually had to go off to the Immigration Service office in San Pedro and prove to people that I was not doing this in order to get people out of the Vietnam War. The best way I could do that, because they wanted to know what my politics were, was to inform them that I had been in the British Royal Navy in my youth and, of course, all theories of that sort went straight out the window! It was the only time I've ever found that to come in really handy. The point is that if you are going to do this, do not be surprised if there's a tremendous amount of suspicion. Because to offer charity, to offer help, without asking something else in return for it, is regarded as very strange. As I said, that's an extremely sad comment on our society and on our government officials.

> *Audience comment:* "When I was training, learning to be a Buddhist, lots was made of learning to be grateful. There is an effort on teaching people to be grateful."

Yes, oh yes, there's quite a bit of effort on that, but do not expect it from people. The reason you teach people to be grateful is to try and help them not to be suspicious, because the opposite of gratitude is suspicion. Quite truthfully, it takes a long time before you find that one out. It never occurred to me that the roots of ingratitude were suspicion. Yes. So, Dogen continues:

> *Scripture:* "There is no need to be concerned about how small the gift may be so long as it brings True results for, even if it is only a single phrase or verse of teaching, it may be a seed to bring forth good fruit both now and hereafter."

In other words, do not be concerned about how small a gift may be, or how little a thing you may do for somebody else. It is important just to do it, and to do it wholeheartedly.

That other people take no notice or are suspicious is not your concern. And above all, do not be covetous, for to be covetous is the exact opposite of genuine charity, of genuine giving. So, when you find yourself being happy and generous, and not worrying about whether people are grateful or not, you are beginning to show one of the four signs that your training is going in the right direction. And it's an extremely difficult thing to do because "Why shouldn't they say 'thank you'?" comes up in the mind. And you do not realize that requiring someone to say 'thank you' is an act of covetousness: you covet their gratitude, you covet their thanks. You are forcing something. It is nice if they know to do it, but they didn't ask you for what you did. Why should you expect them to be grateful for it? This thing touches on the most simple things of all. So often someone hands a cup of tea to another person, and we look around and say, "Well, why didn't they say 'thanks'?" Did they ask for the tea, or did we just offer it? It is not important: the point is the offering. I have had people say to me, "Well, I cleaned up the ceremony hall; you could as least say 'thank you'." I hadn't asked them to clean up the hall. I'm glad they did, but I did not ask it—and I do say 'thank you'. But the point is: to expect it is a sign of covetousness; true charity has not yet been understood. We make offerings without ever expecting thanks. And it's a very hard one to learn, because you think, "Oh, how good I am; look what I'm doing (and you're really patting yourself on the back) because now just think of all the gratitude I'm going to get." That is not charity; do not make a mistake on this.

> *Question:* "This is really a hard one for me because, in the world and working in a normal job, hopefully our employees, employers, and customers recognize,

you know, what you're doing. And it certainly turns the whole thing around when you do the best you can and it's not appreciated or not seen."

That's when you need to train as though your hair's on fire. I mean that. In the world it is much, much more difficult for any person than it is in a monastery. Because in the monastery at least everybody knows, roughly, what they're supposed to be doing, Although some of them seem to go around with their head in a sack. (I have a saying, "So-and-so is walking around today dragging his brains in a sack behind him", and they know exactly what I mean by that statement). But in the world, for the average lay person (and this is why we try to have the retreats for the laity, as much as possible), it is much more difficult. And you have to train all that much harder; there's not very much you can do about that.

> *Monk's comment:* "Just another thought on that, too: the origin of suffering being attachment, what's the idea of expecting anything? It seems like expectations are just attachments."

I learned this particular one the really hard way over in Japan. A couple of Swedish people wanted to come and study in Sojiji, and they'd got no cash. But they were saying (one was a bricklayer, and the other one, I've forgotten what his job was), "We'll gladly lay bricks for you in return." And Koho Zenji made me write a letter saying, "I don't want any bricks laid." They were really upset, I mean, "Here we are giving up our jobs to come to you, and you don't want our bricks!" And I had the unpleasant occupation of explaining, "We didn't ask you to come." They thought we were being incredibly rude, but we weren't—we were telling them the truth. They had asked could they come and lay bricks. Well, we didn't want any bricks laid. It's very difficult to try and get it through the mind of a person who does not understand how charity works what genuine charity is. And equally more so to get it through the minds of people who are coming out of a Christian background, where such a thing is regarded in a totally different way. But what a Buddhist is aiming at is giving without ever expecting thanks, help, gratitude of any type, or reward. And, at the most difficult level of all, thanks is the one thing that everybody feels they can't give up: "At least they can say 'thank you', even if they can't give me any money for it." No: that is still attachment.

The other way they teach you this in the East is when you're out digging up weeds. It's very, very easy to pull up big weeds in the garden. You can go around, you can have a nice looking garden, except there's all these little ones. And, you know, those are the back breakers: it doesn't look as though much is happening, but they're the back breakers that you're picking up one by one; they're all the little "thank you's" you're expecting and these other little things you're expecting. And until you really clean the garden—which is the garden of the mind—of those tiny things, you are not going to find the perfection of this one of the four wisdoms: charity.

> *Question:* "I can imagine many situations in which there are no overt plans, but nevertheless one finds oneself enjoying the act of giving. Is this all right?"

I have done this and it hasn't done any damage. The main thing is not to expect anybody else to take pleasure in it.

That's the thing. "Well, I like it anyway" is what I periodically say to myself, and I go off: I don't find any problem with that. But if you expect somebody else to like it, then you're in trouble. It literally is a razor's edge that you walk along. You were going to say something, I think. . . .

> *Monk's comment:* "I'm chuckling about 'how much more difficult it is in a non-monastic setting' and I would like to say '*au contraire*'. Picture that you've been working in this setting for ten years, no one has ever paid you a cent, you're working twelve, fourteen hours a day—and you come up with the thought, 'Well, at least somebody could say thanks once in awhile!' I'm not so sure it's any easier!"

That's true: it just takes a bit longer for it to sink. Yes, go ahead. . . .

> *Question:* "First of all, I thank you for addressing the thing that's been disturbing me the most the past few months; it's amazing. Okay, my difficulty is: my heart says to give to the Abbey, which is absolutely where my heart is, but 'I should' says, 'Oh, no, you must give to your children.' This week I gave something to my daughter, and it was accepted in the ugliest possible way; I mean, it was just tearing me apart."

But she's still your daughter, and you still love her; worry not about it. Your heart doesn't say, your greed says. Your greed says, "She should at least have been grateful, not ugly." That's what's talking. Don't worry about it: you did what you felt was right. But don't expect gratitude. And don't be greedy for something other than the ugliness. This is a very hard teaching—it's very hard indeed. But as I said, this is for spiritual adults: you can't be a spiritual child here. Children expect, "Well, why can't you say 'thank you' to me for what I've done?" But as you get older, and deeper into spirituality, you have to realize you're not going to get any thanks at all. In fact, you might get kicks for telling the truth. I have had a good many. I have frequently told the truth to people, and they've not wanted to hear it, and they've gone off in tempers. And, as some people here know, then they've written about me in newspapers afterwards. So, don't expect thanks, sometimes expect vilification; or . . . don't expect it, but don't be surprised by it. It doesn't matter: you give because it is good to do so; it's that simple.

Audience comment: "I was surprised by it."

Yes, well that's another sign: not being surprised; don't be surprised at anything. After I had been at Sojiji half an hour my surprise pretty well reached saturation point. I didn't think it could get any deeper. You see, here was I: I had given up a first-rate job in London—a darn good career—to go over to be with someone to study Buddhism, who had invited me over. And I was being asked, "Well, what did you come for? He never sent you an invitation." "What?" "Well, I mean, this is all men: you can't come in here." And for two months they wouldn't let me in, while all the officers fought like blazes—and forgive me for using such terms—over whether or not the abbot had the right to have me in. And then none of the others would teach me. It would have been very easy for me to have got taught with the other monks, but at first they wouldn't do it. As if, "Well, the archbishop invited you over: he's the one that's going to have to do the job." But you needed forty-seven seals on a piece of paper to get to see him. You got to go through each person above yourself, and it was a fuss all the way up. And there was no way I was going to get to see him. I said, "All right, I'm going to break the rules. He lives across the garden; well, I'll walk across it." And I'd walk straight across the garden and into his house. I did not want to break the rules. I hate breaking rules; I'm a very law-abiding person. What else was I going to do? I burned all my boats and all my bridges. All I wanted to do was to go along to lectures that were held for the two hundred monks studying there, but only one person allowed me to go to his lectures. That was the disciplinarian, who said, "If the archbishop says it, it's done. *Hai!*" And that was the long and short of it as far as he was concerned; there was no problem. He has remained a good friend all down the years. The others sat there arguing with themselves as to who could and who couldn't: "But the rules say. . . ." The disciplinarian said, "Yes, let me have a look in the books", and he went through the archives (literally stacks of stuff) and said, "But in Twelve-something-or-other, they let a woman into Eiheiji, so I'm letting her in here." He literally went hunting for a precedent. He didn't say, "It can't be"; he went looking for how it *could* be, and there's a tremendous difference in the mind of someone who does that and the mind of someone who is prejudiced and says, "No." There wasn't prejudice in his mind; he was just up against keeping the rules, as disciplinarian. And I've always loved him for it. He gave me a very rough time, and he and I understood each other perfectly: that's just how it should be. I didn't ask for special treatment: I asked for fair treatment; that's what I got from him. And that is how you have to understand charity and covetousness. Any other questions on charity before we go on with the passage? Right, let's have a look.

As it says, "Even the slightest verse or a single phrase or word may be a seed to bring forth good fruit both now and hereafter." That is certainly true of myself, because I remember asking Koho Zenji, "Well, I've done all this—look at how people are behaving!" He said, "I told you not to expect too much." And as I was going out the door he said, "Later on, I'm going to tell you to expect nothing." It was the "expect nothing" that gave me the clue to finding the Unborn, because what I found is that nothing "matters". So he'd actually given me the two finest clues he could as to how to find the meaning of one of the four truths, the four wisdoms: charity. So, just one or two words: you don't need a whole long talk. Some of the things he did didn't help at all, like having me photographed sitting beside him on the same cushion, which infuriated some of the people who'd longed just to be able to get into his room. He didn't help matters all that much now and then, but that didn't "matter" either.

> *Scripture:* "Similarly, the offering of only one coin or a blade of grass can cause the arising of good, for the teaching itself is the True Treasure and the True Treasure is the very teaching: we must never desire any reward and we must always share everything we have with others. It is an act of charity to build a ferry or a bridge and all forms of industry are charity if they benefit others."

Here he is speaking of the importance of doing any work that helps another person and expecting nothing in return. One of the strangest things I can remember was at Ipoh, in Malaysia, where there was a little monkey chained on a wall. It obviously loved fruit, and there was a fruit tree, and something in me knew it was longing for it. I'd got a small box of dried apricots that I had bought, and I walked up to it and offered it one, and it ate it. It was so obviously hungry for fruit that I gave it some more. And suddenly, after about the fourth apricot, it grabbed my hand in both its hands. I have never felt gratitude like that. I'd have loved that monkey for a pet. If creatures can feel that gratitude, what can humans do? Just think about it. This was a tiny little monkey, no higher than a foot, with a huge heavy chain around its neck. It just clutched my hand: I have never felt anything go through my body like that—from no human, ever. So I gave it the rest of the packet and walked away. And I felt well fed—oddly enough, I felt very, very well fed. It sat there holding the packet in one hand and eating them out; it was just a tiny little box. So, don't be surprised if you don't get gratitude, and be pleased when you do because somebody else is showing the real signs of enlightenment. Showing gratitude of that sort is a real sign of enlightenment. It was the first thing that made it clear to me that animals weren't nearly as dumb as people gave them "credit" for being. And they genuinely did have the Buddha Nature, as my master pointed out to me many years later.

Don't think that because an act does not appear to be religious, like building a ferry or a bridge, as it says, that it is not going to bring forth good karma: it will. But if you only build something that causes damage to others, because you have not studied it carefully enough or taken enough trouble about it, then do not expect good results. Whatever you do has to be done one hundred percent as best you can: a hundred percent good job irrespective of whether you're being well paid, well rewarded, or thanked. Only then is it a genuine act of charity. Only then do you, as it is stated metaphorically, "create true meals for true monks." This is in this sense that the cook of a monastery creates food for the monks, using the finest effort possible to make even the poorest ingredients into heavenly food.

TENDERNESS

> Scripture: "To behold all beings with the eye of compassion and to speak kindly to them is the meaning of tenderness. If one would understand tenderness, one must speak to others whilst thinking that one loves all living things as if they were one's own children."

This can be extremely difficult, especially when someone very drunk turns up at the Abbey gate and requires to sleep it off. A Buddhist is not required to be a fool: whilst making it clear that you love and accept the person, you must still make it clear that it is advisable that they sleep off their drunkenness somewhere other than the meditation hall. You are not required to be a fool, because then you are not expressing tenderness, you are expressing stupidity. A lot of people find it very difficult to find the dividing line between the two, and because it is so difficult, very many mistakes are made. Many mistakes are made, but they are made with the best of intentions. There used to be an old saying in the East that no Zen master knew their stuff until he or she had ruined at least two people. And it was pointed out to me that this was probably a better percentage than the average medical doctor. I didn't get into that one, because I don't know. But it was said that you definitely ruined two before you really learned your job, and I'm inclined to agree with them.

Tenderness, then, is being able to look at everyone and anyone and see the potential of the Buddha Mind: the Buddha

Nature, the Buddha Nature being that which l⟨
with the Unborn and the Undying. It is to see th⟨
others no matter how they're dressed, or their colo⟨,
former creed, present creed. . . . A lot of people come to Zen⟨
who had peculiar, perhaps, theories or political affiliations;
none of these things are of importance. If you allow them to
get in the way, you will not see a Buddha, you will see your
own prejudice; it is very important not to be caught up in that
prejudice. If someone comes to you who is mentally ill, as
sometimes happens, then your job is not to see someone who
can't train, but someone who will be able to train in the
future. Find them the best way to get the necessary help so
they can train in the future. One of the beauties of this is that
what we are trying to do is find the Unborn, the Undying. And
as such, whatever a person's affiliations were, whatever their
mental state, whatever their sexual orientation, none of this
matters for all of this comes out of opposites and discussions.
What you are there for is not to become sane, not to become
heterosexual (or homosexual—or whatever happens to be the
one not in ascendancy)—it is to find the Unborn. As such,
none of this stuff comes into it. Since it doesn't bug the
Unborn, why should it bug us?!? This is one of the stupidest
situations that ever comes up, but a lot of people place prejudice in the ascendancy and then make prejudice part of their
religion. In Zen the only thing that you are required to do is
search for the Unborn, so stop the arguments in your heads! It
sounds much nicer to say "Get beyond the opposites", because
that gives you a little more fancy wording, but really it is just
stop the arguments in your heads—this, that, or the other
which causes inadequacy or pride—and just go on and look
for the Cosmic Buddha, look for the Unborn. No matter
what a person looks like or their state of mind, see in them the
possibility of the Unborn.

There's a rather amusing incident a year or two ago in a Christian monastery over in England where a film crew from the BBC had turned up to shoot some video footage, and one of them thanked the monks afterwards for allowing them in. And the abbot looked at him in amazement and said, "But, my dear man. . . ."* The expression on the man's face as he went out—this was on TV—was rather interesting. But even the BBC was regarded in the same way, and that is how a true Zen Buddhist must look at anyone who comes to their door.

Whatever their prejudices or state is, that is their state of karma, which they have to deal with. All I ever feel is compassion for a tremendous number of people who have karma that they have nothing they can do about, except train to deal with it. I have great respect for people who are lugging around these huge lumps of karma. So understand the meaning of tenderness: it is not treating people in a babyish way; it is recognizing that here walks a future Buddha, and doing everything you can to enable that future Buddha to find his or her true potential.

> *Monk's comment:* "If I could comment on this whole line of thinking: prejudice as to what someone should or should not be like can be a large part of our

---

* This is a British expression meaning that the speaker is amazed that anyone would even consider the possibility of doing something else: in this case, something other than treating the television crew with respect and allowing them free access. The quote is faintly humorous, implying as it does that even BBC crews have a soul and should be treated with Christian charity, at a time when TV crews were not overly loved, especially when they turned up on one's doorstep. The humor is heightened by its parallelism with a famous quote of Dogen Zenji when he was asked if all living things had the Buddha Nature. He is reported to have replied, "Even horseflies!"

expectations about religious people. We expect
priests or teachers to fit into a certain mold. But
they're simply human beings who strive to find
Something beyond their own humanity. That doesn't
mean that they will cease to be human or that they
will become some sort of transcendent being. They
will still look exactly like human beings and show all
the signs of it, including the frailties and mistakes.
And what you have to see is evidence that they are in
touch with That which lies beyond it. That requires a
much subtler way of observing and requires you to
become in touch with That yourself in order to recognize It in someone else. And that is the essence of
the religious transmission from person to person: the
recognition of the Buddha in someone else."

I can remember taking a walk in '76 when I was fairly ill,
not far from our temple in Oakland, and we met a really
huge man who was very obviously "stoned" out of his head
on something or other. And he and I looked at each other,
and I was literally looking at a Buddha. I could see it: there
was all this—all the drugs and everything—working in his
head and body, but what I saw, very clearly, was a Buddha.
And he must have seen it in me, because we stood and
talked to each other. I remember the monk who was with me
standing there looking terribly worried, with his hand in his
pocket, almost looking as though he got his "piece" there,
ready to shoot him in case he got up to anything. And the
man and I were having this wonderful talk with each other.
Then he walked on; the body was in this dreadful state, but
the spirit was shining through.

This is why it is so important to have a different outlook—
a Buddhist outlook I would perhaps say—on crime and

punishment. Because the one thing that the Western world does not understand, or doesn't seem too willing to admit to, is the doctrine of change: anicca. One starts in Buddhism with the fundamental faith that every single human being is born with the potential for knowing the Unborn and the Undying. There is no such thing as original sin which has to be cleansed. There is no such thing as a person who is stuck for eternity, once they have committed a crime, with being a criminal. Yes, sometimes one does a wrong act, but that was yesterday, it's not today. I have been wanting to write a book on this subject for the last four years. I haven't done so because I don't think that the world is ready for it, or could handle it, yet. But if you really understand tenderness, and if you really learn to look at people—which is something you must do, and, I assure you, you will be able to do it if you study meditation very deeply—you'll never be able to place a label on them again, ever. For what you will see is a potential part of yourself, and you and they are part of the same Unborn and Undying. And when you see that, then you will never be able to place the label. This does not mean to say that if somebody has done a wrong act, they do not necessarily need to go to jail; I'm not talking about that. I am saying that once that is dealt with, once the karmic consequence has been dealt with, then the only thing such people deserve is our respect. We must go on looking at them not as criminals, not as this, not as that, but instead see someone who is as we are: looking for the Cosmic Buddha.

This is why tenderness, in this sense, is one of the signs of enlightenment: when you can look at people in this way, no matter what state they're in. It's one of the reasons I was so overjoyed when I found I'd got a monk who was also a psychologist, because then he could help people who were mentally ill to get to the state where they could be normal in this way. And I knew that he wouldn't be looking at them as people who were sick, but rather as people who had karma that needed to be helped: it makes such a difference. But our whole society would have to be re-educated, as it were, in this way if everybody were to be helped. And that is a long ways off, so it's not easy for lay people, as our friend here has pointed out, dealing with the world in this way, because the world just doesn't think that way.

I put myself through what I call "my private hell" for a couple of hours each day, which is watching the news just to see how far, backwards or forwards, the world is progressing. Because if you get out of touch with it, you can't help the world; you've got to be in touch with the state that it's in. And, yes, it isn't pleasant, but if you get out of touch with it, then you will never be able to help anyone because you won't know where they're coming from or why. So that, also, is included in tenderness: being aware of what is going on. That does not necessarily mean that you have to watch the rubbishy programs that have been on in the last year; it does mean that at least you have to be aware of the news, however unpleasant. Any questions on tenderness, while we're on the subject?

> *Question:* "On this issue of prison, it seems to me that our prison system cuts the convict off from feeling, or sort of paying off, his karma."

It does, but there's also another problem. There was an issue that came up on the local ballots, which was whether or not to give money, if you remember, for the prisons. I wanted to vote no, because I thought that if it were defeated they'd be forced to find a better system than just sticking people in jail, but then I realized they were just going to keep on over-crowding the places. So, very sadly and against everything that I believed to be right, I voted yes. I knew that I was doing the wrong thing in voting yes, but I was doing an even more wrong thing if I voted no. Because in the overcrowding, only harm could come. That's not an easy way to have to live: "Yes, I know; I accept the karma that I have done wrong, but I didn't have an alternative." So you do as little harm as you can. It's very important for Buddhists to vote on every issue, and think of it from the finest and deepest point of view possible, because only by so doing will we eventually change the system. To use such methods as riots and this sort of thing only creates more problems: you have to do it from a sensible, responsible mind. I agree with you on what you just said. But until a few more people, until a majority of people, start seeing that this is not the right way, nothing is going to happen. And the way to change their minds is to start with one or two who see that it's not the right way: it's our duty to change it not by forcing, but by making it obvious that it's not the right way. Not very comforting, but fact.

Question: "What about civil disobedience?"

Civil disobedience? Well, I gave you an example by walking straight across the garden into Koho Zenji's house: that was civil disobedience, with a vengeance. And, I'm still carrying the karma for doing it, and I'm not complaining about it. If you feel that that is the only way to go, then you, as a competent spiritual adult, will make that decision. And if you get lugged off to jail, then you'll say, "Thank you; this is my karmic consequence." I mean that and I'm not being silly: you have to make your decision as to the right way to go and take the consequences of doing it. If the intention was good—the whole point here being intention—then there will still be karmic consequence, but there is no deliberate attempt to do evil, fair enough? How to work out the Three Pure Precepts—it's not comforting but, by God, do you grow up fast and truly grow up! You really become in charge of your own mind. We'll talk more about this tomorrow; anything else on tenderness while we're at it? Okay.

> *Scripture:* "By praising those who exhibit virtue, and feeling sorry for those who do not, our enemies become our friends and they who are our friends have their friendship strengthened: this is all through the power of tenderness. Whenever one speaks kindly to another his face brightens and his heart is warmed; if a kind word be spoken in his absence the impression will be a deep one: tenderness can have a revolutionary impact upon the mind of man."

I know it can. It can also have a revolutionary impact on the social system. When it has been used properly, I have seen it take all the snideness and nastiness out of a situation. It is very difficult to continue to dislike another person who is not deliberately going along with dislike or hatred or sneeriness or snideness. It is very difficult to do that. Let's have a look at the next one.

BENEVOLENCE

> Scripture: "If one creates wise ways of helping beings, whether they be in high places or lowly stations, one exhibits benevolence: no reward was sought by those who rescued the helpless tortoise and the sick sparrow, these acts being utterly benevolent. The stupid believe that they will lose

something if they give help to others, but this is completely untrue for benevolence helps everyone, including oneself, being a law of the universe."

If you think about it, very few people realize that benevolence is a law of the universe. We never think about air—be grateful for it—until somebody has stuck too much pollution in it; then we complain about the pollution. We don't give thanks for the fact that the air is there anyway. These are the reasons that you bow to your seat and you bow to the wall before and after meditation. If it wasn't for the carpet and the floor, you would have no place to sit; if it wasn't for the wall, you would have no place where to rest your eyes quietly while you meditate. It is not a benevolent act to look at the carpet and say it's dirty, or to look at the wall and say it's spotty. Just as with the news, which only ever seems to print bad news and never prints good, so also with us: we never give thanks for what we've actually got; we are never grateful for what we have got, we only complain about it. Benevolence is the opposite of this: creating wise ways to help beings. In some respects, cleaning the carpet is a wise way to help beings. But at a later date, one must realize that it doesn't matter whether the carpet is cleaned at all. It's just a place to sit; it is, of itself, benevolent.

Benevolence is perhaps one of the most difficult of these four wisdoms to understand, for everything in nature is at all times helping beings, yet, man is usually unaware of the fact. The trees are helping us, the flowers help us, not just by their beauty and their shade, but by what they do to the air. Our children and our animals are helping us. What are we doing in return? The trees have given us wood upon which to sit. We've just taken them; we haven't thought that the

tree lost its life to give it. As you get deeper
benevolence, you begin to look at a cabba
acceptance of the thing, which is to be willing ι
so we can continue to live. Then you start looking aι ι.
scriptures (for lunch and supper and the like) are the wa,
they are: "We must think deeply of the ways and means by
which this food has come. We must consider our merit
when accepting it." Have we really, truly realized what we are
doing? We are killing things so that we may stay alive. So
what are we doing, what are we giving, in return? What are
we actually offering? Or are we just taking, are we just greedy?

"We accept what we eat so we won't become lean and
die": that's the reason we eat, not so we can hack some poor
frog's legs off because we think they're tasty. I put something
in our quarterly *Journal* about this once, about the way in
which India is killing off all its frogs and then complaining
that it hasn't got various crops which the frogs ate the bugs
from, and we then have to give them aid. What we are really
doing is supporting the habit of certain people to eat frogs,
but it takes a long time before you can look at it from that
angle. There are very few frogs who actually make it: I think
it's one in five thousand eggs makes it to full frogdom, and
then we chop off its legs as soon as it's made it! "Think
deeply of the ways and means by which this food has come.
Consider your merit when accepting it." Remember that
you're only eating so as not to become lean and die. Don't go
around destroying things because you want taste. But, if
your body needs meat because it's the only way you can sur-
vive, because you are sick, then Buddhism has always said
that this is fair—because you may not commit the greater
crime of causing yourself to die, because then, and only then,
would you not be able to find the Unborn. And perhaps if by

eating the meat you can stay alive, then you can help other people to find the Unborn. Then something has sacrificed itself for a great cause and has, in fact, become a Bodhisattva. But you do not go out in order to get a steak because you fancy a steak. "We eat so that we will not become lean and die." And we eat also so that we may become enlightened: "We accept this food so that we may become enlightened."

"The five thoughts" at mealtime (which actually give us the whole of the meaning of benevolence, the purpose there, the making of offerings): everything is offering itself to us; what are we doing? When we start thinking that way, we start making the offering of benevolence to other things. Make your life have a purpose, then everything will offer itself to you with joy, and you will make your offering with joy. The whole universe will blaze up in joy! I have felt it do it, and it's exquisite! But don't be surprised if then your body is happy with the same meal every day of the week because it knows the purpose of the meal: that you eat solely for the food value and the good of your health. And, yes, the taste buds won't be satisfied as they were before. What's even funnier is they don't want to be, because the purpose for eating is now clear. The same thing applies to making too much in the way of clothes or furniture or anything of this sort: you need just enough and no more.

Now, you should not make yourself—as the world regards it—weird in this sense. We are not here to become strange; we are here to find the Unborn. We accept the benevolence of all things so that we may find the Unborn, and we give benevolence so that all things, and all beings, that have not yet found the Unborn may find it. In this place, "the wooden figure sings and the stone maiden dances." That is the meaning of those two lines in the morning scriptures. Anybody got anything they want to say about this one?

Audience comment: "It doesn't seem like there's much of a difference between charity and benevolence."

There actually is; there's quite a bit, because charity is something that we ourselves do, and benevolence is recognizing something that everything else is doing and then going along with it. In charity you don't recognize it, you just *do*, but in benevolence you've got this two-way thing going very beautifully. And in charity the feedback the self wants is gratitude and, when charity is done correctly, the feedback you get naturally *is* gratitude. But in benevolence, because it is the two-way thing, the feedback you get is joy. There is a difference: they all interact on each other, but one seems to "blaze up" in a different way, and it is essential to have that difference. Anybody else?

So you all understand benevolence? Right, we'll look at the next one. It is important, by the way, to realize that benevolence is a law of the universe, whereas charity is not. Benevolence is obvious in every single thing, even in things that humans have made—like the road out there, for example. The sun bakes it, the cars go up and down on it, the drunks and the dogs do various things on it, we walk on it, and it does the very best it can of being a road. Sometimes the strain is so great that it cracks, and then we have to be benevolent to it and mend it. Everything is doing the very best it can at all times to help us find the Unborn, and that is what makes it a law of the universe. So keep that well in mind. The road that you travel is one of the finest Bodhisattvas you've got: it is just being itself, the very finest road. Don't swear about its potholes; get out and mend them. If all you see of the road is its potholes, you will never see its Bodhisattvahood, and you will not understand this law of the universe.

SYMPATHY

> Scripture: "If one can identify oneself with that
> which is not oneself, one can understand the true
> meaning of sympathy: take, for example, the fact
> that the Buddha appeared in the human world in the
> form of a human being; sympathy does not distin-
> guish between oneself and others. There are times
> when the self is infinite and times when this is true of
> others: sympathy is as the sea in that it never refuses
> water from whatsoever source it may come; all waters
> may gather and form only one sea."

"If one can identify oneself with that which is not
oneself"—the danger in this is of leaving oneself out of it
altogether and only seeing others. A lot of people do this and
think they are identifying with others, whereas they have not
really seen that what they've done is become do-gooders
instead. To identify with another is to see, "There, but for the
grace of Buddha, go I": to recognize identically the same
thing in yourself that is going on in another person. I can
remember someone being very horrified to realize (and this
was someone who had been very much against gay people)
that what he was afraid of was that he might be the same
way—to be able to identify with them, as a possibility: "Oh
my God, I could be that way." Yes, you could, and there's
nothing wrong with it, because your job is finding the Eternal. Sympathy is based on knowing oneself intimately: "Yes,
I have aspects of bigotry." And, given the right circumstances, "I could murder somebody." Think about it from
that angle: have a good look at yourself, and see the poten-
tials within yourself. Then when you see someone else you
won't judge that person, but realize that you could be in the

same situation. Understand his situation: look well at his situation, or hers, and realize, "Yes, I could be that way, and would I want this to happen to me?"

Judgmentalism is the big opposite of genuine sympathy: judging others. "I am not like that" can be a judgmental statement, but if you say, "I pray that I may not be like that", you are recognizing that you could be. There's just a different, tiny, little shift in mind in the way in which you look at it, because you are recognizing you could be that way and wishing to help rather than to judge and push out of the way.

I believe in the old King James version of the Bible what is said is, "Judge not, lest ye be judged" rather than "Don't judge others." And it is much more important (this "Judge not, lest ye be judged") if you would understand Buddhism, because what Buddhism says is there is absolutely nothing preventing you going straight to the Eternal at death other than the way you judge yourself at the moment of death. Now, we know that at the moment of death things that really worry people come up. We've seen it happen. Anyone who has ever been present at a death knows that this can be so, and the job of a Buddhist priest is to say, "Don't worry about any of this; just go straight on to the Eternal." Don't create clouds at the moment of death to hide you from the Eternal. Now, if you've cleaned up your karma, then you're not likely to produce clouds at the moment of death. This is one of the main reasons—this is a terribly important point, friends—this is the main reason why people who want to make a good death meditate: to clean all of that up so there is no obstruction in the way when they die. But actually it is not the Eternal who puts up the obstruction, who does the judging: we judge ourselves. It is we who do the judging of us, and we who turn away from the Cosmic Buddha. And this is why you have the Buddhist exhortations during and after the time of death: we tend to think that things "go out like a light" and everything snaps off; Buddhism says it takes forty-nine days after death. And for those forty-nine days, the priest is constantly warning, "Don't turn away; there's nothing that can get in your way; go straight on. If you've made a mistake the first time, don't worry: you will have another chance on such-and-such a day." Buddhists in the East have actually proved (although no scientist here would ever accept such proof) that on certain days at certain times, these things come up again for the spirit. The important thing is: don't turn away, go straight on; don't let the clouds get in your way, go straight on! No, there's no judgment in that, and that is why this is such an important matter.

It's terribly important that a person should truly have faith in the Unborn at the time of death, because if they do, then they are not going to judge themselves. But some people still judge themselves: "No, no, I've done too much; there's nothing I can do." Do you know Marlowe's *Faust*? Have you ever seen (there's a wonderful film of it done by the Oxford University Dramatic Society)—have you ever seen Marlowe's *Faust*? Very interesting! At the very end as Faust is going down to hell the angels are exhorting him: "Look up, look up! You don't need go down there." And he says, "I'm damned, I'm damned: I have to go." So he goes. And the angels are saying, "He's mad. What's he doing this for?" But he is the one that turned away. And Mephistopheles, in that particular version, is equally beautiful in that when he is asked what it is like to be in hell, he says, "To be in hell is to be cut off from God by one's own will." The willingness to cut oneself off.

This is one of the big dangers of coming out of a Christian-Judeo background because you feel you've got to be judged, because of guilt. Buddhism says, "No, you weren't guilty by being born in the first place: all you did was just pick up some karma. So what are you judging yourself for now? Since you weren't guilty in the first place, why do you need to be judged later on?" But if you don't clean up the karma, yes, then you're going to come back again, or something will come back again. Keep on cleaning the stuff up. Buddhism's very beautiful in that sense, quite totally different, but it all comes out of not having original sin.

To continue with the last of the signs of enlightenment that Dogen mentioned, sympathy: take, for example, the act that the Buddha appeared in the world in the form of a human being. Sympathy does not distinguish between oneself and others. At all times, Shakyamuni Buddha had the form and figure of an old monk. He was born and He died. At all times He was human; He was never a god. There have been many attempts, both by the Chinese and the Indians, to deify Him, but at all times He had the form and figure of an old monk; Zen makes this very clear.

You read the *Denkoroku*,* the story of the Transmission: at all times every one of them, every one of the Ancestors, had the form and figure of an old monk. And at some point in their lives each one of them was a good candidate for the job of world's prize rat! It's very encouraging to find that out: that they were all incredibly human. One was definitely the world's prize drunk. It is a most fascinating book to go through; those of you who have got copies, I suggest, read the *Denkoroku* with great care. There is no way you will not find one of those Ancestors who does not become your particular

---

* Keizan Zenji, *The Denkoroku or The Record of the Transmission of the Light,* trans. Rev. Hubert Nearman, O.B.C., with Rev. Master P.T.N.H. Jiyu-Kennett, M.O.B.C., as consultant and editor (Mt. Shasta, California: Shasta Abbey Press, 1993).

"patron saint", because every one of them was as we are now. As the ceremony which you do for Jukai says, when you take a thorough look at yourself, you become one with the Buddhas and the Ancestors, "for they were as we are now, and we will be as they in the future." The promise of Buddhism: if you do something about yourself, yes, you are as they were, but you will be as they in the future. So, have a look at yourself, and find which one you are in the *Denkoroku*, and recognize it honestly. They were all very human, but they all had one thing in common: they all had this little thing that told them, "There might be something better than what I'm up to right now." They heard that little voice which said, "You could do better." And when they saw it, they grabbed it and they did it: they didn't sit around and wait; they got on with it. In other words, they were in a mess because they couldn't see anything better right then, and as soon as it was put in front of them, they got on with it. As I said to you on the first day, there is no excuse for anyone to remain in the state that he or she is in; if you really want to change, you can do so. Do not be satisfied with the brick wall. Go on beyond it. Don't be afraid of it: go on beyond. The Buddha Nature is everywhere! It does not discriminate between male-female, black-white, rich-poor, old-young. Yes, go ahead.

> *Monk's comment:* "I wanted to say something more on one of the comments I heard awhile ago, the comment that someone had noticed that the same people who are capable of incredible good are also the people who are capable of committing a crime. As that was being said, I was thinking, 'Yeah, those people are you.' If you truly accept the proposition that everyone is capable of doing the ultimate good, guess what: everyone is also capable of every atrocity known to man."

Yes, and that's the meaning of sympathy: the recognition that "I could be Hitler."

> *Same monk's comment:* "And the more you meditate, the more you realize that's true."

That's scary. It is the fullest and deepest acceptance of the meaning of sympathy, and therefore you can never blame anyone. That doesn't mean to say you shouldn't do anything about it, but do not pretend to be superior. "Do not be proud of yourself and devalue others" . . . along those lines.

These signs of enlightenment are four very important things, and there isn't one of us who can't make use of them in our daily lives: with our families, with our friends, with our employers, and with our employees. If you really want to follow the Buddha's teachings, if you really want to find the Eternal, you have to emulate the Eternal before you become totally one with It. And this is how it's done: by awakening and following the mind of the Bodhisattva. The last section tells you of the way in which you live, and feel, and know you are, as a result of doing this and keeping the precepts. Would you care to continue?

THE LIFE OF GRATITUDE

> Scripture: "Putting the Teachings into Practice and Showing Gratitude."

Now, we have been speaking of gratitude all along, as an aspect of other things, but now I want to concentrate on it by itself, for gratitude is the main sign: gratitude for the teaching, for the Eternal—for the Buddha—for everything which shows us the Eternal, and for that which comes from the Eternal—the Buddha Nature or the "spark" of the Eternal, whichever you like to call it.

> *Scripture:* "The Buddha Nature should be thus simply awakened in all living things within this world for their desire to be born herein has been fulfilled: as this is so, why should they not be grateful to Shakyamuni Buddha?
>
> "If the Truth had not spread throughout the entire world it would have been impossible for us to have found it, even should we have been willing to give our very lives for it: we should think deeply upon this: how fortunate have we been to be born now when it is possible to see the Truth. Remember the Buddha's words, 'When you meet a Zen Master who teaches the Truth do not consider his caste, his appearance, shortcomings or behavior. Bow before him out of respect for his great wisdom and do nothing whatsoever to worry him.'"

It's very important to remember that. I've been hammering away the last two days: don't worry what other people get up to, find someone who teaches the Truth, learn from that person, and go on. And don't copy their mistakes. A friend of mine, a fellow Buddhist teacher who I knew both in Japan and here, as he was getting sick, started having difficulty getting up to go to morning service. One of his disciples, whom I also knew quite well, decided that he needed to copy his master, and started being late. My friend took him into a room afterwards and said to him, "Take your robe off; you're not fit to be a monk", and the young man started doing that. And he looked at him and said, "Whatever are you doing?!? No one can tell you to do that; put that robe back on!" So he did so. He then took him outside, back to the hall where everybody was wondering why they'd disappeared, and said, "Now, this is an example of what *not* to do. You are supposed to learn from your master and not copy his mistakes. Now try to be up in the morning." Keep this in mind, when you bump into a teacher. Yes, because they are human they are going to make mistakes. And some you're going to hate, and some you're going to disagree with. What are you hating? It's not *your* mistake that he or she is making: they're the one who's going to "carry the can" for it, karmically speaking. Here's Dogen in the thirteenth century telling you the same thing. It's very interesting: as you go through the history of Buddhism, you discover they've been doing this since the beginning.

> *Scripture:* "Because of consideration for others on the part of the Buddhas and Ancestors we are enabled to see the Buddha even now and hear His teachings: had the Buddhas and Ancestors not truly Transmitted the Truth it could never have been heard at this particular time: even only so much as a short phrase or section of the teaching should be deeply appreciated. What alternative have we but to be utterly grateful for the great compassion exhibited in this highest of all teachings which is the very eye and treasury of the Truth? The sick sparrow never forgot the kindness shown to it, rewarding it with the ring belonging to the three great ministers, and the unfortunate tortoise remembered too, showing its gratitude with the seal of Yofu: if animals can show gratitude surely man can do the same?"

Remember the story I told you earlier about the monkey in Malaysia? It was pure, unadulterated gratitude: it was so pure it rather put humans to shame. And that was just for giving him some of the fruit. So, don't think these things you do are not worth doing: they are. Go ahead, friend.

> *Scripture:* "You need no further teachings than the above in order to show gratitude, and you must show it truly, in the only real way, in your daily life; our daily life should be spent constantly in selfless activity with no waste of time whatsoever."

This means that (and I know it for a fact myself) once you find this place—this Third Position,* the Eternal—the gratitude flows out like a river. A lot of people call it the "water of the spirit", or the "water of the Eternal" or, as you see in some statues, Kanzeon pouring the water of compassion out. It's also the water of gratitude.

From this "Third Position", it's just not possible to think of doing something contrary to the precepts, because you can never imagine how you would be crazy enough not to be in this wonderful state. But you can't meditate in order to "get" that: you meditate for the sake of meditating—because you long to be one with the Eternal, because you are not satisfied with you—not to "get the benefits". I've said this to you several times: if you do it in order to "get the benefits", self enters into it and it is not pure. There is a story in one of the scriptures which is not known very much, but which is

---

* The "Third Position" is a phrase Rev. Master Jiyu often used for That which is beyond the opposites (a "position" and its opposite being the first "two positions").

very valuable on this. It speaks of someone who kept coming 'round, being reborn, being reborn, being reborn, hundreds and hundreds of times. He was always giving things to monks, always giving things to the poor; he was sharing everything, and "I'll be a Buddha soon." And that was why nothing happened. Finally one day, after millions and millions of years (and this is a lovely Buddhist allegory), he finally gave something without thinking that he'd become a Buddha, and guess what: he wakes up a Buddha! Don't give with the thought of getting; don't meditate with the thought of getting. To long to be one with the Buddha is one thing, to long to be one with the Eternal is fine, but if you sit down in order to "get" the Eternal, you're wasting your time and you're spinning your wheels.

> *Scripture:* "Time flies quicker than an arrow and life passes with greater transience than dew. However skillful you may be, how can you ever recall a single day of the past? Should you live for a hundred years just wasting your time, every day and month will be filled with sorrow; should you drift as the slave of your senses for a hundred years and yet live truly for only so much as a single day, you will, in that one day, not only live a hundred years of life but also save a hundred years of your future life."

That's what Dogen is referring to in the chapter I mentioned of the man who kept coming back, and back, and back, and back. That is a reference to it in this scripture.

> *Scripture:* "The life of this one day, today, is absolutely vital life; your body is deeply significant."

And it has rights. Don't try to force it to do something it really can't do without serious injury. That's asceticism: it is not religion.

> *Scripture:* "Both your life and your body deserve love and respect for it is by their agency that Truth is practiced and the Buddha's power exhibited: the seed of all Buddhist activity, and of all Buddhahood, is the true practice of Preceptual Truth. All the Buddhas are within the one Buddha Shakyamuni . . ."

And all of you are within That.

> *Scripture continues:* ". . . and all the Buddhas of past, present and future become Shakyamuni Buddha when they reach Buddhahood. This Buddha Nature is itself the Buddha and, should you awaken to a complete understanding thereof, your gratitude to the Buddhas will know no bounds."

The Buddhas are all those who went before, who found the Unborn. "They were as we are now; you will be as they in the future."

Finding the Unborn is so incredibly important, so crucial to everything. You know, next time we bring this meditation booklet out, I'm going to put into it that part of the *Udana Scripture* which speaks of the Unborn. The *Udana Scripture's* not as short as it could be; I will just put that part into it that is relevant, and we might also include the Five Laws of the Universe. You see, this particular set of classes has been very useful, because it is essential to find out what people really need to know if they're starting, like many people are, from scratch. If you don't know that such a thing as the Eternal exists in Zen, you can get really confused when you are told this sort of nebulous "x-y-z": "It", "That", "suchness", and all the rest of it. You know, you're sitting there literally "thinking the unthinkable".* What am I thinking about? (laughter) Since the Buddha clearly said it, and everybody in the Far East knows it, it never occurs to anybody to explain it to anyone. Why should it? "Everybody knows it." I can remember saying to Koho Zenji once about this, "Why don't you teach it?" And he said, "What's there to teach? It's known to everyone." Then I realized exactly what the problem was: we Westerners were all starting from the premise that there was an "Emptiness" that was totally, negatively empty. And it wasn't. So next time we bring this out, as I said, we'll put that in here.

What questions have you got?

QUESTIONS

> *Question:* "I'm wondering about proper behavior around people who have just died, or even if you come upon an animal that's been dead for awhile, but in particular people who've just died. Can you do anything, can you try to help them go to the Eternal?"

Just wish them as well as you can; always want the very best for everyone. One of the teachings for officers in the temple is that it is your duty in your office to make every

---

* "Think the unthinkable" is one frequently used translation of the passage in the *Rules for Meditation* that was translated by Rev. Master Jiyu and her teachers as "Do not try to think; do not try not to think."

other officer and junior in the temple as much of a success as possible. In other words, you must never think in terms of your position being more important than another, or getting power over another by doing something or other. Your job is to make everyone else a success, and, of course, yourself. That's what you do when you come upon a dead body or a dead animal: you want the very best for it. And in that sense you bless it so that the very best possible may be for it.

> *Question:* "When you said that the Buddha was a human being, does that apply to His life after enlightenment, as well?"

There's a thing that very few people know about the Buddha, and that is for about a year after His enlightenment, He almost starved. It's actually historically correct: not everybody was one hundred percent eager to follow Him. The actual history is quite interesting. There is also the fact, which is also a little known fact indeed, of a very heavy mistake that He made, which nowadays would make every Sunday paper from Sydney to London, and that is that He was extraordinarily tired on one occasion and said to His monks, "I'm going off and take a couple of weeks to meditate and while I'm gone, I want you all to meditate on the unsatisfactoriness of the body", and when He came back, He found the Order was remarkably smaller: many of them had committed suicide, having totally misinterpreted His teaching on nonattachment to the body.* And that fact is kept very

---

* See F. L. Woodward, trans., *The Book of the Kindred Sayings* (Samyutta-Nikaya), Vol. V (London: Pali Text Society, 1979), pp. 283–299.

quiet. Even when you know the Eternal and are enlightened, you can still make mistakes.

> *Second monk's comment:* "You can still have a bad day."

He was human; He wasn't a god. And you may think I'm crazy for what I am saying here, but the fact remains that I can make mistakes, and nobody's more aware of that fact than I am. And that is true of all of you: however much you may know the Eternal, because you are *not* the Eternal (but there is nothing in you that is not *of* the Eternal), you can make mistakes. Don't try turning the Buddha into a god. One of the blessings of reading history is finding out how very dangerous that is. It's like what I was saying about World War I: we need to read our history much more to see how dangerous it is, what we are doing right now. If you do not want to leave karma behind that has to be dealt with the next time around, you have to be very careful, you have to view things from the mind of the Bodhisattva. It's a very good point, what you brought up there.

> *Question:* "Can one be spiritually taken over? Can your reliance on teachings and teachers turn into a form of self-brainwashing?"

It depends, it depends how it's done; the answer is yes. If you do it right, it won't take you over. The way in which you prevent it from taking you over is by not being
word—not becoming heavily doctrinal and
way on other people, because then it's take
Remember what I said in the first lecture: real

insist on truth. I can look out of this window and there's a pole out there, and from here I see it at one angle, the gentleman over there can look out of his window and he sees it from a different angle, and this other person looks out here—she sees it from a third angle. We're all seeing the same pole; we're all seeing it from a different angle; and we're all "right". But I have not got the right to say to the gentleman over there, "Your angle's wrong, mine's right." Mine's right for me, because this is where I am. His is right for him: that's where he is. You can make anything take you over. The kaleidoscopic mind, as Dogen calls it, is all important: the willingness to be able to see other people's opinions, to understand other people, to have sympathy. Realize that other people have the right to their point of view. The fact that one person calls It "God" and another "Allah" and a third "the Eternal" or "x-y-z", that's all right too.

Dr. Raymond Moody wrote a book* which was talking about near-death experiences, and all of them had visions at the time, and one was a doctor who was an atheist. Instead of seeing a vision of the Buddha or Christ or something like that, he had this lovely, warm, pinky-gold blob that came to embrace him. And the effect it had on him was exactly the same as what the religious visions had on the other people, but because he was an atheist it just turned up as a lovely pinky-gold blob. And they said, "Oh, you imagined this; it was hallucinated", and (this was really delightful to me: I almost spluttered with glee) he gets as mad as anybody else has ever got when you tell them their visions aren't real; he says, "I know when I'm hallucinating; I wasn't hallucinating:

---

* Raymond A. Moody, Jr., M.D., *Life After Life*, 38th ed. (New York: Bantam Books, 1986).

this was real!" It was so delightful, because it didn't happen exactly the same way.

The kindness of the Eternal is unlimited. Think of the incredible love and longing for we "sparks" to return to It: It is willing to appear in whatever form will not be offensive, so as to be most embracing at the time of death; it's exquisite! Think of what we're aiming at when we try to meditate! No wonder when you forsake self, you realize yourself to be this minuscule thing (less than a grain of sand; even at that, that's miles too big) in this incredible scheme of things. Just try to imagine a love of that type! And don't set up cardboard facades of doctrine and say, "That's mine, and that's the only right one", because then you've drunk the wine of delusion like you wouldn't believe!

5.

The Ceremony of Household Life

Today we are going to have a look at the first of the two great ways of putting all of this into practice in daily life: the way of the householder. The Buddha taught, and Soto Zen maintains to this day, that both the way of the householder and the way of the monk are necessary and are complementary to one another. If you wish to know the perfection of the household way, study Vimalakirti, who is the prototype of the greatest of all lay people. He is pictured here* in his house with his wife. Always he was being asked questions. He was a "true man" in every sense of the term: people came to talk to him as to a priest; he was regarded as very, very knowledgeable. And he was always ill. The reason was simple: people made so many demands on him he was sort of on a smorgasbord, and they came in and "ate him", you know, every day of the week. The *Vimalakirti Scripture*† is probably one of the finest scriptures that lay trainees can read. It's also one of the finest that a monk can read as well, but I'm saying this from the point of view of a lay person

---

* This lecture series on living the Way of Zen as a householder was originally accompanied by slides.

† Charles Luk, trans. and ed., *The Vimalakirti Nirdesa Sutra* (Boston, Massachusetts: Shambhala Publications, 1990).

Vimalakirti and his wife.

who really understands Buddhism. It's an incredibly valuable scripture, for it shows the pinnacle of training for the Mahayana Buddhist householder. I will not be referring to it in detail during these lectures, because I want to discuss foundations rather than pinnacles, but I do recommend that you read it, for it shows you where all of this is leading. What I will do over the next few hours is to look at various aspects of daily life with you and see how the ceremonies of Soto Zen can show you that what appears mundane is, in reality, sacred. And by the end of this I hope that you will also see that the whole of life is a ceremony: dignified, worthy of respect, and religious in every aspect.

YOUTH

There is a scroll that was given to me (it was one of about thirty or forty prints that were made of a very famous picture) by Koho Zenji. It depicts the story of an old man who's got his "fire"—the fire of ardor and zeal to find the Eternal within him—but he's older than anybody else and says, "Which way? Which way?" And a little boy looks up and says, "That way: that's where it is, down the road." This was given to me when I first went to Sojiji and was put in my room because I was about twenty years older than the monks there, and I had come with a fire and zeal saying, "Which way?" and these young monks helped point for me. Do not despise the young. And when I learned not to despise being told what to do by seventeen-year-olds (which isn't very easy when you've been teaching them in high school and you're thirty-eight years old), I got another picture.

Your own children can be excellent teachers, you know. They know exactly where to catch you in your training, and they do study you to see if you are really training. I recall a three-year-old who looked at her mother (she'd been taught to meditate and the like, just to sit with her mother, and her mother had said that she sat to meditate because it was a quiet place within) when her mother got mad with her on one occasion, and she said, "Mommy, you've left your quiet place." (laughter) So, they're much more honest about it than we are. They can actually keep you well in training, or they can drag you all the way out of it, depending on how well you yourself are training.

When it comes to educating a child in the Buddhist religion, the first and foremost thing is that the child must be cherished—not merely looked after, or even loved, but cherished. However foolish its comments, however childish, however silly, however babyish, the child is trying to express itself and must never be thought of as something that is *needing* to be educated, but rather as that which has within itself all the knowledge that matters. And it is our duty as religious educators to unlock the doors of that knowledge so that the child may experience and express what it already knows.

In a very real way, the religious education of the child starts prior to birth, on the very night of its conception. The attitude of mind of the parents—whether they are in a selfish mood, simply wishing to gratify their own pleasure, or whether they are wishing to produce a child which both of them will love—will affect the child at a later date, for there is that in a child which somehow senses whether they were wanted, whether they were cherished, from the start. Do not make mistakes that will cause a child to ask at a later date, with genuine grief in its heart, "Why did you beget me? Why was I born?"

Of course, Buddhism, unlike some other religions, does not believe in original sin. Therefore it places no guilt on the child from the moment he or she is conceived. Instead, it says that we are simply born, and later, as a result of what we do with ourselves, of what happens to us, and of our going into dualistic thinking, we educate ourselves out of our original oneness of mind into a duality which we then have to transcend if we are to be able to do anything whatsoever to overcome the spiritual illnesses our education has generated. The Buddhist teacher therefore says, "This child knows all, as indeed I know all, but they cannot yet express it (and I can only express it partially). Therefore we are both on the same road. I have been going along it for a little longer than they have and I will try to go at the speed they are going so that they may catch up with me and, perhaps, be able to surpass me—who knows?" So it is the duty of one who would teach Buddhism to a child to get their egocentric self out of the way to a very, very great extent so that the education of the child may be a free and beautiful thing, untrammeled by "Look at what *I* have achieved in *my* educating of this child!" It is the child that does the educating of themselves by using their experiences to fall back on later; the child makes the running; and it is the child that matters—we are all children in the Buddha Nature. When we say, as adults, "I know and you do not", we are really saying, "Our Buddha Nature is better than your Buddha Nature"; thus is set up duality, self, fear, and inadequacy. If, on the other hand, we say, "Your Buddha Nature and our Buddha Nature are one, but there is a difference between us because you are smaller than us and we are older than you; therefore we have run a little farther but we will come back to help you run as far", the difference in our attitude of mind, and the difference in the attitude of the child to learning, is phenomenal.

I am often asked, "How do you teach meditation to children and what is the best age to start at?" In the East, the

Lay minister meditating with her children at home altar.

average child is taught to meditate as soon as it is possible for them to sit upright, i.e., around one or two years old. No doctrine is put into the child's head. The mother and father, and the rest of the family, will sit quietly in front of the family altar; the child, without being restrained, will either sit for a few moments or roll around on the floor with the parents taking no notice. The parents thus express their knowledge of the child's latent understanding and do not treat it as less than themselves. In a very short time the child wants to sit like the parents, as do, interestingly enough, the dog and cat. I have sat down to meditate and my cat has come up, looked at the wall, and then sat down to look at it with me. Thus, if the parents meditate, the child will meditate, too.

I have seen children at the age of two and a half doing formal meditation in the lay meditation hall in Sojiji—and doing a wonderful job. These children do a meditation so pure and exquisite it is unbelievable to watch; but they would not be able to discuss the Buddha Nature with you, nor would they be able to put into words the doctrine of the Trikaya,* nor would they be able to explain the "all is one and the all is different" that their little bodies express. Their explanations are not as the world understands explanations. And yet every part of their bodies will express the "all is one and the all is different": they will express the Buddha Nature for they have learned to meditate with their whole being untrammeled by duality. They are indeed whole creatures and can teach us much.

A bit later in childhood, one can begin to teach simple Buddhist concepts, but you must keep in mind: no indoctrination; allow the children to bring it out for themselves. You could show them, shall we say, a doll which has two faces. "Do you know what a two-faced one is? Do you know what someone is who is not quite telling the truth? It sounded so good, their story, and yet something in you, inside your guts, tells you it's not quite right." You've always got to encourage the "gut feeling" (for lack of a better word), the innate inner sense, within the child so that it gets to know its own Buddha Nature. As you know, the answer to every koan—to every religious problem—comes from one's own faith within one's own guts, and a child grows this faith by discovering that he or she does know what is truly right and that there is something they can trust within themselves, not from some nebulous heaven outside in the sky or some demon that's going to come up with a big pitchfork. If a doll helps with

---

* See footnote on p. 261.

this, or a story, use it: you can use anything under the sun that works.

They know by instinct, but they do have to be channeled, if you like, into right action. They know what is instinctively good because it makes them peaceful within. What is instinctively bad makes you feel awfully ill within. So allow the instinct to show, and help them become more aware of it so that they can distinguish it from other things and thus learn how to trust its guidance in life. Thus, you do have to guide the child; you have to give it the chance to see that what it was doing was wrong from a Buddhist point of view, without belaboring the point and making it feel guilty or small. Everyone knows that if you don't have some few rules for the kids, they're going to leave their toys on the top of the stairs and mother's going to break her neck falling down it. And somebody's going to trip up on what little junior has built on the sidewalk. Small children (and some adults) simply do not understand the consequences of their actions, so rules (and laws) are necessary: you can't do it by any other means. But you're not doing it to take people's freedom away; you're doing it so they can have it. Above all, when doing this, you must never humiliate. Because what you are encouraging is the Buddha Nature to grow within, and if you are humiliated—the Buddha Nature is a very delicate thing, incredibly strong and also incredibly shy—It will not show Itself all that clearly.

Now don't be surprised, by the way, that if you teach them to trust their Buddha Natures and take responsibility for their actions, once they start taking responsibility they really take it. And there is always a natural respect and gratitude for the parents. There must always be the sense that the parent is someone whom they respect and whom they will look after in the parent's old age. Not necessarily in their own house, as is done in the East, but always there will be recognition that there is a responsibility to that parent. And, if you allow a person to grow up normally in this way, one seldom finds there'll be a real fight at a later date. Of course, every child has their "rebellion sword", especially as a teenager; you have to expect that. In my day and age it was very easy: all you did was forget to wear a hat and gloves, and people thought the Empire was falling! It's much more work nowadays to have a good rebellion: you know, you have to stick a safety pin through your nose and turn your hair green. I'm glad it wasn't that difficult in my day. (laughter)

At the conclusion of childhood, between the ages of fourteen and sixteen in the Far East and perhaps a bit older over here, Buddhist young people are then ready to take Jukai. Jukai, the formal first taking of the precepts, is the equivalent of a Buddhist coming of age ceremony. After taking Jukai, a young person may indulge in proper pleasures with a male or female. It is the time in the Far East when they are allowed to meet members of the opposite sex, when they can go to dances, theaters and the like—because they have found out what they are doing it for. They can then enjoy their young adult lives, and also in the Far East, if someone has taken the precepts and he or she wants to marry, the church will always marry them. So to do Jukai is to be accepted into the church as a full adult; if there are committees, they can be elected to committees; if there are meetings, they can attend meetings. They are no longer children because they have taken the responsibility of recognizing that they themselves wish to keep the precepts, but not because some god has said they must and not because some devil has said he'll drive them into hell if they don't. They do it because they want to.

Question: "I have a nine-year-old son who is interested in coming with me to the meditation group; is that okay?"

Yes. They can join in if they wish, but they should not be required to. There is no requirement. Children are also welcome to attend ceremonies. At Buddhist "Sunday school" in Japan, I saw them being taught about ceremonial as sort of games, dance games and the like. And they just realize that religion is a natural part of life and it's something that they can join into. And then, too, sometimes they just played baseball with the monks.

Monk's comment: "If a child is interested in participating at home, you can always offer them the opportunity to meditate with you, give them a place to meditate and things like that. And also, if you have some sort of a small altar, you can always have them help look after it, keep it clean, and explain to them about offering incense, and have them do that when they're old enough."

Question: "Do you think we should give children vegetarian food at home but allow them to eat meat at friends' houses and school?"

The ideal thing is to let the child decide. I realize that this may be dangerous, especially when there's an illness which requires a specific diet. In that case, of course, the child must always be able to eat what is necessary so that he or she may live and continue their training. That's one very important point. In general, however, I would say that I would discuss it with the child, if they're old enough to know what seems good. You may find that vegetarianism is quite natural for the child, and in that case they will turn vegetarian, and fairly fast; don't be scared if that happens. And they may not.

> *Question:* "How can we teach gratitude to our children without sort of forcing them into external forms of politeness rather than developing inner charity? Or is it that we need to learn how to recognize the natural gratitude that's already there?"

Yes, we do: because we want to find out what's going on inside them. I've often said we educate our children out of enlightenment and then they have to educate themselves back into it. But I don't know how else you can really help them. I'm not saying that this is wrong; I do think that we should not be too surprised if we don't get gratitude for what we give, especially as they get older, because a lot of children have to put up with an awful lot from parents. There's the old saying in England that "A sweater is something a child wears when its mother feels cold." And it's perfectly true: don't expect gratitude for that; take into consideration that the child may have a totally different metabolism from yourself. I've never yet met any English mother that understood that. (laughter) So, it's not that simple, and you do want feedback.

I have got to the state with children that I talk to them very much as I talk to adults, but perhaps in somewhat simpler English. And that way I can get feedback on what's really going on within. So, if you do treat children in that way—if you think of them as just small adults rather than as children—you get a much better feedback. You also find out if they really need the sweater! And not insisting on it is very, very wise. Creating the parent-child gap is very easy by insisting on gratitude for things that really a child knows they don't need or want. It's not very comforting, is it? But it really is: communicate—just talk to the child, and not as if they know nothing or are stupid. They get really mad if you talk baby talk to them or treat them as if they're stupid, 'cause they're not.

I can remember, in London, having a bunch of children that I was teaching in the Sunday school of the Buddhist Church, and Koho Zenji, who I was corresponding with, wanted some pictures of the Sunday school. I arranged with the parents that the children could come nicely dressed and we'd group them around the statue. There was a seven-year-old who hadn't seen one very pretty little girl before, and he kept eyeing her thoughtfully, and as I was about to set up the camera, I saw him wink solemnly at her and say, "Later?" And that's when you start thinking: who is the child and who is the adult? (laughter) So, don't do it the other way, and, above all, don't expect thanks. But it's nice when it comes naturally. If you do it this way, I've found that children give thanks naturally. The important thing is not to require it, but to have it come out naturally. As you know, that is the true meaning of gratitude: giving thanks without ever being required to, just because one's whole being is so full of thanks. And that's how you can bring it out. In doing it this way you can get genuine gratitude out of your fellow adults, too; you are not requiring it, and if they are rude or coarse with you, just don't be coarse back; you don't have to be. If they don't wish to change, they will eventually go away and leave you, and you'll be with the people who want to be different. It does happen; it takes time. You'll always find one person around you who bugs you, of course. For some reason, the Buddhas and Ancestors seem to think that's necessary—maybe just to keep you on your toes.

MARRIAGE

For a good several hundred years after Buddhism came to Japan, probably at least until the time of Keizan, weddings were never done in Buddhist temples. They were done in Shinto shrines or in other faiths, but not in Buddhism. This is because of an erroneous belief that, since people were reborn, if you were constantly having children then you were encouraging people not to train but to get themselves reborn, and therefore you should not get married because then you would not encourage people to be reborn. They failed to notice, of course, that people are going to have children whether they are married or not, and if somebody hasn't trained properly in this life, they're going to get reborn in any case. This is one of the innovations of Keizan Zenji in the fourteenth century: he decided that it was not wrong to have a wedding ceremony in a Buddhist temple. There was just some erroneous thinking on the subject of birth and rebirth, and so Soto Zen has an actual wedding ceremony, although a lot of the other Buddhist churches in the Far East do not.

Now, a Buddhist wedding in Soto Zen is a very beautiful thing, and I have tried to translate it in a way that conveys its true meaning to Westerners. It is two people coming together, making a contract in which each one guarantees to make the other a complete and absolute success in his or her own way, as much as it is possible to make that person a success. That is the main vow they exchange: "I guarantee to make you a success in your own way." So everything is geared to doing what one can to help the partner in every way possible. The first Buddhist wedding ceremony that came out was slightly different. It started off with the husband guaranteeing to love and to cherish, and then to keep

Wedding ceremony: lighting the wedding candle.

and to guard; and for the wife to love and to cherish, to cook for and provide children, and to guard what he brought home. Then Soto Zen realized that what really mattered was not somebody keeping to the letter of tradition in this way, but making everybody in the family, and one's partner especially, a complete and absolute success, as much as it lay within your power to do so. As such, I think the Soto wedding ceremony has come as close to the ideal marriage ceremony as possible.

It's extraordinarily beautiful: there is not only the exchanging of rings, but also each comes to the altar carrying a candle, signifying that they are two of the lights of the Buddha's crown. Together they light one candle from their two, signifying that they wish to become one with the Cosmic Buddha and one with each other. And they are. They then have their hands bound by the rosary of the priest, signifying the oneness of their union. And people make some strange comments sometimes when I'm doing this, because the lotus blossom scepter is then placed on top of the bound hands for the pronouncement that they are husband and wife, and people say of me, "She's using the cosmic welding torch again today." (laughter) It's actually not a "cosmic welding torch": doing this symbolizes the seeds of the lotus blossom dropping on the marriage and blessing it so as to make them able to make themselves a complete and absolute success, each in their own way. And up to now we have found that this type of marriage ceremony seems to hold people together a lot better than some of the others we've bumped into, simply because of the intention of making the other a success.

But it is essentially a temporal ceremony, and one should understand quite clearly where Keizan is coming from with regard to rebirth and children. For some it is good to enter a monastery and be celibate. For others it is good not to enter a monastery but to remain single. And for others again, it is good not to enter a monastery and to get married and have children. None of these things are contrary to the teachings of the Buddhas and Ancestors. The only reason why some people get stuck on the idea, "Well, I'm missing out on something if I don't become a monk, if I get married", is pure self; they are saying, "What have they got that I'm not going to get?" Because every single person, whether she or he is in a monastery or outside it, can get to the Cosmic Buddha. They're going to go by a different road, but they're still going to get there. One is not going to get something different from the other. One may get there faster than the other because they're "at it" full-time, but the place they're going to get to is going to be identically the same one. So, there is not a heaven for the monks and a heaven for the lay people: it's just how long you are going to take and which road you are going to go by. And it should also be understood that people who have children may very well be doing a complete bodhisattvic act. If I were a being who needs to be reborn because of past karma, I would prefer to have a really good pair of Buddhist parents who were helping me find the right road. And for some Buddhists this is the right road, this is their way of training: to help the young, so that they too may find the Buddha. So, do not think that Buddhism is against marriage.

Now we're going on to the next topic, but before I do that, does anybody have any questions they want to ask on weddings? I think it's all fairly clear.

Question: "What about the Buddhist view of divorce?"

That's another matter; that's another matter entirely. Once a pair have been married, they have united their karma, and, as far as Buddhism is concerned, they may live apart, they may think they're not together, but they're still linked together. Hmm, maybe the "cosmic welding torch" *is* a cosmic welding torch after all. (laughter) There's no way to undo what has been done. The partners can live apart; if they wish to collect up the karma of living apart, it's no skin off Buddhism's nose. We're not going to get into an argument of whether you should or shouldn't. As far as Buddhism's concerned you're hitched, but if you want to complicate your karma by getting hitched to somebody else, that's your problem. We're not going to have a fight on it. The beauty of the Cosmic Buddha is that It just sits there and says, "If you wish to complicate your life, please be my guest."

Monk's comment: "It's like any other karma: you can't undo it as if it had never happened. You can do some other act; you can add some other karma or merit to it, but you can't simply make it 'unhappen'."

Question: "Do you have any kind of premarital counseling such as some of the Western religions do?"

We can have, if someone thinks they need it, but we've not done it on a regular basis. We've not had the necessity, odd as it may seem: this thing of making each other a success seems somehow to help that quite a lot. It's not two unequal partners; it's two people trying to do the best they can for each other. And, after all, what else is love?

PRACTICE AT HOME

First of all, you must understand that, as Dogen says in his instructions for meditation, "The koan arises naturally." Now, the koan is your fundamental question, the driving force of your Buddhist practice. And, in the beginning, you may think it is merely "My feet hurt during meditation." So, you fiddle them around until you find where they don't. And then you just sit again. And you realize that the purpose is not to sit there in pain, but to find the Unborn. So fiddle your feet until you've got them right; it's very simple. If that's the first koan to solve, deal with it and then you go on from there. And the natural koans soon get out of the practical and the mundane and are lifted to much greater things and much higher things.

But don't despise the worldly, don't despise the mundane. As Dogen himself said, "Remember, it is by the aegis of the human body that we can find the Truth." If you're in any other body, how can you find the Truth? We can't talk to

Winnie, my bulldog down on the floor here; we hope she's found the Truth. You and I can talk to each other; I can tell you what to do. If you're dead, I can't tell you what to do: you're not here. Don't despise the human body and, above all, don't ill treat it. Remember the "three lacks": your body deserves food; it deserves rest; it deserves clothing. It does not deserve excess: "Six parts of a full stomach support the man; the other two support his doctor." Don't become a glutton, and, above all, do not turn yourself into an ascetic. The Buddha Himself warned that it was wrong; every one of the great ancestors have warned that it is wrong. Any extreme is wrong, and it will do harm, so don't let it happen—under any circumstances. Not if you want to truly know the Cosmic Buddha. And a properly trained Zen layman, or laywoman, understands this, and uses it in their own daily life. It *is* their daily life.

Now, one of the things that is most helpful in reminding yourself of this Middle Way between indulgence and asceticism is the mealtime ritual, which I mentioned earlier. The mealtime ritual is solely to have a good look at one's self and see the reasons for which one eats food. It starts by asking us to "think deeply about the ways and means by which this food has come." Most serious Mahayana Buddhists are, of course, vegetarians, because one does as little harm as one can. But there is the harm of pulling leaves off the lettuce and cutting into root vegetables and this sort of thing, so one has to be sure that one is making use of one's life properly. Otherwise things should not be sacrificed for you. Why should things be sacrificed if you do nothing of benefit in this world? So, we recite what we call "the five thoughts": first, "We must think deeply of the ways and means by which this food has come." What has been sacrificed, where has it come from? Then, "We must consider our merit when accepting it." What have we done; have we been useful, have we been lazy, do we really deserve all that we've got; how well have we trained? Next, "We must protect ourselves from error by excluding greed from our minds." In other words, don't be so ravenous to attack the food out of sheer greed that you forget to think about these other things. There's plenty of time; you are not starving. I don't think I need to go into that one any further; you know what I mean. "We will eat lest we become lean and die." I have interpreted that as eating for the food value but not for what one fancies all the time. This is something that I am not always agreed with by the people that are with me. But I eat now solely for the food value and nothing else; that and the keeping of my body healthy. In other words, I think of food as medicine and medicine as food—not as something that is just to be enjoyed and taken lightly. And finally, "We accept this food so that we may become enlightened." I think you can see that all the "five thoughts" are really connected very much together. You eat so that you shall not become lean and die. You eat for the food value so that you won't sacrifice more than you need, nor will you become greedy, and also so that you are able to train much better than you otherwise would. That's the way I work it out. And if you recite these "five thoughts" before each meal, you will soon see how they reverberate all through your life, because the attitude of mind behind them applies to many things, not just food.

The same is true of meditation: make it part of daily life, not just when you are doing formal sitting, but bring it into all of your life. You do this by bringing your mind back to just what you are doing at the moment. It's the same mindful awareness: you use it in the ceremony hall, in the meditation hall, and you use it when sitting in your car. We used to do a brochure on sanctifying the mundane which showed somebody sitting at a red light with a seat belt on, paying attention to the road, and a child in a child-restraint beside them. And another car alongside this one, where the person had the radio blaring, a coffee in one hand, and was talking to their neighbor. This is how to sanctify the mundane and, at the same time, help everybody else around you. Now, obviously there are going to be times when you need to talk to your neighbor in the car. The point that we were trying to make was: if you can be as alert and mindful in your car as you are in meditation, then you have taken the meditation out of the meditation hall and put it into the car. And you have made it possible to find the Cosmic Buddha, the Eternal, just as much at the red light as inside the temple. That is what you should be doing with all aspects of your practice: finding uses for it in your everyday life. You can do this not only with meditation but with ceremonial, iconography, scriptures . . . everything.

One of the things that can help with this is to have a home altar. Now, there are many variations that you can make, and we will look at some of them, but a few things are basic. The altar should be arranged as a series of steps. On the highest one you have your scroll or picture of a Buddha, or your statue of a Buddha or a Bodhisattva. On the next one down you have a candle on the right side and flowers in a vase on the left. I always recommend to people not to use cut flowers but instead to have a living plant or artificial flowers. As you get deeper into meditation, your sensitivity will become much more alive, and just looking at the flowers with their cut stems can start causing you pain because you know that this destruction of living things was not necessary. I know one person who went through a forest after trees had been cut down there, and her ankles were hurting. So, you can become extremely close to the rest of living things, and

A typical home altar.

if you want to meditate, it is best not to have cut flowers. It is best to have a very alive plant, if conditions for it are suitable, preferably a perennial. A green one that is always growing is an excellent idea—just something that is full of life. I've often said to people at our various temples, "Please don't bring us cut flowers" because of this problem, but live plants we love. And, of course, we love flowers in the garden; you just don't cut them.

If you have a third step, then here, in the center, you would have an incense bowl with a stick of incense in it, or you can put that in the center of the second step if you only have two. It is nice to have incense, but be careful of what sort you get. The Indian incense can be much too pungent for safe meditation, in that it'll be getting on your nerves after a short time. And it also seems to create a lot of allergies. I don't know what they put in it, but your purpose is not to sit there and sneeze for half an hour. So, find an incense with which you can safely live and which you really like. On the same step as the incense you put your offerings. Always one should make an offering of some sort. And then somebody in the family should eat it: you don't put it there to waste; it must never be wasted. It's usually fruit. You sometimes have a couple little lanterns here too, one on each side. The reason that the items are placed as they are is because they form a circle: a circle of offering and receiving. On the way up the circle (it always turns from left to right), we make the offering of flowers and incense, and what we receive in return is the light of understanding, the light of the Unborn. Those are the basics.

Now, you also can have a small family tombstone or a family death book, actually called a "Family Book of the Buddhas". In the Far East these books have a page for each day of the month, thirty-one days. Then you have the "Buddha of the first day", the "Buddha of the second day", the "Buddha of the third day", etc. Supposing your great-grandfather died on the third: you put his name on the page for the third, and he's the "Buddha on the third day of the month". And perhaps your father died on the fifth day: he becomes the "Buddha of the fifth day", to whom you offer gratitude. And so it goes on, and sometimes you've got two or three people who died on one day: "The Buddhas of this day are. . . ." You can recite a scripture for them, you do your three bows of gratitude, you then recite the offertory: "We offer this incense and these offerings to the Buddha (of such-and-such a day) so that we and they and all beings may be able to obtain the Truth." It's a very beautiful thing. Your relatives are still with you, very much so in reality, in

Two types of memorial tablet (small wooden
tombstone): individual (left), family (right).

this spiritual place where you find yourself in your meditation. That's a very exquisite thing.

Now, as I said, you can also have a family tombstone,
which is very difficult to describe. Imagine a box of wood sitting up on end, which is hollow with an open front, and it has
a bunch of slim pieces of wood which fit snugly inside, facing
the opening. It has doors on the front, and on the little pieces
of wood you write the Buddha of the day on each piece. And
you just lift them out and put the one for today in front so that
the name can be seen. You can stand this beside the Buddha or
on the second step at the center rear so that it is in line with
the Buddha. "The Buddha of such-and-such a day is . . .", and

there's the name. The whole thing should be beautiful and dignified; often there is a top crowned with a jewel, the jewel of the Cosmic Buddha. And you do your meditation in front of this altar, with the candle and the incense stick.

And you can do your own memorial services right there at your home altar. There are specific dates when it is best to do memorial ceremonies. This is because of the belief that mourning takes place over a period of three years, and also the full working out of one's karma takes place over a period of three years after death. This being so, memorial ceremonies are said at specific times: the day of death, three days after, five days after, then seven days after that, and then after the first crucial forty-nine days it gradually changes to every six months, then every year, and then three years. And then, if you want to go on giving thanks down the centuries, it goes to whenever you want to do it, or, if you do it at a temple, at least every twenty-five years. Temples vary on that one: it can be every twenty-five, fifty, or one hundred. In the end, you know, it does have some rather amusing results in the Far East, because you get little old ladies coming along on buses (there will be a busload come in from a village), and you'll see some tiny little old lady with a huge sack of wooden tombstones, because she's got one for each person instead of one of these family boxes. They come into the temple carrying this huge bag of tombstones over their shoulders and hand them to the monks for a memorial to be done for the whole family. The whole lot will be put on the altar: the "Buddhas of such-and-such a family", not of a specific date. And it gives a much greater sense of family than we have over here—certainly much greater than I had in England. It works very well indeed. It also works excellently from the point of view of giving you a chance to be grateful for everything that has gone on. Gratitude is so important in this.

The memorial ceremonies that you do at home are really the same as those that are done in a temple; the only thing that is done differently are the actions, because you have a different setting. The actual basic ceremony is identical. First you have your offering of incense and the naming of who the ceremony is for. Then the recitation of the scripture of your choice, followed by the offertory in which you offer the cakes and the food and the incense to whoever is being offered to (grandfather, grandmother, whoever), wherever they may be. Then comes the final dedication to Buddha, Dharma, and Sangha at the end of the ceremony. Now, Buddhism does not doctrinalize about what happens after death. Buddhism has always believed in rebirth, but we don't necessarily know where the residual karma has gone. So, the offertory at a memorial ceremony says, "I offer this to John Doe, wherever he may be." That is what is known as a transfer of merit. We have made offerings; if one person makes an offering, another person may receive the benefits. That is the belief. So something is offered in memory of the dead, and the merit of the offering is passed on.

Now remember that it is the merit that is passed on, not the offering itself, and the karmic residue that receives it, not some individual soul. People seem to get confused about this, with some rather amusing but sad consequences. For instance, one of the practices that happens a lot in the country districts in Japan is to make offerings of things that the deceased really liked. Imagine what it's like if you've got a drunk that's just died. I can remember a number of ceremonies in which there were enough bottles of sake on the altar to slosh the entire Japanese army! And the families believed that the priest had to partake of this to prove that he or she was really passing on the merit. I can remember sitting at a funeral on one occasion with five bottles of sake in front of me and saying, "No!" And they were saying, "But how will he get the merit if you don't drink it?" I came up with something that was perhaps slightly wicked, but I've since thought it was slightly ingenious. I told them that I had five friends, which was true, who loved sake and who were great monks, and that I would send them a bottle each, so that the dead would get far more merit. They loved the idea, so that's exactly what I did. What else could I do? Have you ever tried drinking five quart bottles of sake? But they are so naive, the country folk. They didn't realize that it was incongruous, and you had to be compassionate enough to realize that they didn't think it was incongruous or impossible. They were grieving over a dead relative, and I would have been deeply wrong and would have injured them if I'd done anything other than that. As it was, it worked very, very well. And the five people were delighted. In fact, I think three of them went into their ceremony halls and recited a tiny scripture for the deceased. So the deceased got the merit of extra scriptures, just because of a bottle of sake. I do not regard that as doing wrong. I regard it as coming under what is called "wise ways of helping beings" in Buddhism. It's the wisest way I could think of for five bottles of sake. I don't drink. Questions? Yes.

> *Question:* "Could you describe more clearly the different meanings of candles and flowers?"

Yes, by all means. We offer the flowers and incense, which symbolize the true spirit of prayer, the true heart, the true spirit of meditation, the longing, the offering up. Which means that we are asking to ascend to the Buddha. We are carrying our offering of training to the Buddha, which brings forth the light of the Dharma, the teaching. It is a circulation, and it is the deeper meaning of the circle, of constantly walking in the circle. To make the offering, the sweet smelling offering of our prayers and our meditation and our life's work, which takes us on our way to Buddhahood, which brings forth the light of the Truth. And that is the meaning of it: 'round and 'round in a circle.

Question: "What about the offering of pure water?"

The offering of pure water . . . ah, I hadn't mentioned that one, had I? There should be a glass or bowl of water behind the incense burner: the water of the spirit, the Water of the Eternal. We offer the water, our water of the spirit, so that it may be blessed by the fountain of the Eternal; we offer up plain water, we receive back the Water of the Eternal. It represents what we do in our meditation, of offering up ourselves so that we may be blessed and we may feel the fountain, know the fountain, of True Life. Okay, anymore on this before we go anywhere else? Yes.

Question: "Who do you include in the family?"

Grandparents, great-grandparents, all the way straight back. As many as you want. Anybody you want to. Quite literally all the way back, as feels right or is useful to you.

Question: "I mean, just parents, grandparents—or is it aunts, uncles . . . ?"

Oh, I've got aunts and uncles and you name it: brothers, sisters. . . . Yes. Yes, go ahead.

Question: "Isn't it also a very close and beloved friend?"

Oh yes. But in the Far East you'd normally have a separate tombstone made for a close friend; it wouldn't necessarily go on the family altar. I don't know that we have to follow the strict Japanese custom on that. We could put our friends on it if we feel like it.

> *Question:* "If a person died a year and a half ago you could still . . . ?"

Oh yes; oh yes, by all means.

> *Question:* "What about people who haven't had parents but had foster parents, or somebody who was a teacher when you were very young?"

That's fine. That's no problem. You see what we're dealing with here is not ancestor worship but an offering of gratitude to those who helped us to train and seek the Truth.

> *Question:* "In other words, it includes all people who guided you?"

Yes. And it brings all of the world into it: it can include the local road sweeper, if he showed you the Truth. It doesn't have to be a specific relative.

> *Question:* "I was wondering about bad relatives or people who were sort of evil or mean to you."

I'd say they need it more than anyone else. After all, they've shown you how not to be. There are Buddhas who can show you what not to be, you know, and they're just as much Buddhas for showing you that. I made that statement once when I was on the campus at Berkeley around the time of the Watergate hearings, when somebody said to me, "Well, what would you do if you had a relative like Mr. Nixon?" And I said, "He's a great Buddha: he's showing me how not to behave." And I was not being funny, he really was—what not to do. There is great gratitude for somebody showing you that, because often we don't know what we shouldn't do. There's nothing wrong with that.

Question: "What is the true meaning of merit?"

Supposing you've got a relative who you really feel worried as to where he or she might have ended up. And I'm sure that all of us have at least someone, friend or relative, who we worry a bit about. Suppose you've got that and you really want the very best that can be done for them. The thought is "I really want the very best for this person. I'm making this offering; I pray that they may be helped, wherever they may be." That's really offering merit: it's trying to help, without judgment and without expectation. And there are people who need help.

> *Monk's comment:* "I view it as an offering of love and goodwill back to the Source of all love and goodwill, that somehow it may be used in whatever way is best to assist the karma of that individual. It's an offering up to the Source that doesn't need it anyway, but in a way somehow . . ."

We both of us know it doesn't need to be done, but we're doing it anyway. It's a rather beautiful act that somehow makes an awful lot of sense the more you do it. But it's a little difficult to put it into cold terms in a university classroom.

Monk continues: "... you can't explain exactly what you do, but something happens when you do it."

Question: "Does time run out, like if you found out about a relative a hundred years ago...?"

Oh no, no, no; it never runs out. I've seen people turn up with bags that went way back to the twelve-hundreds. They've been a bit eaten and chewed by the mice, but they're still there. It makes all of life so much more really and truly alive.

WORK

Don't despise any occupation. All is the work of a Buddha, especially if it is offered for the benefit of other people as well as self. You must never cut self out of this, by the way. We train for self and other. I remember saying to the person who was teaching me, "No, we don't: we train for others and self." And he said, "Well, you may, but I don't and neither does anybody else here. And if you take the trouble to think about it, you'll find that you're wrong." I thought about it and I was wrong: we train for self and others. But we do not make self with a capital "S" and others with a small "o". We are both equal in this; we are all training for the same reason. But don't think that you do not count in this; don't always put yourself down. And if you do always put yourself down, you will not find the Eternal because you will always think you are no good, that you're not capable of finding the Eternal. "It's not possible for me to find the Eternal: I'm a female, I'm a this, I'm a that; I couldn't possibly find the Eternal."

The Cosmic Buddha doesn't care two hoots what you are. Pure Love can only be interested in the fact that you want to find It. So don't put yourself down and don't give yourself the idea that you are only doing something for everybody else. We're all in this together, both self and others. Now, this may not seem to be all that relevant to the work we do, but stop and think about it: what is the purpose of our livelihood? Is it not the mutual benefit of self and others?

> *Question:* "Next week at work I must choose between nine people who want the same job. How do you not hurt eight people?"

Well, you choose the best person for the job, the one who will be the most compassionate and the most efficient, and you hope that the other eight will get work. You see, the danger in what you're coming up against is that you (forgive me, it may sound a little harsh but it's not meant to) are really saying, "I would love to be God, because then I would have enough jobs for the whole lot." But you're not, you're human; you've got one. So you do the very best you can and, as a human, you wish the very best for the other eight. And tell them if something comes up that they're suitable for, you'll think of them. That way even if you can't spread jobs, you spread love. That's doing the best you can. But if you get emotion in it ("Oh dear, I so want to give work to the other eight, what can I do?"), you've wasted a wonderful opportunity of giving what you actually can give. There's no simple answer, and there's no avoiding the taking of the karma. And you will be taking the karma, because one or two of them are going to hate your guts (I guarantee you that one) however much love you give out. But that's not your problem; that's their training, not yours. You will have done the best you could.

Question: "I've been meditating for a few years now, and I find that it's harder to do my work than before I started. Not that I'm not as good at the job; if anything, I seem to be better at it, or at least that's what I'm told. The problem is that I seem to be so much more sensitive to the pain around me, in my fellow workers and our clients, that I get really tired and drained. And when I ask for help with this, the pain does not seem to go away, but somehow its 'darkness' is filled with 'specks of gold'. Is this making any sense?"

Any time someone, whether a lay member of the sangha or a priest member of the sangha, tries to do something about themselves they will find themselves burdened with other people's grief unless they really know that they themselves are not the Cosmic Buddha and that there is nothing in them that is not of the Cosmic Buddha. One of the sad things for members of the helping professions is that too many of them take onto themselves the suffering of others and make themselves eventually ill with it, instead of realizing that they are not the Cosmic Buddha and must ask for help from the Cosmic Buddha. This person, when asking for help, is shown the suffering and is shown it "shot through" with the golden points of light, the little moments that make one dance, the essence of the Buddha. One has to look at those little moments, one has to be willing to cry, "I am not sufficient. I cannot do it." But it is exactly these little glimpses of something greater that make it possible. These are the little moments of faith. The deeper we go into meditation, the more suffering becomes apparent, therefore the more important it is that our faith shall deepen and we shall learn to recognize the little golden moments that point the way to the Cosmic Buddha. We have to stop trying to hold on to being able to do something ourselves about that very suffering. For we can do nothing of ourselves, if "we" are in the way. If all we see is suffering, we ourselves are in the way. And if we are in the way, we cannot see the Cosmic Buddha working through it.

This is a very, very hard lesson to learn; for a layman or a laywoman it is even harder. But all the signs are there. This person is never truly apart from the temple. The "presence" is always there. Perhaps they need to study more deeply what the real temple is. For the real temple is the temple of one's own body, and the real cloister is everywhere. This does not mean that one should not become a monk, if one has a calling to do that. Nor does it mean that monks should all go out into the world. It means that the real cloister is everywhere, and the real "presence" is everywhere. We enter into a monastery—we retreat, as it were, in order that we be able to advance. We can only advance if we do not become caught by the hindrances. If our grief over the suffering of the world is constantly hindering us, we will not advance. If we cannot look at the suffering and see the "golden moments" and recognize what they are, recognize that they are the Cosmic Buddha shining through that suffering, and have faith to hold on to that, then nothing can help us. Thus, what was originally a dark and seemingly grieving and despairing place becomes the garden of the Bodhisattvas, the waveless sea of the saints, both before what is known as "death" and after what people call "death". The spirit of truth is within all these situations; the Buddha Nature is within all things. The world is a rough place to those who do not know this. The advantage of coming to a monastery for retreats is that it is a place in which one can set the world somewhat aside for a little and get closer to the little golden moments, to the Cosmic Buddha. Thus, they are the more easily recognized, not only in the monastery itself, but also in the world outside.

To see the Buddha in suffering, in pleasure, in pain, in joy, in sorrow—this is one of the greatest gifts of enlightenment. But faith is much needed to be able to do this, and you have to do a lot of work upon yourself before faith is a fully understood concept. Far too few people know what faith really means. In one sense, every one of us has incredible faith: we all believe that we will waken in the morning, though we have no proof of it. We also have no proof that we won't. We believe that we will, but one day we will not. Neither of these ideas terrifies us. It is with this attitude of mind that one must go through the world and the monastery. It is absolutely imperative that we feel the cloister beneath our feet wherever we go and the presence of the ceremony hall within our hearts wherever we go. Then, however much grief and suffering others try to lay upon us, or try to bring into us simply because in some cases the person concerned is looking for a sympathetic ear, or simply because we happen to be more open than others and therefore can feel it more clearly—whichever way it is—if we have found how to carry that "presence" in our hearts from the temple, whether we are here or whether we are sitting in the dining hall or working in a hospital or in a hospice or sitting in an office or driving a bus—no matter what we are doing—whatever the suffering that we see or that may come into us, we will see the Lord's work within it. And we will learn to accept that this is the way it is, because this is how karma works. And in accepting karmic consequence, we will find the Lord in all things and be able to work peacefully and effectively. This is to fully accept our humanity. And from this place you can actually do the very best that is possible about that suffering, although it is not "you" which does it.

COMMUNITY INVOLVEMENT

So many people feel that "getting into a flap" over something is to get involved in it, but it's not. To be truly involved is to be doing something wholeheartedly and yet to recognize one's own limitations. Not to try to do everything oneself, not to try to do the impossible, is to be concerned but not emotionally involved. Do not allow emotion to become the central theme of your life; do not be a slave to it. Emotion is important, but do not become emotional. There's nothing wrong with emotion—everyone feels emotion—but to become emotional is quite a different thing. To become emotional is to become so wrapped up in something that you can't see beyond it, and you can't really work with it. Not only can you not see beyond it, you can see no way out, 'round, or under it. And then you go into anger or despair because of it. Frequently, people are so overwhelmed by what is going on that they cannot see beyond it, and that is called "to become emotional" in Buddhism. Obviously a Zen master can breathe, they can love, and feel all the emotions of every other person; she or he is just not a slave to them.

Emotionalism is one thing to be careful of; idealism is another. Koho Zenji told me to be "very careful how I went with the Truth under my coat". Now, much as I love America (and I think she's got the best system going at the moment) she isn't exactly famous either for gentleness or total forgiveness, and I don't want anyone going off saying, "We've seen the ideal of Buddhism in action; let's go back and force it to work in our own communities." Ideals are lovely; don't get me wrong. And Buddhism has always said, "Work towards the Buddhist ideal within the framework of what is real", and that includes the laws of the country. A Buddhist is an extremely law-abiding person. And if there is something that is vicious, like the death penalty or something of this sort, then Buddhists work within the existing law to get the law changed. We do not go off and hide the murderer and get ourselves and Buddhism into disrepute. Do you understand what I'm saying on this? I am not teaching you to break the law; I am teaching what is the highest in Buddhism, and then, within the existing system, we work towards that highest ideal. Now please (and I love the enthusiasm that most Americans have) do not go rushing back to your cities and start forcing it into practice, because most Americans aren't ready for it yet.

There is an interesting piece in the "Record of Self-knowledge" Scripture,* which is really a "tariff board" of how many loads of merit you get for doing each right thing, and you get a hundred loads of merit for saving one person from the death penalty. You get fifty for working towards the removal of the death penalty. You get, I think it is, twenty for saving one man or woman from receiving the heavy bamboo (remember this goes way, way back). You get, I think it is, ten for saving a man or woman from being lightly bambooed; and so it goes on. What you are working for is to bring about the magnificence of the Buddha. But remember that you have to not break the precepts in bringing it about. And going off and doing what some people have complained to me that I don't do—which is civil disobedience and going out waving banners and all the rest of it—going off and doing that creates considerable karmic consequence. And, if you'll forgive me for saying so, I do not intend to end up either like Socrates or a few other people of fame in this

---

* Chun-fang Yu, trans., "The Record of Self-knowledge" in *The Renewal of Buddhism in China* (New York: Columbia University Press, 1981), pp. 233–259.

business, just because I have taught you the ideal. There is a difference between knowing the ideal and being attached to idealism; do you all understand what I'm saying? Ideals are great as descriptions of how we want things to be; when they are used as descriptions of how things are or "ought" to be, they become idealism, a form of delusion. So, I love you all: be very careful how you go with the Truth under your coats, as Koho Zenji told me. Especially in what he called "barbarian lands", which was his way of thinking of the West.

I will finish with a little story that you might find very interesting. This one (I hope I've got all the facts accurately because I think the person who told it to me is here but I'm not certain) took place in Cambodia not too long ago, maybe a year or a few months ago. I think it was an American reporter who was in a village, and there was a man there living as a perfectly ordinary person with his family, and this was a man who had caused the deaths of hundreds of people by torture to make the Communists happy. The reporter was absolutely horrified: "Why wasn't this man executed; why wasn't he at least in jail, etc.?" And the people said, "But he did sange (true contrition); how could he be in jail, let alone executed? How could we execute him?!? He is contrite." Now, the reporter got more and more furious and said they were all fools and idiots and dopes and everything else he could think of. But he came out of the American system, and they were coming out of a Buddhist system. And I want you to think about that story because that's a true story. In a Buddhist country many things can happen.

So, you will never see me out waving a banner or walking a picket line, because that is not the way of our tradition. There are some Buddhist traditions which do indeed make a practice of social activism; that is their way and I have no argument with it. It is not mine. And each of us makes our own karma, and so must you: one does that which has to be done and takes the consequences of his or her actions without complaining. This is the true way of Buddhist action. And actions in the political arena rarely "come out clean": they partake of both a Buddha act and a deluded act. How to escape from the consequences of the latter is not a thought for a Buddhist to have; it is our duty to accept the consequences of our actions and, if we truly believe them to be right and so have done them in full innocence of heart, whatever those consequences are, we will take them. All-acceptance is the non-existent gateway to enlightenment. But whatever you decide to do, above all "be careful how you go with the Truth under your coat." Remember Koho Zenji's words; they have far more meaning than most people think. So, is that clear enough?

Question: "Not entirely. (laughter) Maybe it's my own illusion, but it seems to me that political struggle has been advantageous in certain circumstances and that often involves becoming emotional about things and sometimes taking steps that do harm in the service of a greater good."

You still take the consequences of doing it. Would you [addressing one of the monks] like to take this one?

Monk's comment: "I'll certainly try. In some respects I agree, I think it has been useful at times. As to what you and I can do, the type of involvement we are talking about does not preclude working in social reform, economics, politics, even the military. Heck, we've got one student who works in the C.I.A.; he figures he can do more good there than anywhere else. So, it doesn't preclude that. What it does say is, for goodness sakes first train yourself as hard as you can to get yourself out of the way before you get involved in that kind of activity."

Question: "You mean, to quell my own emotions, for example?"

Monk continues: "To learn how to handle them. Not necessarily quell them, but learn how to handle them. To learn to let them come up and go by without catching them, so that when you do act, you do it without self, you know what I mean? And you may well have to act. When you do act in this way, you do it with a better understanding of the way things actually are, and therefore you have a better likelihood of being able to do something with true benefit rather than simply muck things up in a different way."

The world is a pretty unsatisfactory place, and the sooner we get used to the idea, the sooner we'll do something satisfactory. When we really get used to the fact that it is unsatisfactory, we'll want to do something about it, and the only person we can start with is us.

Question: "I have a difficult time deciding what the most compassionate action might be when I feel a lot of anger over things that are inflicted on people."

I asked that question of the Kanin (the Director or Prior) of Sojiji, and I got mad as heck at him when he told me that the only answer, the only real answer, was all-acceptance and education. I said, "Sure, when I get back to the West I'll be sure to tell the blacks that they mustn't be miserable about what happened to them because they've got to learn all-acceptance and be educated!" And then I went off and I meditated on it and I thought about it. What other alternative is there? Yes, it's lousy, but unless there is constant work toward education and mutual acceptance on the part of all sides, it will remain lousy. Just killing people off, or putting people in jail or doing all this sort of forcing of things, is only going to make it worse, because it's going to make tempers get hotter; they're going to flare higher.

I can't give you the whole conversation, but I remember that I had turned up in his room in a prize rage: I had just discovered what the Japanese did with the Koreans. It went something like this: they had kidnapped the royal Korean potters in the 1500s, took them to Japan, and forced them to make their pots. The style they created is now known around the world as this exquisite "Japanese" pottery, about which the Japanese make such a noise. Not only was it not theirs at all, but the descendants of the Koreans are still there. They are not allowed passports; they are not allowed birth certificates; they are not allowed in the public schools; they may never leave the country; they may not mix; and the only jobs they can have is working on the roads. These are the descendents of the royal potters, and Sojiji was telling me how open-minded it was and how marvelous it was and how the Japanese loved foreigners and how they let them mix; one day I just "lit up". It had gone just one step too far. I had been out that day, and I was watching a bunch of really nice-looking women mending the road with tar and spades and shovels, and being almost kicked by the Japanese as they walked by, and I just blew up. And then he gave me this answer; I wish I could remember it fully. God, I was mad! But acting out of anger or righteous indignation isn't the answer. It's just very sad, and acceptance and education really are the key.

> *Question:* "Speaking of the abuse of women, I know that you have faced some fairly major gender discrimination in your life. What advice would you give to your fellow women when we encounter this in our religious lives?"

Don't believe the brainwashing. There was a feminist in the mid 1880s in America whom I read an article on recently, which was very interesting. She made one comment that really unsettled the men: "Women *have* rights. We've got the whole lot; all we have to do is take them." The brainwashing was out of the way there. You see, everyone was assuming that women had to fight to get rights, as if they didn't have them and only the men could give them to them. But she knew that human rights were inalienable; they didn't come from men, they came from God (as she would have put it). So women already had the rights, all they had to do was use them. And the amazing thing was that she not only went ahead and did everything, but they let her.

And if that applies to political and social rights, how much more does it apply to religious ones! Now, when I first got to Sojiji, some of them treated me abominably. They treated me so badly, in fact, that I said, "The hell with it! I'm going to do it, whether they like it or whether they don't!" I did exactly what she did: I *took* the rights. I said, "I've already got them." And immediately the men agreed to it, because they didn't know what else to do. What were they going to do? Here was a female that had taken them; she was already doing it. See what I'm saying?

Questioner: "Uh-huh."

Of course, this approach takes a bit of courage, but it is worth it. It stops the problem right there, and immediately you take it, you can go all the way. If you're stuck with what other people think, then you can't move. If you simply stop believing the brainwashing, you can go all the way—straight to the Cosmic Buddha. And you don't need any help from anybody whatsoever. So that is how I have approached it when I was treated badly: I said, "Phooey to you, if that's how you want to be. I'm going to do it anyway." And, you know, I got the most delicious grin, the most complete gurgling laughter, from my master. And that was fine; and I went all the way. It's the same reason that you sit looking like a Buddha in the meditation hall: we become what we seem. You fill in the rest of that one.

A big part of the brainwashing is that we women are taught that we are somehow inadequate spiritually because we are female. Well, we are not. I know I'm not inadequate; I refuse to behave as though I'm inadequate. And if you've got any sense, you'll refuse to behave as though you're inadequate. You'll be amazed how fast the male sex will jump when you do that—cures it in seconds! (laughter) That gal in the 1880s was right: women already have every human right; all they've got to do is behave like it. I'll tell you a little story along these lines. It doesn't have to do with women, but you'll see the point. When I was in Japan towards the end of my stay, I had to go into hospital for major surgery. There was a young sailor in the same ward, and also an old Norwegian ship's captain. Now this kid badly wanted to be an officer on board ship, and he kept grouching and grouching about the fact that he couldn't become an officer: nobody would let him. He didn't know that the old man on the ward was a captain. And one day, the "old boy" stretched and said, "Well, son, if you want to be an officer, you've got to behave like one. Then they'll make you one."

That is why I am not a feminist in the usual sense of the term: the "struggle for women's equality" doesn't go far enough; it doesn't step outside the brainwashing. Behave like an equal, dammit, and then they will stop. You have to *do it* before it will be cured. You have to say, "Yes, I have a soul, and I know I have a soul" (if you are Christian); "Yes, I have Buddha Nature, and I know I have Buddha Nature."

And, you know, approaching it this way leads to great compassion for the men. In one respect, we are much luckier than they are because our conditioning has forced us to trust something else other than our selfish self, something we call "women's intuition". In the end, this turns out to be a doorway to the Lord of the House. And the male gets very upset about this, because he's had to live much more on the outside in order to maintain his position in the herd. Now, mind you, women's intuition is a doorway; it is not a "private pipeline to God" that the male doesn't have. Sometimes it is baloney; we do go wrong. But I do know this: as a result of the way in which they have pressed us throughout the centuries, we have had to rely much more on what is within and much less on either "self" or externals. So, spiritually speaking, in this respect we are much better off because the average woman is more used to listening to what's inside her than the average man is. In some other respects, of course, we're much worse off. There is a big problem, for instance, in the way many Western spiritual traditions teach that we cannot have a spiritual life except through a husband, that we cannot live except through a male. And nothing is more false, because women can go all the way spiritually. So here we have both men and women stuck at the entrance to religion: the woman feels she can't move 'cause she can only do it through a man, and the man is saying, "Why the heck should I move? I've got it all anyway." Of the two, we are better off because we have got our greed up enough to want to do it: "Dammit, why can't we?!?" Which is much better than being complacent and thinking you've already "got it". Do you see how much more subtle and much more dangerous the latter way is? It undermines the determination we talked about at the beginning, the determination to really get going wholeheartedly in training. Now, once you can get a woman's greed up enough, she says, "To hell with it this way! I'm going to do it, like it or lump it!" And she does. Another area in which men are at a disadvantage is that they are taught to be unaware of their inner life and feelings, not just out of complacency but also because of the social necessity to "put a brave face on it", the "stiff upper lip" attitude of mind. And that is very, very sad, because most men are just as human as are most women. Note that I said "most" men and "most" women: I made them perfectly equal on that one. You always have exceptions in both.

And, treating one another with equality and respect does matter: don't get me wrong on that. One of the things that I love about Soto Zen Buddhism is that, even though some individual priests are narrow minded, it is one of the few major religious traditions which have steadfastly made it quite clear that a woman can be a priest, and it allowed me to become one and gave me the certification necessary to do the job. And by recognizing my spiritual equality with that of men, it helped make it possible for me to cease from the hatred, jealousy, and desire that had eaten away at me for

Rev. Kojima Kendo Roshi, one of the foremost female masters of the twentieth century, offering her congratulations to Rev. Master Jiyu at the conclusion of the ceremonies of becoming a full priest, which took place at Rev. Master Jiyu's small temple in rural Japan. The two of them then discussed the role of women in Zen.

years. Above all, it gave me the ability to really love men in a way I never had before. My relationship now with members of the opposite sex is exquisite: there is never any doubt in my mind, or theirs, of our being equal with each other. We are totally equal—so much so that the subject never needs to be raised—and we are also different. Buddhism recognizes that all is one in the Buddha Nature and all is different simultaneously. Sometimes a Buddha is tall or short, sometimes fat, sometimes thin, sometimes male, sometimes female; all is Buddha, and all exists within the Buddha Mind.

As you know, gender discrimination in religion is not limited to just the male-female dimension. I was having a discussion with someone the other week with regard to homosexuality, and the person was asking me if I would be upset if there were a person of gay or lesbian orientation in my monastic community, would I be worried about it. And as I told this person: we do, and I'm not. When I look at one of my monks walking down the path, I don't say to myself, "Here comes my heterosexual monk." So why would I say to myself, "Here comes my gay monk, my lesbian monk"? We've got to stop paying attention to things that are not important. The person coming down the path is my monk: he's George or Fred; she's Sue or Betty. Do you see what I'm saying? Don't get gender mixed up with things where it doesn't matter; it's one very tiny part of a huge thing. Somehow we've got the two incredibly mixed up, and we have to stop believing that brainwashing.

> *Question:* "I'm a person who at times feels that you just have to plunge in and throw yourself into a situation because it's urgent and you can't hold yourself back."

If you do, then you must take the consequences of doing it. If you don't run it past the Three Pure Precepts, if you just jump right in there, and the consequences are not very pleasant, don't grouch about the consequences. We're not saying that you have to sit there inert, staring at your navel for ten years, before you take a step and do something. We're not saying that. We are saying "be a woman" (or a man) and take the consequences of what you do. Try to do it in the mind of meditation, and know that you'll still make mistakes.

> *Monk's comment:* "Guaranteed you'll make mistakes, okay? Relax: you'll make mistakes, no problem; accept the consequences."

For example, a common problem that comes up here is what do you do in the case of a war, and you are called to serve by your country. To which my answer is: if you go to war, you will kill people; you will therefore break the precept against killing. If you do not go to war, you must take the consequences that the country hands you, which may be to go to jail. And, if you do not go to war, you may allow someone like Hitler to kill millions of others. Now, settle down and have a good look at that, and see where is the true responsibility? What must you do to be responsible, to do the least karmic damage?

Perhaps it is to go to war. And perhaps it is not. Only you, as an individual, can decide. There is no God and no savior that will tell you what to do; you will carry your karmic consequence (or whoever picks it up when you're dead, if you haven't cleaned it up). Remembering that, be very careful what you do, be very careful what you choose.

But, the main thing is intention. If your intention in going to war (I've often mentioned the case of Sergeant York, an American pacifist who went to World War I in order to shorten the war as much as possible and became a great hero in doing it), if your intention is to stop evil and you are willing to take the consequences of doing some evil in order to stop evil, then perhaps it is right to break that precept. And you're still going to take the consequences of having broken it, and don't pretend that you're not going to. Don't think, "Well, I can make the excuse that I did it for the best of reasons." Yes, we know you did it for the best of reasons, and here's the consequence. There's going to be no way

out, 'round, or under that: you're going to get the consequence. But just think what the consequence could have
been if you hadn't done it. The precepts in Buddhism are not
nearly as simple as they look!

Question: "I just want to mention, I think one of the
greatest threats today is that of nuclear war and I was
wondering if Buddhist teaching can promote the
sanctity of life and the generosity of benevolence?"

It can; it can. The tragedy is that we've got to change the
social order somewhat first, and the only people who can
change the social order is us and all our friends and neighbors. And the only way you can make your friends and
neighbors change is by making it obvious to them that
there's something a lot better than the way they are,
because you can't brainwash them or do something to
force them into it. What they have to do is see it as a more
desirable situation than there is now. But, you know,
there's considerable hope. Imagine what it was like two
thousand years ago: the world was a very dangerous, very
very rough, place.

Audience comment: "It still is."

But not in the same ways. We still have a lot of delusions,
but I think they've improved a little. It seems that the human
race goes with the speed of an unenergetic snail, but it does
move, even if not very fast. I can see you want to get in on
this; go ahead.

Monk's comment: "I'd like to address this issue from
my own point of view as a priest. It is this: that an

issue, such as the nuclear situation, can be observed from a Buddhist perspective. And it has many different meanings, if you look at it that way. You can understand a lot about what's going on if you look at it from a Buddhist perspective. And yet, in one sense, right action with regard to the situation is the same as keeping the precepts in a situation: what's right for one person to do might not be right for someone else to do. What we have tended to do—and I think it's very good—is, as priests, not to actually very strongly take an active stand on an issue like that, the reason being that the most important thing that a priest can do is to be seen to stand for That which lies beyond these issues. When you look at a priest what you see is if he or she is in touch with That which lies beyond their personality. A person must feel, when they go to a monastery, that the monastery's purpose is to be in touch with That which is beyond it. The more a monastery or a priest becomes involved with social issues, the more entangled they become in worldly matters. Although as individuals they may have very strong feelings on it, if the priesthood itself becomes associated with political interests, then the purpose of the priesthood becomes confused. If someone has strong feelings about it and it's important for them to take action which they feel is right, as priests you can encourage people to do that, to find their own mind and act. But as priests, for many of us (for other priests it can be very different) it's best for us not to too closely identify ourselves with issues in this way. Do you understand why?"

Audience comment: "Well, I look back at the Second World War and I look at everybody closing their eyes to Nazis. . . ."

I agree with you on that. I know that many people were not happy with me for saying that maybe in those situations for some Buddhists the best choice would be to go to war, but I come of that generation that went through World War II, and if only people had believed what was going on in the thirties, just maybe somebody could have said "stop" earlier. Yes, it would have meant interfering in the private affairs of another country, but perhaps had we done it that early, a tremendous number of my generation would still be alive. Just maybe, now and then, one has to do things like that. It's a very sad situation, yes? I believe there is a time when you do have to make a stand. I believe that, but I think you have to weigh it incredibly carefully, because you can really make some dreadful mistakes on this.

One of the things that Dogen said on the issue is very interesting. He said to find peaceful places—waterfalls and high mountains—to train in; stay away from politics and people in high places. But he never said, "Stop politicians visiting you", and hundreds of them did. His advice was always the same thing: find the Pure Place and act from the Pure Place. A lot of people will misunderstand what you are doing, and sometimes you will seem to do evil for the right reasons, and you will have to carry the consequences of it. And sometimes you will seem to do good and it will appear bad at a later date, and you will have to carry the consequences of that. But whatever you do, if you are a politician, act from that Pure Place and then take your lumps as they fall, because that's the problem of being a politician. So what he said was stay away from it as a priest, which is really what we are talking about. Don't get active in politics, but by all means be willing to counsel politicians to do the right thing. And that I am perfectly happy with and willing to do, but I think somebody has to stay in touch with the Eternal, otherwise everybody goes flying down the hill with the speed of the Gadarene swine* because there's nobody sitting there at the brakes saying, "Now let's, before we release the bomb, see if this is the one and only means."

As to World War II, when World War II started I was a pacifist. I watched what was happening (I was fifteen); I said, "This is madness; somebody's got to stop this", so I got into it as soon as I could. There is a difference when you look at it from that angle, but that doesn't mean that every time somebody says go out and fight "so and so" you should get up and go out and fight. You've got to sit down and find out if it is in fact doing something that is going to cause a ceasing from evil. As I said, we have a copy of a film on Sergeant York. I don't know if any of you have ever watched that; it's a very wonderful film about a man who started out exactly the same way, as a pacifist, in World War I and then, realizing that the only way he could save thousands of lives was by killing someone, he went ahead and did it. It's very sad, but he saved thousands and became one of America's greatest heroes. He has to carry all the karma for doing that, but what else could he do? It's a very difficult line to walk.

---

* A Biblical reference (Matthew 8: 28–34) to the herd of swine into which Jesus put a demon which He had cast out of two men on the road to Gadara. This caused the swine to panic and run headlong down a hill and over a cliff, hence the reference is to any rapid, disorganized, and short-sighted behavior that produces disastrous consequences.

There's an old Zen story, which some of you may or may not know, of a Zen Master who heard there was a war going to take place not too far off, and he thought, "This is dreadful; something's got to be done." He was rather good with his siddhis of doing rather remarkable acts: one of the things which he could do was fly. He thought, "Well (and he was very peaceful in his cave), somebody's got to stop this bunch", so he flew over the battle field. Everybody was so startled they put their arms down and watched him. He flew 'round and 'round and went back to his cave, and when the flying was over they didn't know who was on which side because they were all so flabbergasted, so the battle was finished. He got back to his cave and he thought, "Well, everybody now is going to think I'm a sorcerer; I'm done for as a Zen master", so he sat down and died. Think about it: did he have any alternative? I told you this is not an easy teaching. But he did stop the battle.

> *Monk's comment:* "That's a perfect example of what I'm trying to say. Perfect example: you stand and make that choice, but you weigh something very heavily when you do it."

As I said, I went into the Navy. I've never regretted it, but I carry the karma for doing it and I'm not going to pretend I don't. This is not a teaching for cowards. This is not a way of getting out of one's responsibilities; one has to be a responsible person. And perhaps one's conscience genuinely believes one shouldn't go to war. If that is so, then one shouldn't: it's very simple. And if one feels that the only way one can do good is by going, then one should go. Either way you're going to carry the consequences of that; there's no way around it.

DEATH

Yesterday you saw how the home altar is set up, and the "Buddha of the first or second day", etc. That is for memorials. Now when a funeral takes place, it is usually done at a temple; the statue is taken off of the high altar of the temple and the coffin is placed upon it. A coffin is placed on the altar as the Buddha of the day. And the ceremony takes place as such, honoring the deceased as a Buddha. The whole of the ceremony is really a series of about four or five small ceremonies, each one of which is slightly different. There is the private ceremony for the family the night before the actual funeral, so that they can grieve in private without people staring or watching. There is the public ceremony the next morning, which is for everyone to come to, all the friends and relatives, and then there is the ceremony that takes place at the graveyard or the crematorium. And finally there is the ceremony of literally putting the earth on the coffin. It is customary in Zen for people to literally bury their dead: you are handed a spade and invited, each of the mourners, to put some earth on the coffin. It has a very remarkable effect on people, in that somehow the truth of it sinks in and it helps the process of acceptance quite remarkably. There is also the fact that the seeming callousness of the average gravedigger, who does it as a profession, is out of the business. I have seen people pouring earth on their relatives with such exquisite tenderness: they are recognizing the necessity of the burial, but you don't hear that horrible sound of the gravedigger, as you drive away, thudding the stuff on the coffin with seemingly not a feeling. You can bury the dead beautifully, and with exquisite compassion, and with recognition of what you are really doing. So these are the various ceremonies at the

A funeral altar.

time of death, and they speak a lot about the Buddhist view of death, and life.

> *Audience comment:* "This is something that is really concerning me since Friday night's terrible disaster in Kansas City where that hotel collapsed. I think about it; in fact I was in there, in that very same hotel, on Mother's Day, and I think, 'Well, it could have happened to me then.' There's something to this business about living your life every day as if it's your last moment."

Well, there really is. You have no proof of anything. That's why it is so important to do your meditation every day, that's the whole reason for doing it. That's what Dogen was saying: train as if your hair is on fire; none of us knows when death is going to take place. So, if you do your meditation every night and morning and live a preceptual life in between, you're at least going to be "in tune", and you're going to make the right decisions when the moment comes. A lot of people in the East regard Zen meditation as a religious insurance policy. After a bit they get out of that, but that's where they start from. And it is a religious insurance policy, nevertheless. It's a lot more than that, a tremendous lot more than that, but that's what it starts as with most people. And Dogen knew it and said so.

> *Question:* "I have heard that it is the custom in some forms of Buddhism to sit with the body all the time, around the clock, until the time of burial. Do you do that?"

Yes, we sit in meditation with it. We sit with it all night and all day, too. The custom is to do a seven-day meditation retreat with the body, if that is possible. The custom is to be with the dead whilst the process of rebirth is possibly taking place, to be with the body so it shall be guarded and safe, and also to help you prepare for when you yourself become dead: for you to not fear it, and recognize what it is, and understand it.

> *Monk's comment:* "There is another aspect of that, which is something that is usually a monastic practice, but I have seen it done a couple of times by the families of the deceased. It's a hard thing to do, but if

it feels right to them I have seen it benefit them considerably. It is, if the person has chosen to be cremated, to accompany the body to the actual cremating machine: not just to the funeral parlor, but to the back room where the burner is. One stays with the body as they place it into the crematory and sits in meditation with it as the actual cremation takes place. This is indeed a hard thing for a family to do, and I would suggest it only if they feel in their hearts it is good. However, I have seen it be an extremely liberating thing: I have seen them come out after that and, well . . . it's over. And it wasn't so horrible, because it takes the total mystery and fear out of it."

This is the same thing as using the spade at the burial. That was what I was trying to explain when I was saying about putting the earth on the body oneself. It takes the fear out of it, and you understand what is happening; it's a normal part of life and one shouldn't fear it. It's a new beginning, a new start.

> *Monk's comment:* "There is also a practical word of advice if you're transferring the ashes or cremated remains from the funeral home or cremation society's container into one of your own. It might help you to know ahead of time what you are going to find when you open up their little box: it's not just ash; mostly it's bone."

You are going to find fragments of bone. When I transferred the remains of Rev. Seck Kim Seng from the ginger jar they brought him over in, I was somewhat startled to discover that I was holding the finger bone of the man who had ordained me, and wondering if it was the finger that had held the razor that shaved my head. I was also somewhat bemused to discover that my dog was interested in it, so please be very careful.

Monk continues: "It looks like chips, fragments of bone. There is, of course, some ash along with it. While in the West you wouldn't usually find an identifiable piece like that, the combustion is not complete either in American crematoria or in the crematoria in the Far East, so the 'ashes' are not really just powdered ash."

Second monk's comment: "Another brief practical one. . . . Are we coming to look like the Abbey undertakers?" (laughter)

No, I just think you are growing a longer nose and looking rather pale! (laughter)

Second monk continues: "It has been our experience that, contrary to the sort of expectation that floats around, a number of funeral homes will be very cooperative. I'm not saying all of them will, but a surprising number of funeral homes that we've had contact with are quite cooperative with Buddhist approaches to the dead, providing you know what you want and you tell them quite clearly, and you are prepared to go elsewhere if they are not interested in providing you what you want. But they are in it, I suppose, as a business, and they want to serve their clientele, and if you know what you want, usually you can get it. So it's not as bad as I expected it to be."

And you've also got to remember that a tremendous number of people just do not know what are the customs of a Buddhist.

Question: "It might be helpful if actual Buddhist cemeteries were available, don't you think?"

Oh, yes. In fact, we've gone to great trouble at both of our main monasteries, here and in England, to do exactly that. So we have Buddhist cemeteries in both countries, as well as parts of the monastery ceremony halls reserved for cremated remains. Or you can have just a wooden tombstone there, if you like. One of the beauties of putting up this new hall at Shasta is that there now is an actual tombstone hall and an actual reliquarium, an actual place where you can put boxes of bones, and people can come there and sit with their dead, if they wish to. There is a place to meditate in there; they look sort of like little private chapels where you can go be with your relatives. There is also a Buddhist cemetery for pets, and a place in the hall for their ashes, too; the whole family can be together.

Now, you might think that funerals are the end of it, as far as Buddhism's willingness to help with one's life, but they're not. We mentioned memorial ceremonies earlier and how they can continue even for centuries if it seems good. And there is a special kind of memorial called Segaki, the Ceremony of Feeding the Hungry Ghosts. Hungry ghosts take many forms and there are many beliefs about this in the East, but the history of Segaki is very simple. Moggallana, the Buddha's disciple who was foremost in psychic powers, came to the Buddha and said, "My mother died, and I saw her in a dream two or three nights ago. It was terrible: she was longing for food and she couldn't take it. She had a huge bloated stomach and a tiny throat, and she couldn't get anything down, and everything she touched turned to fire. What can I do?" And the Buddha said, "Well, the best thing you can do is make a great feast, for she has become a hungry ghost. We will offer the merit of it to her, and then all monks will partake of it and give their merit so that she may be able to hear the Truth and open her closed mind, and thus be able not to have fire in the mind and in the stomach." And they made this great feast and much ceremonial, and that very night Moggallana dreamed again. And there was his mother, no longer in this situation, able to eat and drink, and giving thanks at the feet of the Cosmic Buddha. That is the history of Segaki, and it has been celebrated ever since: it is one of the oldest ceremonies in all of Buddhism.

Whenever you have had someone who you really feel was . . . how to put it politely . . . lacking in merit, a downright louse or any variation thereon, this is the ceremony you have done for them. You also can do it for anyone who was not meditating, or not peaceful, at the time of death, just in case they made mistakes at the time of death. Generally, Segaki is celebrated at large temples once or twice a year for everyone whose relatives or friends request it. You also do it for suicides. For a suicide, however, you do it immediately after the funeral ceremony: they have a separate one all to themselves because they need all the help they can get, and fast.

The ceremony is literally what I said. You offer them this food, a huge feast; you recite to them all the best scriptures you can lay your hands on. You offer all the sincerity and love you can find within yourself and ask that the merit of all this be transferred to these people who have had no advantages, no opportunities, or who just were too narrow-minded, or too mean, or who went so much into despair that they killed themselves. There is a very famous picture of

Segaki, which if there's a good artist here somebody could paint one day; I've been trying to get a copy of it for years; it's very rare. It shows a Segaki altar with three Chinese priests in front of it, and there are little "gakis", you know, with their big fat tummies and their thin throats, climbing around. There's one peeking 'round from the side, stealing a fruit from the side of the altar, and there's one lying on the altar: he "got religion". You know, how you see these posters of people who've "got religion": well, he's lying there happy as a lark, with fire going on all around him, just gobbling everything he can see, and one priest is standing there so happy, just looking at him. You know, "It worked, it worked; this one's got religion!" (laughter) And there are the others, carrying stuff away; you see them scurrying and carrying it. It gets the point over, very, very clearly and very beautifully. In other words, it's an extra funeral ceremony, if you like, for anybody whom you can't feel certain about.

Literally everybody brings food. You should see the altar: it's out of doors, and it is covered in food. I went to help at one at a Rinzai temple to which thousands of people came, and they built this altar: it was just a bunch of trestles in the garden and wooden boards. As it got close to the time for hitting the gong for the "gakis" to come, I noticed that all the monks were sort of withdrawing carefully into the temple and closing the doors; and when the gong was hit, the entire congregation, about four thousand of them, swooped onto the altar. Some got a little trampled, and they got covered in rice and a few other things, and the boards collapsed and things like this. But they had a wonderful time, and they were getting food for friends who had died, and they would eat some for them. You're not supposed to have a free-for-all, but it does turn into a good-natured one occasionally in the East. It's rather fun.

A Segaki altar.

Question: "What if the relative has requested no funeral service or memorial of any sort?"

An awful lot of dead, I suspect, have changed their minds and wish they'd not said that. (laughter) I don't know; I can't give you a formula for that; you have to trust your own heart. If it seems good to offer it anyway, I would actually say, "Well, I know you said that, but I've found something

better than what you knew about, so maybe you'd like this."
They don't have to take any notice of it if they don't want it.
That's one of the nice things about all this: it is just offerings;
no one is being forced to do anything. You aren't trying to
convert someone to Buddhism after their death or anything
like that: it's just an offering. So, if you sense that it might be
welcome, I would go full steam ahead.

> *Question:* "Is Segaki something that we can do at
> home, like memorials?"

> *Monk's comment:* "It's one of the few ceremonies that
> I think would actually be unwise to do at home, sim-
> ply because to do a Segaki properly you have to be very
> open to all kinds of needy spirits, as it were, out there."

Yeah. Especially I wouldn't do it in San Francisco!
(laughter)

> *Monk continues:* "And you may get a little too open to
> some of them interested in, sort of, "munching" on
> you instead of what's on the altar, okay?"

In the Far East, they say that even a priest must never do
a Segaki alone unless you are absolutely forced to, and when
I was in Umpukuji,* I was forced to do Segaki by myself for
a number of years until I got the priest from the neighboring
village to come along and help me, and even with two he was
worried about it. And, I mean, these are experienced priests.

---

* Umpukuji is the name of the small village temple in rural Japan
where Rev. Master Jiyu-Kennett served as the parish priest for several years
before returning to the West.

> *Monk's comment:* "And in general, we find it is useful to have the most experienced priest available be the celebrant at the Segaki, even when you've got a bunch of them."

Yup. A lot of them love doing ceremonies in Shasta, but when it comes to Segaki they usually look to me. (laughter) But I understand the reasons why; it's good sense. You literally are opening the door to everything and saying, "Come on in, all ye who have not made it, or who made mistakes, come on in. Come and listen and eat."

> *Monk's comment:* "After all, you are dealing often with things which are somewhat deluded in some sense; they sometimes get things backwards."

> *Question:* "In Segaki, is the offering made to all beings, inclusive of the particular person that it is being offered for?"

Oh yes. All; the whole collection, yes.

> *Monk's comment:* "That's where you get into trouble. (laughter) But you can't really do otherwise with a good heart."

> *Question:* "When you do Segaki at the Abbey, can people come and give offerings for a particular person?"

Oh yes, yes, yes, yes. That's the idea.

> *Audience comment:* "I don't believe any of this stuff about ghosts and 'gakis'." (laughter)

That's fine. That's fine. One day, maybe. It's not my problem; I don't have to worry. As a matter of fact, neither did I for quite awhile.

Audience comment continues: "I mean, I am sitting here, letting it all sink in; I don't know that it isn't true, but I don't have any conviction."

That's fine. No problem. That's the nice thing about Buddhism: you don't have to believe it. It doesn't insist. This is okay, this is good for now; it goes "on the back burner", and then, if someday something comes up along these lines it's "Oh yes, I remember; so it is of some use." The beauty of the Buddha was that He Himself said, "Do not believe anything that I have told you because I have told it to you; you can only really believe it when you know it's true for yourself."* I am sharing with you what I know is true for me. If it at a later date is true for you, that's just fine.

Monk's comment: "I'm not sure what to believe about all this, either. The Buddha talked about it, and He also made it pretty clear that it isn't the Important Thing in His teaching. What is vital are the Four Noble Truths, which, of course, include the meditation and precepts that we have been talking so much about. But I will say that I've seen enough weird stuff to know that there's more to this side of it than my scientific mind would like to admit."

Hmmm, I think we're making progress! (laughter)

---

* See footnote on page 30.

Monk continues: "Another point is that some people seem to be much more sensitive to this particular realm of reality than others are. If you happen to be, any of you, particularly sensitive to this naturally (as it were, 'tuned in on this particular wavelength' is the only way I can put it), it may be helpful to be aware of the possibility that this stuff gets very interesting. It gets very fascinating, indeed. And, if that happens, then you can get 'hooked' on it; you can get 'hooked' on the fascination of exploring these dimensions. And that can do real damage. So that's another reason we say, 'Do not try this at home.'"

It is much more dangerous than drugs, when you get "hooked".

Monk continues: "That does happen to people, and they can get in over their head, and don't know how to get back out. So, if you happen to be a person who has what is actually a natural gift or sensitivity for these things, please understand that you run a risk if you deliberately get involved with it."

Especially if you try to encourage it. This is one reason why Buddhism warns against spiritualism, channeling, and the like: it is an endless distraction from real training, and a dangerous one at that.

Monk's comment continues: "Well, fortunately, I guess I'm not that sort. And I was just thinking that if Einstein explained to me the theory of relativity, I wouldn't have any conviction of it, either."

Which means that you are a nice ripe plum to be picked. (laughter) Do you remember what I said about the people without convictions on anything being the ones that the Buddha "picks off the tree" first? You can think of the reason why: "Oh, there's nothing there; oh, but I don't believe; oh . . ."; you can just sit there, not bothering with beliefs about anything in particular. You're just being a nice ripe plum. It's the ones with the set convictions that have the problems. They're the ones that have the big koans and who take a long time to wake up. I have had people come to study with me, and one is eager: he's got his books on Zen; and the other has been sitting there, sort of looking around doing nothing in particular: and she's been "picked off" like this, and then the first one comes to me, "How come she's got a kensho and I didn't?!?" Well, I tried telling him and it didn't help all that much; he had his books on Zen.

So you see, or should see, from what I have been saying today that there is absolutely nothing that is outside Buddhist life. You do not have to feel you have to do something strange: you don't have to use chopsticks, you don't have to go around with a funny haircut, you don't have to be an unnatural human being. Buddhism permeates the whole of daily life, and you are just a normal human being. There is nothing weird or strange or mysterious. And you are not an atheist just because you refer to the ultimate things of your religion by using words like "void, unstained, and pure"; simply you are saying, "I can tell you what the Eternal is by telling you what It is not", instead of, "I can tell you what the Eternal is because *I know.*" I much prefer to say, "I can tell you what It ain't"; I feel a lot safer doing that, much safer.

6.

The Way of the Monk

A DAY IN THE MONASTIC LIFE

The first thing a monk hears in the morning is the wake-up bell. It is important that this shall not be an electric type bell, something that is going to cause startle or nervousness. It has to be something that is very alive and definitely held in the hands of a human. If you have the other type, the mind is too frazzled at the time of meditation. All of the monks are lying in their beds; we have men on one side of the zendo (the meditation hall) and women on the other. They are all facing the same way; they are all on their right side, which is the way the Buddha slept. This is because the Wheel of the Law, which is the symbol of Buddhism, always turns to the right, never to the left. One is showing, even as one sleeps, one's willingness to go in the direction of the Wheel, not against the Wheel. Everyone's pillow is just simply his meditation cushion, or hers. The Head Novice is the one who, being anxious for everyone to be up and alive and meditating, runs around with the bell. He or she runs around the zendo and then runs around to the officers' rooms.

The only accommodation a novice monk has is the one platform upon which they sleep, sit, and eat. There is a cupboard behind the seat: the food bowls are on top, a bottom shelf for bedding, and a top one for clothes and possessions. The meditation hall platforms are about three feet wide by six feet long. Here again you see the frugality of life when one is a novice monk: one place to eat, sleep, live, die. And that's really all one person needs; the maximum space they can occupy, alive or dead, is about six feet by three. And that's their space. It helps one to meditate wonderfully, that realization. In the Far East the platform is covered with a thick straw mat; we use carpet. And we have now arranged something whereby you can pull part of the platform out, if you have bad legs or can't twist yourself up for meditation, and you can put your feet down through the seat and just sit there, and not look as though you're different from other people. You're just sitting on your meditation place with your feet down through a hole. And you put the piece back in again when you want to lie down, or if you want to sit differently, and you put it in a different place if you're turning around to have your meal and you want to sit facing out. In other words, we've made them versatile. This is us; this is Throssel and Shasta. It is not the way of Sojiji, and it is not the way of Eiheiji (the other great training monastery of the Soto School in Japan), and yet it is identically the same Way. We're all doing identically the same thing; we're just finding our own best method of doing it.

There is one person who was already up when the bell sounded. In big temples, the officer who goes around the temple after "lights out" in the evening to make sure that there is no fire then sits down in meditation in one of the shrines and meditates throughout the night. Thus, there is eternal meditation, day and night, in a monastery.

The assistant to the Head Novice then hits the wooden block to tell people that it is time to go to the bathroom and cleanse themselves. It is their job to notify everyone that the bathroom is ready, that water is ready, that everything is clean and prepared. As you go and clean your teeth, so you recite the scripture which says, "May I cleanse myself and crush delusion as this toothbrush is crushed in my mouth." Now in ancient days the toothbrush was a stick that you crushed in your mouth, and you would crush it under the eye teeth, which are called "the eye teeth of delusion". So brushing the teeth is made a religious act. Going to the bathroom is made a religious act: one prays that there shall be no disasters. Buddhism is a very realistic religion. (laughter)

Then everyone comes to the meditation hall and sits upon their seats. On the altar of the meditation hall is the statue of Manjusri, the representation of True Wisdom. He sits upon the beast of self. Self should be portrayed as very much alive, very much awake. He's also got one eye going in one direction and one in the other (self is not known for being all that together). In the temple where I trained in Japan, he had very big eyes, and they seemed to follow you all around the room.

For meditation, most of the monks sit facing the wall in Soto Zen; those who face outward are certain officers that have work in the meditation hall. One of their jobs is to make sure that people are not sitting incorrectly, for fear of harming themselves. Whilst the meditation is on, one of the monks rings the meditation bell in the ceremony hall. Between each ringing of the bell, there is a bow. This bell rings throughout the first period of meditation. It is also sometimes called "the bell that rings but once". At the end of meditation, this same monk hits the morning drum, which signifies that the dawn has broken. And the first words on everyone's lips are the kesa verse, the short verse we recite when placing the monk's vestment over our robes for the first time of the day, which expresses the willingness to undergo training for that day.

The bell is now rung for Morning Service. The procession of monks is led into the ceremony hall by one of the Disciplinarian's Assistants, with his bell. On our main altar at Shasta is a statue of the Cosmic Buddha, which is the representation of the Unborn. And in front of it is a smaller Buddha statue that represents that which comes forth from the Unborn to the born, the "Unborn within the born" if you like, such as the historical Buddha, Shakyamuni.* It's the best way we can demonstrate how the Unborn is found. The altar is sixteen feet across and eight feet wide. Behind that big altar are two small shrines on either side of the back wall, the one on the left being dedicated to Bodhidharma, the monk who lost the use of his legs from sitting looking at a wall for nine years. He shows us that it can be done, no matter how grueling a time one puts oneself through. On the other side, the altar to the spirit that guards the grounds. Now, you can put any statue you want here, to represent any deity or divinity (just in case there happened to have been one) that might have been upset because you took this place over and turned it into a Buddhist temple. Whereas that may look like superstition to a lot of people, it is very comforting to some, especially in the early stages of training: that you just didn't

---

* Behind the head of the large Buddha statue is a circular mirror. This mirror is hard to see from most of the hall, although its ornate frame serves as a halo for the statue. Now, a round mirror has sometimes been used as a representation of the Absolute, the Truth, the Immaculate Void; so experienced Mahayana Buddhists may recognize in this altar arrangement an expression of the Trikaya: the clear, round, mirror of the Dharmakaya (ever present but not generally visible), the great golden-hued body of the Sambhogakaya, and the human figure of the Nirmanakaya.

grab the land away from whatever teaching had been given there prior to its becoming a temple. And so, there is a shrine to whatever other deities may once have represented that area. As I said, you can use any statue you want for that job. It was suggested by some to use various statues of other religions, but I felt that might not be understood, so chose a statue of Confucius, because nobody knew a statue of Confucius or would be upset by it. And he was perfectly willing to be the representative.

Behind the main altar is what can best be described as the "reliquarium" of the priesthood. Here you have the ashes of the founder of the temple, which for us would be my own Transmission Master, Rev. Keido Chisan Koho Zenji of Japanese Soto Zen, and of the various monks of the temple who have died. There are also statues or portraits of the founder and other great monks in your monastic lineage. So we also have here the ashes and a likeness of my Ordination Master, Rev. Seck Kim Seng of Chinese Buddhism. On the central altar of this shrine are icons of the two great founders of Soto Zen in Japan, Eihei Dogen Zenji and Keizan Jokin Zenji, and a third icon representing Manzan Dohaku, a great reformer of Soto Zen after whom is named the line through which I trace my own lineage to the Buddha. A special ceremony is done here at the end of Morning Service: a ceremony of thanks for all the teaching that they gave, and all the monks join in it, for giving thanks and meditation are the two main occupations of the monks.

Everyone having got into the hall, we now have Morning Service. First there is a set of bows. No one has eaten anything yet, by the way, or drunk anything; this is all before breakfast. For the first thing that one must do is search for the Unborn, and be still to be with the Unborn. After the bows are completed, the incense offerings are made at the

*Abbot and community bowing during a ceremony
at Throssel Hole Buddhist Abbey.*

altar, whilst people sit still in meditation, waiting for the ceremony to continue. Then we recite scriptures (we do them in English, which I have set to plain song) and offer the merit of the ceremony to all living things, that they may find the Truth. We then do the ceremony to the founders, which

I just mentioned, and conclude with more bows before recessing back to the meditation hall.

The temple is then cleaned, breakfast prepared, and the community meets together for a silent breakfast. The Head Novice's assistant rings the bell for breakfast, although "bell" is the wrong term for it. It is a large wooden fish drum; a fish was chosen because in the East it is believed that fish never sleep, so it represents eternal mindfulness. Before breakfast is served, a food offering is made by the cook, who has just finished cooking breakfast while that last part of Morning Service is going on. They make the offering of a meal and place it in front of the Buddha statue. You should understand, this offering is not being made to a statue: it is being offered to the Buddha That Is To Come, and when the ceremony is over, when breakfast is over, it is the duty of the Sacristan to eat that food. It must not go to waste. The offering is made of exactly the same things that everyone has for breakfast.

Now, depending on the monastic schedule, meals are either served in the refectory, where we all sit down at tables, or they are served formally in the meditation hall. When we eat in the meditation hall, everyone sits in meditation at their seat, this time facing forward with their set of monk's bowls in front of them. Everyone waits quietly for breakfast. Before the food is served, we remind ourselves of the purpose of partaking of the food that has been offered to us. "I am about to feed my body. I pray that I may truly feed my spirit with that which I do this day. I must think deeply of the ways and means by which this food has come. I must consider my own personal merit when accepting it." Am I worthy of eating? What have I done today? What will I do today? Will I be worthy of the food that I am about to receive? "I will eat lest I become lean and die (and thus be a nuisance to everybody

A formal meal in the meditation hall.

else), because I wish to stay alive in order to find the Eternal, to find enlightenment." That is the meaning of the mealtime offering, one of the most important offerings of the day. Only then is the food served. Monks take turns to serve food to the community, and each one, having got their bowl full of food, blesses it before starting to eat. Everything is carefully laid out. We don't use chopsticks, because it was too difficult for people, but we do use spoons.

> *Monk's comment:* "It's pretty hard to eat granola with chopsticks." (laughter)

Once they have been served, each person puts out a few pieces of granola, or whatever it is they're eating, to help feed those not so fortunate. These pieces represent the Dharma, the Teaching, the willingness to give Teaching and substance and food. They are offered at a later time on an altar outside. They are offered to the Hungry Ghosts, the "gakis": that is, anything that longs for teaching and either can't get it yet or can't accept it. As I said, this is placed on an outdoor altar, and it is left there for the "gakis", who look remarkably like squirrels, birds, and the occasional temple dog. (laughter)

All of the meal is, of course, eaten in silence, except for the recitation of certain prayers. After the meal is over each person receives so much water, again the person indicates how much they want, and they wash their bowls carefully. The monk's bowl must be thought of as a monk's mind: pure and clean. It must be shining, glistening almost, within, in its purity. As the bowl appears, so must be the mind. We eat the food from the bowl, we take notice of the Truth with the mind; we are careful that we do not eat wrong things from the bowl, careful that we do not drink the wine of delusion with the mind. Thus, every day you are taught to look closely at all that you are doing. You clean everything up. You take a look at the dirty washing-up water in your bowl and say, "Yeek, is that what I've got in my skull?" And you start thinking about some of the ideas you've got, and, you know, perhaps some of them look worse! Thus every-thing is connected with everyday life. And then, when we have cleaned the bowl thoroughly, we dry it and wrap it up in its cloths, that it may stay pure and clean. You see how everything in monastic life is an indication of meditation? And the same is true of the water with which the bowls have been cleaned. Monks either drink it (there's no soap in it: it's just hot water), or it is collected and taken outside to the gar-den. You do not throw away the washing-up water: every-thing is of great value. Even if it's dirty water, it can keep a plant alive. Everything is of great value.

Working meditation.

Breakfast over, the next thing that follows is the morning lecture. Again all the monks sit in their places in the meditation hall, if the lecture is a formal one, or in chairs in the monks' hall if an informal one. The mind in either case should be the same: the mind of meditation, the mind within the Unborn, the mind which realizes the importance of purity of body, mind, attitude, and intention. After the end of the morning lecture, there comes community work. The monks do work together, such as clean-up in the garden; this is followed by individual work in one's monastic department. The work of the day is many things: perhaps it's working in the kitchen, perhaps it's in the library or in one of the offices or the gift shop. Perhaps it is looking after the graves.

At eleven o'clock every morning, the temple is officially open to all comers: tradesmen, people who wish to do business of any sort, guests who wish to go around and visit or

Ringing the great bell.

who wish to take tours of the buildings. The opening of the gate is announced by the ringing of the great bell. This bell is rung again, later in the day, when the gates are closed to the world outside. Around mid-day, we have our main meal, served like breakfast, either in the meditation hall or in the refectory. Then follows a time of rest, and back to work.

As soon as the great bell goes for the second time, for the closing of the temple to the world in mid-afternoon, Evening Service starts. This is done in the meditation hall. Everyone's sitting in their places for meditation. First thing you do, when you've got the world of business out of the way, is get back to the Unborn as fast as possible. This is why I say that being in a temple is much easier than being in the world outside.

When evening comes, there is a light meal followed by rest and, of course, more meditation. If it is the end of the monastic week, which is the night of the third or eighth (any day with a "three" or "eight" in it—third, eighth, thirteenth, eighteenth, twenty-third, twenty-eighth—there being five days in a monastic week), then there is a ceremony symbolizing the fact that the temple must be cleaned thoroughly and therefore the meditation hall will be closed officially for one day while that cleaning goes on. That doesn't mean to say that you can't meditate. It means that the actual meditation hall should not be used for that purpose because the cleaners will be in. And the cleaners are, of course, all the monks; so you make a meditation of the cleaning. The bell is rung, summoning the Buddhas to be present at the cleaning, so that we can know what it is that really needs to be cleansed, for we are dealing here with our karma. On these evenings the schedule is relaxed, and the monks enjoy a social tea together before bed.

The following day, there is shaving of the heads and bathing. In our bathhouse we have two huge bathtubs, blue tile: one warm, one hot. We do not have communal bathing. We do have a large number of showers, and I deliberately alternated it: men had a chance at the tubs first one day, and women had it first the next day. And I hope that nobody argued as to which got it first. But, on the very first day, fortunately they didn't. (laughter) However, we can take four people showering at one go, and then you can have one in each tub, if one wants it warm and one wants it hot. But there is no communal bathing, in the sense of mixed. I have to make that very clear because of the size of the tub: some people thought that this was what took place. It actually wasn't; the tubs are large so that you had a tub in which you could really soak. I don't know how many of you have got the opinion that I have, but how can you ever soak in an American bathtub? I have not found out yet how you do it.

(laughter) And in these you can. You can sit in it up to your neck and really get a soak. Everybody has a specific time and that's it. And as you go into the bathroom there is an altar outside: Badarabosatsu, the Bodhisattva of the Bath. "I am about to wash my body. I pray that I might cleanse my heart," you recite. And when you come out of it, you bow again—you make three bows to the altar outside. "I have cleansed my body. I pray that I did cleanse my heart." And you can do that at home every time you wash. You're not just a body that needs to be kept clean and helped with antiperspirants and heaven knows what else that comes out on the TV ads. You have to do something about the spirit. And if you do not use every worldly thing for a spiritual purpose, how will you ever be able to use this worldly body to find who is its true owner? How will you ever be able to find the Eternal if you do not realize that all worldly things do lead to the Eternal if they're used properly? Anyone can use their bath hour, or half-hour, or however long they have, for this purpose.

Now, once the monks go to bed again, then the senior monk whose duty it is to go off to check for fire that night will start the process all over again by sitting in the eternal meditation in front of the statue of the Bodhisattva of protection until the daylight comes again and everything starts again. So, from eleven to three-thirty the world may enter and business may be done; from three-thirty till eleven we search nonstop for the Unborn.

MASTERS AND DISCIPLES

Buddhist training is not something that someone else can do for you. It is not something that you can get from a book. It is something that you, as an individual, do. People tend to think only of masters: "I must go to a master or I can do nothing." Phooey! If you really want to do something, you can, right now. All that a master does is point the way.

One of the things that was really interesting when I first started in the Far East was that I kept thinking various of my seniors were hindering me, and they'd keep saying, "I am doing nothing; I am merely following you." And after a bit I realized that they were running beside me, and every time I seemed to be coming off the rails, they would shunt me quietly back onto them again. But they didn't push me, and they didn't pull me, and they didn't order me. I went—just they helped me: they nudged me back on every time I was likely to fall off. "Remember thou must go alone, the Buddha does but point the way." That's all He's doing. The Buddha is not a savior. He is saying, "I did something about myself, therefore you can do something about yourself; I'm the proof of it. Now why don't you get on and do something about you?" And that is what a master does.

Now, it is important to remember not to judge a master's acts or their sayings by your yardstick. In the scripture most used in the Soto School there is a warning: "Do not judge a master by your standards; do not worry about his caste, his sex, or his shortcomings." And in some versions of the *Shushogi*, which is the scripture I am speaking of, it also says, "and don't worry about his mistakes. If he teaches the Truth, follow him and never worry him." Now, masters do make mistakes, as I have pointed out before; if you worry about the mistakes of a master, then you will eventually lose your faith because, if you are always thinking about their mistakes, then you will start wondering, "Well, if they make mistakes like that, maybe they could be teaching wrong." And as soon as you have made that connection, your faith in the master is already damaged. So please do not worry. The master is always human, from the time of their birth until the time of their death; they are going to make mistakes. They are going to make mistakes because they are "not God", but because they have trained themself, there is nothing in them that is not "of God". You must not think of him or her as God; you must think of them as someone with more experience than you have, who has been on the road a bit longer, digging through the valleys and climbing up the mountains perhaps a few years ahead of you, but they can still make mistakes. And, if you do not trust that their heart is good, then you will be making a mistake, too. And you will prevent yourself from ever studying with a good teacher. This is not a new problem, of course: if you look back in the days of the ancients, you will find the same thing happening. A monk would leave his monastery in a temper and go to see another master. And the master would ask, "Are you a new monk?" "No." "Where did you come from, then?" "Master So-and-so, but he didn't teach me properly." "Oh, so you've come to look for a really good master have you? Well, there are no good masters here, but I've heard there's one across the river. . . ." And so the monk would get passed from one master to another until he realized what a fool he was being. I've actually seen this done in the Far East: I saw one American tramp from one end of Japan to the other, looking for a master. I'd better not use his name; he's a university professor— fairly well known. And he came back having concluded that there were no good masters. Indeed, of the type he was looking for, there were no masters, because he was judging. In other words, he was saying, "I am Buddha; I know what a true master is. And unless you conform to what I believe a master to be, I will not study with you." So each good master said, "Fine. There are no good masters here."

So, masters are human; do not expect otherwise and do not judge. I am reminded of something that my own master told me on this. He said that if the abbot or abbess of a monastery, if a master, lives their life in public, they will both strengthen the faith of their real monks and damage the faith of those who are possibly on the brink and not too strong. This is because he or she will live their training in public, and their mistakes will be clear, and their misjudgments will be clear, and if the monks cannot see past that, then their faith will, in fact, be damaged. I choose to live that way rather than to be the great secret abbess living in my own house, defending myself with a long length of kyosaku every time someone dared to question my authority, because, although it seemed to me to be a more dangerous method, I had the feeling that the results would be a lot more lasting and a lot more real. I suppose, after becoming the head of a monastery like Shasta Abbey, I should take the "bone" out of my head that requires me to explain why I do things. I still think it is necessary sometimes to make such explanations, however.

There was a fine example of my own master living openly as a human being in this way. When I first came to Sojiji, they had a big, round communal toilet which was simply a great big hole with a fence all the way around it. And at eight in the morning everybody sat over the fence. I'm not fooling! At first I was shocked to discover that Koho Zenji came and joined us. Why was I shocked? The Zen master needed to go to the toilet. Somehow I had got it into my skull that this man was so great that he didn't have normal functions. And here he was, sitting over the "honey pot" with all his juniors. That was an important thing for me. Don't ever turn masters into gods: they aren't. And don't judge them and make them less than they are, either. Just make them fully human. Fair enough?

Rev. Master Jiyu sitting beside her own master,
the Very Reverend Keido Chisan Koho Zenji.

It is also important to know that the master can tell a
monk something which he or she honestly feels to be true at
the time and which they feel in their instincts and their
"guts" is likely to happen, and the master can be wrong. The
master is fully aware of this. They are not saying to that person, "God told me that such-and-such will happen." They
are saying, "I feel in my guts such-and-such will happen."
The monk may, or may not, take notice of what was said.
But if they confuse it with "This is what God says is going to
happen", then they have already set the abbot, or master, on
a pedestal, and trouble will follow. If the monk understands
that what the master said is the master's honest, private

opinion, then it is another matter. I have said to people on many occasions, "Please be careful on the road; there could be an accident; I'd rather you didn't go." This does not mean I have got a private line to God which has told me this is going to take place. It means that I'm looking at the weather and I've got a funny feeling inside. Everybody has funny feelings inside; do not confuse that sort of a thing with teaching. It has nothing to do with it. I am not a sorcerer; I am not God, and there is nothing in me that is not of God.

People who have not studied Zen deeply have this problem to a very, very grave extent, and this is why Dogen says that a master will have their teaching limited by such thinking. It is why Soto Zen has difficulty telling the whole truth to masses of people: you can really only do it one-on-one. So, when a master is with people who think in ordinary ways, that master's teaching will be completely obstructed by the selfish desires of those people, for they will perceive it as they want to perceive it. If they make the mistake of putting the abbess in the place of the Cosmic Buddha, or of putting the master in the place of the Cosmic Buddha, then everything she or he says has to be the word of the Cosmic Buddha, and when it does not work out that way, then faith is seriously damaged. But if you understand that the abbess, or the Zen master, is on the same road to enlightenment as are you and your next-door neighbor, simply that she or he has been "at it" a bit longer, and if you do not hold the master's mistakes against her because you know that she is not God and that there is nothing in either her or you that is not of God, then we can all train together very, very safely.

Question: "Would you say something more about the master's mistakes and how you learn from them?"

Well, you have to be very careful what you say, you know. For instance, take *The Wild, White Goose*,* which we have published recently. I did not want to publish it for years and years, because it was all my mistakes and how I learned from them, and we had a couple of idiots (I can't call them anything else) who read it and said, "Right, now I've got to make the same mistakes." That was not the purpose for which *The Goose* was published! It was to show that, in spite of your mistakes, you can make it. And so *The Goose* has now been published with a whole collection of annotations at the back and little numbers underneath various passages. And periodically you'll see number "4", for example. You check up "4", and I've written, "This is non-Buddhist thinking." And then you get "5", and you check up "5" and it says, "Don't do this", or something like that. (laughter) It's the only way I could publish *The Goose* safely, or somebody's going to go off half-cocked and do exactly the same things. It wasn't published to say, "This is the way in which it must be done." A lot of people make mistakes; you learn from them, you don't copy them.

One of the interesting things in that book is how it teaches you to be a jiisha (or chaplain or personal assistant, whichever word you prefer) to an important priest. Every one of them (as I was explaining to my own chaplain yesterday) had something or other that usually the chaplain couldn't stand. For example, one of the officers I was working for loved to get drunk every night. That did not mean that I was to get drunk: my job was to learn Buddhism from him, not to get drunk with him. But it also meant that I was not to sit

---

* This is the two-volume set of Rev. Master Jiyu-Kennett's diaries in the Far East. Rev. P.T.N.H. Jiyu-Kennett, Roshi, *The Wild, White Goose*, Vols. I & II (Mt. Shasta, California: Shasta Abbey Press, 1977 & 1978).

there and criticize him. If he wanted to make a mistake, that was his headache; I couldn't stop him. My job was to make sure that I didn't make the same mistake. Now, it was very worrying and very frightening at times, because sometimes he got very drunk. But, after a bit, I discovered that he could translate an awful lot better when he was slightly "topped up" than when he was sober, so I started making good use of it and the result was some of our scriptures. (laughter) Think about that. The Lord of the House can use everything, if you go about it with the right attitude of mind, but that does not mean to say that somebody who is about to translate should say, "All right, now I need to get drunk." This monk's mistake was his mistake; it is not somebody else's mistake. And it is not for me to say that I am any better, because I have a love of watching a soap opera at lunch time. And there are certain members of the community who can't stand soap operas, and one of them happens to be my chaplain. We've sorted it out now: he goes off and does what he feels like while I watch my soap opera.

Koho Zenji was a little more wicked. He absolutely loved Sumo wrestling, and he was convinced that everybody must love Sumo—it was terrific. The entire temple used to stop, as far as he was concerned, from four to six every afternoon while he watched the Sumo matches and bobbed and weaved in front of his TV set. And all the time his poor chaplains sat there with polite grins on their faces, hating every minute of it. That does not mean to say that if you want Koho Zenji's enlightenment you should sit down and watch TV every afternoon from four to six, watching Sumo. There is nothing particularly Zen in Sumo; it was the old man having some relaxation for a couple of hours in the middle of the day. Don't suffer from the idea that everything the great Zen master does is so marvelously esoteric. All Koho Zenji was doing was having thorough fun because a number of his relatives had been Sumo wrestlers. It used to get rather funny because, of course (uh, this is a slight digression), he was Archbishop of eastern Japan, and they (the Sumo wrestlers) knew he loved it. So they would always send him tickets, and he would march off, dragging his retinue behind him, to go to the matches. And, of course, they'd give him these lovely front seats, and there was one of his chaplains (who was a little like mine), who was rather fastidious in what he looked like, nice and clean and graceful and the like, who would sit there in terror as these great big bladders of lard would throw each other around and would periodically land in his lap in the front row. (laughter) And he still had to do it with exquisite good countenance, all the while Koho Zenji was delighting in it! (laughter) There was nothing esoteric in that: the old man was relaxing.

You see, a lot of people cannot understand that a Zen master is human and that he or she has desires to be human occasionally. Yes, maybe they know God better than a few other people, but they still use the toilet and they still like to watch the TV set and they still have fun watching Sumo. And maybe even occasionally one of them hits the bottle, and they're going to pay for everything they do wrong. Being a Zen master does not give you automatically a right to "enter heaven" straight away that nobody else's got. It merely means that you know better, you have the certainty, you know the Unborn exists: you have seen It, you have met It, you know It. That is what it does, but it does not make you God so that you cannot have faults and failings as an ordinary human being. Do you understand the difference? Be very careful of that. It's very dangerous, because a lot of the trouble over here stems from the fact that people think that an enlightened person is virtually the equivalent of God. She or he is "not God and there is nothing in them that is not of God", but then *you* are not God and there is nothing in *you* that is not of God. Keep that well in mind, and, as you search your hearts for all the things you've done, set right as much as you can (and if it's not time yet to set right some of the things, then wait until the time is right), but above all admit honestly to yourself, "Yes, I have done this-that-or-the-other." Don't try to pretend. Remember that you have to sit up straight in the presence of the Buddhas and Ancestors and say, "I don't intend to do anything else wrong; I'm going to do everything I can not to do anything else." Now, obviously you will do some more things, but each time they happen, try to stop it happening again. And the teacher, the master, does the same; fair enough?

> *Question:* "So, you mean that not everything a Zen master says is to be taken as teaching?"

I have to be very, very careful what I say sometimes, because the Zen master, if they say something, immediately in the minds of some it is taken as infallible teaching, and that is a very dangerous situation. I can remember on one occasion being rattled like mad about a cat that was constantly making a mess in the house. I said, "That so-and-so cat shall never come into a house again!" Now, of course, I did not mean that the so-and-so cat was never to come into a house again, but two years later I heard that there was a scratty cat shrieking outside with almost no food and no fur left on it. You see, you see what I'm saying? Somewhere there was a mess-up of communication. If that happens please, please see my chaplain, okay?

Question: "One notices that a monk will come up to a lay student and say, 'The master said that we do it this way', and then another monk will come up to you and say, 'No, the master says we do it this other way', and then by the time you get three or four monks saying it. . . ." (laughter).

Yes, I know that headache. You've got to remember that I probably spoke to them in spring, summer, autumn, and winter, for example. And in summer you do it out of doors, and in winter you do it in the tool shed, and if it's raining you don't do it at all, you see. They've not known, or they've forgotten, what the rest of the story was. One of the more humorous applications of that which I can remember was in Sojiji. There were two chief monks, one who sat in the back of the hall and one who sat in the front. When we were doing walking meditation, everybody was walking around with their hands in one position in the front of the hall, and then I noticed that as they got to the back their hands changed to another position. And as they came back to the front their hands reverted to the first way. I said, "What's going on?" And then they explained to me that of these two chief monks, one had gone and said it was one way and one said it was the other, and the bunch of novices were not going to get into trouble; they merely swapped hands as they went around the corner. (laughter) At a later date this came to the ears of the abbot, who "blew his nut", blew up the pair of them, and said everybody had got to be the same. But he didn't say which way! (laughter) And for the next five years we went around doing the same swap. (laughter) You see, you have to remember that temples and their "contents" are human, and common sense is not as common as one would believe. It is not nearly as common as is given out to be believed. I have told my monks many times that a temple can only function as well as its worst monk, which is very sad but it's true. So, if that sort of thing happens, my sincere apologies. Um, do it the way of whichever monk you happen to be with, and don't worry about it. It was the only way I learned to do it in Sojiji, how's that? It saves a lot of aches, pains, high blood pressure, squabbling, and a number of other things. All right? You were going to say. . . .

> *Monk's comment:* "I was just going to say, 'So one monk tells you to do it this way, another one tells you to do it that way: that can't stop you from finding the Truth. So one monk tells you the master says this and another one says the master says that . . .'"

It's the kaleidoscopic mind.

> *Monk continues:* ". . . none of that can stop you from finding the truth. *Nothing* can stop you from finding the Truth!"

Not even if you have to sit outside the zendo in the snow it can't stop you; not even in the bottomless pit of hell can it stop you. What matters is your training, not theirs.

> *Question:* "Do you think that masters are necessary for all Buddhists, or is training sufficient?"

Since Shakyamuni Buddha didn't have one, I think you've got a pretty good answer.

> *Questioner continues:* "But is He the only one?"

There are hundreds of people who haven't had them. And there are hundreds of people who wouldn't make it unless they had them. It's an individual thing. It's the fact that some people are tall, some short, some fat, some thin . . . ; they are all Buddhas. There are times when you need a teacher and times when you don't. Make use of one if you need one and go on when you don't. I remember after I had been Transmitted and was a full priest being told by my own master, "It is time you went away and sat beneath your own Bodhi Tree. You have said yes to me. Now do you say yes to the Cosmic Buddha?" Free will still existed, and I had to say yes every moment of the day, every day of the week. I could still turn away. You could do it completely on your own if you were lucky and had the time. I don't know any reason why you should refuse the collective experience of several thousand years of people who have done it. But you can if you want to. And you might succeed, although generally those who insist on doing it all by themselves do not, because their unwillingness to take refuge in the Sangha is based upon some sort of attachment, some sort of delusion.

Question: "What are the manifestations of a good teacher or a good master, so you'll know one?"

Well, I'll quote you Dogen; I am not going to tell you, he does it much better than I do. I think it's in the *Gakudo-yojinshu* (I should know, I've translated this stuff). Ah, just a minute; sorry about this . . . [pause while she looks in her book] . . . here we be: "The necessity of finding a true teacher." It comes in the *Gakudo-yojinshu*; * I was right.

------

* See *Gakudo-yojinshu* in *Zen is Eternal Life*, pp. 162–178, op. cit.

Scripture: "A former Ancestor once said, 'If the mind that seeks is untrue, training will be useless,'—this is utterly true and the quality of the training inevitably depends upon the quality of the teacher. The trainee is as a beautiful piece of wood which the teacher must fashion as does a skillful carpenter; even beautiful wood will show no graining unless the carpenter is an expert, but a warped piece of wood can show good results in the hands of a skilled craftsman. The truth or falsity of the teacher is in ratio to the truth or falsity of the enlightenment of his disciples."

So, it's by the disciples you know if he or she is any good. When anybody comes to me and says, "Whom do you suggest I go to?" I say, "Well, go and talk to any of their disciples. Don't talk to the master; go and talk to the 'kids'. If they are any good, if they exhibit what you would like to be like, that's the person you're looking for." If they don't, go elsewhere. I'll finish this off, because it's rather fascinating.

Scripture: "Understand this clearly and become enlightened. Yet for centuries there have been no good teachers in this country (this is the Thirteenth Century in Japan, understand; it sounds very much like the present day)—how do we know? Just look at their words: they are as people who try to measure the source of flowing water from a scooped-up handful. Throughout the centuries this country's teachers have written books, taught trainees and given lectures to both men and gods, but their words were as green, unripe fruit for they had not reached the ultimate in training; they had not become one with true enlightenment. All that they transmitted were words, reciting names and sounds: day in and day out they counted in the treasury of others, contributing nothing whatsoever thereto of themselves. There is no doubt that this is the fault of the teachers of old, for some of them misled others into believing that enlightenment must be sought outside of the mind, and some taught that rebirth in other lands was the goal (in other words, they taught you to look outside, instead of inside, of you); herein is to be found the source of both confusion and delusion. Unless one follows the prescription on the medicine bottle, an illness may be made worse by taking medicine; it may even be the same as drinking poison. For centuries there have been no good doctors in this country who were capable of prescribing correctly, and of knowing the difference between, true medicine and poison, therefore it is extremely difficult to cure the sufferings and diseases of life: since this is so, how is it possible for us to escape from the sufferings brought on by old age and death? Only the teachers are to blame for this problem; it is certainly no fault of the disciples. Why is this so? Because the teachers are leading others along the branches of the tree and ceasing to climb up the trunk to the source (which is always much more difficult to climb than the branches). They lure others into false paths before they have their own understanding based on certainty; they therefore fix their concentration solely upon their own selfish opinions: it is indeed terrible that teachers have no perception of their own delusions. Under these circumstances, how can disciples understand what is right and what is wrong? (How can they see a true teacher?) As yet Buddhism has not taken root in our tiny country (this is the thirteenth century still) and thus true teachers are still to be born: if you truly want to study the very best Buddhism you must visit the teachers in China, which is very far away, and you must think deeply upon the true road which is beyond the mind of delusion. If a true teacher is not to be found, it is best not to study Buddhism at all: they who are called good teachers, however, are not necessarily either young or old (male or female) but simple people who can make clear the true teaching and receive the seal of a genuine master. Neither learning nor knowledge is of much importance for such teachers have a characteristic in their extraordinary influence over others and their own will power: they neither rely on their own selfish opinions nor do they cling to any obsession, for training and understanding are perfectly harmonized within them. The above are the characteristics of a true teacher."

That's the most perfect description I've ever read. Go and look at the "children"; don't look at the old monk, fair enough? Dogen does it much better than I would have done.

MONKS AND HOUSEHOLDERS

Now, the Sangha consists of four sections: the male monks, the female monks, the male lay Buddhists, and the female lay Buddhists. I use the term "monk" for both men and women not because I am a feminist or anything of that sort, but simply because if you translate the words accurately, osho means "monk and priest" and ni-osho means "female monk and priest". There is not the difference in Buddhism that there is in Christianity: everybody starts as a monk or a nun (as some would call it) and ends up a priest in Soto Zen, whether they are male or female, unless they specifically decide they don't wish to go any further. (I have yet to find anyone who did that.) Whereas in the West the term "nun" implies that one is not, and can never become, a priest. So, while in the early stages in the Far East it looks like there is a gender difference, or at least a separation, because women and men are usually segregated during their training in different monasteries, in actual fact once they have become full priests there really is no difference at all. Our school of Buddhism treats men and women equally because the Buddha Himself made it very clear that there was no difference between the meditation of a man and a woman, nor of the end result thereof. He couldn't do much about the local customs: customs are far harder to change than are religious teachings! So, in early Buddhism you do have some distinctions made between men and women, but we don't have to follow those customs.

So, you have male priests, female priests, laymen, shall we say, and laywomen. These are the four orders, and they are all equal, and they are all equally good, and they all equally go to the Eternal. The difference is how long it takes: monastic training usually goes more quickly. We have to face the fact that it is much more difficult to train in the everyday world than it is in a monastery, where everything is laid out to make it possible for you. It is much more difficult; I'm not going to pretend it isn't. As I said before, the end product's the same, but it's still much more difficult. It's like everything else: if you go to a college to study a subject, you are going to get there a lot faster and get your degree a lot faster than if you go to a night school because you are working full-time. But, of course, if you go to college and just sit there, then the person who really works at night school may well pass you, and there are plenty of very famous lay people who did rather better than some monks. If you think of it that way, then you can understand what is the real difference between the two from the laymen's point of view (in "laymen", I am including women). So if you keep that in mind, you can understand why it is necessary not to think you are going to lose something if you don't become a monk. When I first came to be teaching this in this country, everybody I met wanted to be monks: they were convinced the monks got the secrets and the laymen sort of got to provide the money to the monks. That was not true, and not everyone is suited to be a priest. Not everyone wants to be a priest and not everybody should be a priest. I know that there are going to be people in the Buddhist Church who will yell at me for the last one. Everybody, of course, has the potential, but there are people with children, people with family obligations: things that have to be dealt with. This does not mean you can't find the Eternal, and it does not mean that the Sangha, which is one and undivided, has privileges for some and not for others. It is very important to remember that.

Another difference between the monastics and the laity is in how they are of benefit to others. It must be understood that someone who becomes a monk does so because he or she not only wants to find the Land of the Lord, they also wish to become a priest so as to help others by holding out their certainty to those people in their own quest for that Land. The lay person, on the other hand, goes on the quest for the Land and incidentally may hold out his or her faith to help others as they journey. But they do not have a specific temple with, so to speak, a "shingle" or sign outside saying that they are there full-time, ready and willing to help. Persons who wish to understand how the householder's training helps others in its highest form should study the writings about Vimalakirti and also those of Layman P'ang.* Now, I am not saying that because someone is a lay person they do not wish to help others. They just do it as they journey through the world in which they live. Like the priest, they are in the world but not of the world. Unlike the priest, they do not necessarily stay in one place and "hang out a shingle". What the lay person understands in training, they show in their everyday life, and in that way they benefit and teach others, although not doing so consciously. They teach by example, simply by going through life practicing the Bodhisattva way, without bugging people and without trying deliberately to teach them. Just by doing that which a Bodhisattva does, you will teach. And this unassuming practice of the Bodhisattva way is the final and great achievement of the lay person, and the purpose for their existence.

> *Question:* "You said once that it is important to fully be lay people and not to imitate monks. And I wanted, am curious about, how to go about doing that and why."

The best way is being satisfied with training the way you are training, not to constantly think, "Well, maybe they've got more than I have." Envy is the big problem, but people don't recognize it as envy. It is "Well, I want to be a householder, but I really want what the monk's got; now how can I wangle it and get that?" And the answer is: you can't. You either have to be a householder, which is a complete and perfectly wonderful way and part of the Sangha, or you've got to be a monastic, which is a complete and perfectly wonderful

---

* R. F. Sasaki, Y. Iriya, and D. R. Fraser, trans., *A Man of Zen: The Recorded Sayings of Layman P'ang* (New York: John Weatherhill, 1971).

way and part of the Sangha. It's contentment: that is the best way, to be contented. Then you become grateful and thankful, and then you are really training; you go just as fast as a monk does then. But if you think you are missing out, then you're actually holding yourself back and then, in fact, you do miss out. But it's not because you are training as a lay person; it's because you are judging yourself again. When you do that, as we've seen before, you've already missed out; you've lost your peace of mind. That's the very best advice I can give you on that: be fully what you are, and don't worry about what somebody else has "got".

> *Monk's comment:* "On this problem of 'has the other way got something better?' I ran into a quote from Socrates. (This is not a new problem!) He said, 'Let a man choose the family life or celibacy, as he pleases: he is sure to repent of it.'" (laughter)

It's a good answer. Yes, go ahead.

> *Audience comment:* "Yet sometimes, for some of us, there is a sort of sense of urgency that is there when you are training that pushes you. Yes, it's fine to be a layman, and yet there is that push to do a little more, which eventually, if you keep following it, ends you up doing it entirely and becoming a monk."

Yes, that can happen. That perhaps has happened for you, but that does not necessarily happen for everybody.

> *Audience comment continues:* "No, what I am saying is how do you find the middle way when some part of you keeps pushing?"

Well, you have to decide what you really want to do. If that part of you keeps pushing, and that is what you want to follow, then that is what you follow. And that will become your Middle Way. I don't know if you understand what I am saying by that. You see, I can't really answer your question. To find the Middle Way does not mean to avoid making a commitment: it means to find the very best way for you. And if you are constantly being urged to be a monk, or to be a layman, perhaps that's what you should be, and that will be the Middle Way for you. But don't try pushing away any part of the decision. Don't try pushing it one way, and don't try pushing it the other: just let it grow naturally. The Middle Way grows naturally; it does not come as a result of forcing a decision. And, when it has grown, then it must be acted upon.

> *Question:* "About celibacy: why is it that the monks of your order are celibate? It seems like most Zen monks in the West are married."

Well, there's an interesting history behind that. Up until about a hundred years ago, all Zen monks were celibate— both the men and the women—in China, Japan, Korea, and Vietnam, just as most of the rest of the ordained Buddhist Sangha has been since the time of the Buddha. Then the government of Japan, in a move to weaken the power of the Buddhist clergy, passed a number of laws, one of which permitted (and actively encouraged) the monks to give up their vows of celibacy, abstinence from alcohol, and vegetarianism. Over time the male monks mostly married, but the female ones, whom the government didn't see as any threat anyway, did not. So in Japan at the present time most male monks are married; the Japanese female monks and the Zen monks in most other countries are not. Thus you will find that those Western Zen groups who were founded by a Japanese male monk generally permit their priests to be married; those founded by a Japanese female monk or a Zen monk from another country generally do not.

Now I, of course, was ordained in Chinese Buddhism, which is celibate, and trained in a Japanese male temple with a male master, so I had both ways open to me and had to decide which way to go. Personally, it has always been clear to me that celibacy was the way for me, as it was for Koho Zenji as well. He was one of the male Japanese monks who made the personal choice to remain celibate. When I first came to this country I was undecided on this, but, coming out of both of these traditions, I decided we'd allow monks to marry if they chose and see what happened. And we did have several members of the community who got married. Then we knew why most Buddhist monastic orders in the world didn't do that. Eventually most of the married couples did have to leave monastic life, not because either we or they wanted it that way, but simply because when the children came they had incredible expenses. They just had to go out and work and earn a living; there was no other way in which it could be done. There was also the fact that monastic training got in the way of looking after the children, and since they had children, it was their duty to look after them. In other words, they had effectively walked back into the household state. But there was something much more subtle than that even, and that was that the Eternal came second, because of the needs of the children and the husband or the wife—the marriage and the children had to come first, which is fitting and proper—and therefore the training of such people became more like that of laymen and laywomen. It seemed that to fully function as a priest, the

Eternal had to be first, that and the ability to respond at a moment's notice to the spiritual needs of the congregation or the disciples. I was very sad that having married monastics did not work out for us, but there was nothing like doing the experiment and finding out what was the best way to go. It also explained to me why (although I should have seen it— I was awfully "thick" not to) most of the male monks in Japan left their monasteries after their initial training and went out to work in banks or in school teaching and the like; the answer was very simple: they had to keep a wife and children. There was no other way they could do it. You couldn't expect a small temple congregation to keep both the priest and his family. The women monks, as I said, didn't marry and therefore they were accepted throughout all the Buddhist countries of the world. The men were treated as laymen when they went to other Buddhist countries, which I always felt was rather unfair, but it was the one circumstance which I encountered in Buddhism in which women had higher status than men. So that is why now, in our Order, if you are a monk, you're celibate.

> *Question:* "I would sort of like to go back to the question that somebody in the back raised, that you just answered, but sort of from a different angle. Okay, there's something that makes a person start to train and something that, say, makes a person meditate twice a day instead of one, and so on . . ."

It's known as "being disturbed by the Truth": there is something that is disturbing you to do more.

> *Question continues:* ". . . well, the question which arises for me is: is this the voice of envy saying, 'Well,

train more; I have something you haven't got', or the voice of Truth simply saying, 'Train more'?"

Yeah. And the answer I have to that is that if something wants me to train more (this is *my* answer, by the way; don't take it as your answer; this is my answer), then it must want my good; therefore it has to be the voice of the Cosmic Buddha. My willfulness would say, "Why don't you stay in bed?" You see, you've got to think about it from a very practical angle. What would want me to train more deeply? Obviously, the Cosmic Buddha. Now, I might also want to train more, in which case I win either way, you see? Whichever way I go with that I win, because willfulness, delusion, would not ask me to do that. And even if it did ask you to do it out of envy, well, there is an old Christian saying, "God writes straight with crooked lines." All right, so you're envious of somebody else, and so you're training: that's just fine; it's a place to start. I know of someone who was so annoyed when he discovered his wife had a kensho that he settled down and said, "I am going to make it." And he did; he was driven into training by envy; there's nothing wrong with that. The training, if it was started out of envy, will require that you give up envy. So, it really doesn't matter, does it? You see, the Cosmic Buddha can use anything. But delusion can only use delusion.

Now, I see that our time together is about up. In conclusion let me just say that you, and only you, can do all of this; you do not need a third party. Above all you do not need me. That's why I named the first book I wrote *Selling Water by the River.* I was quite honest about it; I'm not a con man. If you want to do this, I can show you how. It's very easy to do, but you've really got to work at it. It's easy, but it's hard in that it takes a lot of time and a lot of willingness, and willingness is one of the things that most people aren't too eager to give, and that's what makes it difficult. Dogen says later on in another one of his scriptures, "Will is a donkey and words are a horse." The will is like a donkey that won't ever go the way that you want it to go, and the words that you tell it are like a horse prancing around in all directions and not giving over-much information. In the beginning you have to do something about that donkey-will, and later you have to change the word "will" into simply *being willing*, and there is a big difference in that. Let me leave you with a final quote from Master Dogen; this one is from "Shoji",* his discourse on life and death.

> *Scripture:* "The Way to Buddhahood is easy. They who do not perpetrate evil, they who do not try to grasp at life and death but work for the good of all living things with utter compassion, giving respect to those older, and loving understanding to those younger, than themselves, they who do not reject, search for, think on or worry about anything have the name of Buddha: you must look for nothing more."

---

* Great Master Dogen, "Shoji", trans. Rev. P.T.N.H. Jiyu-Kennett in *Zen is Eternal Life*, pp. 196–198, op. cit.

About the Order of
Buddhist Contemplatives

The Order of Buddhist Contemplatives is a religious order practicing Serene Reflection Meditation (J. Soto Zen) as transmitted from The Very Reverend Keido Chisan Koho Zenji, Abbot of Dai Hon Zan Sojiji in Yokohama, Japan, to Reverend Master P.T.N.H. Jiyu-Kennett. Rev. Master Jiyu-Kennett came to the United States in 1969 and established Shasta Abbey in 1970. She founded the Order of Buddhist Contemplatives in 1978, serving as Head of the Order until her death in 1996. In North America, the Order now has Priories (congregational temples) in Albany and Maricopa, California; Eugene and Portland, Oregon; McKenna and Seattle, Washington; Edmonton, Alberta and Vancouver, B.C., Canada. In Europe, Throssel Hole Buddhist Abbey in northern England was founded in 1972, and O.B.C. Priories are located in Edinburgh, Scotland, and Reading and Telford, England. There are also meditation groups affiliated with the Order in Great Britain, Canada, the United States, the Netherlands, and Germany. The Order has male and female monks; women and men have equal status and recognition and train together in the Buddhist priesthood; they are referred to as both monks and priests. The monastic order is celibate and vegetarian. In addition to monastics, the Order includes lay ministers throughout the world. The Head of the Order is Rev. Master Daizui MacPhillamy. The Order publishes *The Journal of the Order of Buddhist Contemplatives* quarterly.

About the Monasteries
of the Order

THROSSEL HOLE BUDDHIST ABBEY

Throssel Hole Buddhist Abbey is situated in a quiet valley in the north of England. It was founded in 1972 by Rev. Master P.T.N.H. Jiyu-Kennett as Throssel Hole Priory, and over the years has become a monastery and seminary for training priests of the Order, as well as a retreat and training center for a large European congregation. Its Abbot is Rev. Master Daishin Morgan, a senior disciple of the late Rev. Kennett.

The Abbey offers for lay guests a full and varied program, to which all are warmly invited. Experienced senior priests teach both meditation and how to use the Buddhist Precepts in establishing a daily practice. Through these means one can find the Truth, or Buddha Nature, at the heart of oneself and all beings. Training shows how to let go of the clinging that causes suffering, thus allowing this inner compassion and wisdom to enrich our lives. Guests meditate in the bright and spacious ceremony hall, and sleep there at night, dormitory-style, with complete privacy between men and women maintained. A large dining hall includes a small library and common room area for guests. By following the monastery's daily schedule, guests experience how it is that all activities of life—working, relaxing, reading, eating, and sleeping—have true spiritual depth and value. For more information, call or write Throssel Hole Buddhist Abbey, Carrshield, Hexham, Northumberland NE47 8AL, United Kingdom; phone: +44 (0) 1434 345204 or fax: +44 (0) 1434 345216.

SHASTA ABBEY

Shasta Abbey, located on sixteen forested acres near Mount Shasta city in northern California, is a seminary for the Buddhist priesthood and training monastery for both lay and monastic Buddhists and visitors. It was established in 1970 by Rev. Master P.T.N.H. Jiyu-Kennett, who was Abbess and spiritual director until her death in 1996. Buddhist training at Shasta Abbey is based on the practice of Serene Reflection Meditation and the keeping of the Buddhist Precepts. The monastery is home to over 30 ordained male and female monks and its Abbot is Rev. Master Eko Little, a senior disciple of Rev. Master Jiyu-Kennett.

Guests and visitors follow a schedule that is similar to that of the monastic community, providing a balance of sitting meditation, work, ceremonial, and instruction in Buddhism. The schedule allows the mind of meditation to be cultivated and maintained throughout all aspects of daily life. Retreat guests stay at the Abbey's guest house, which accommodates about 40 people. All meals are vegetarian and are prepared in the Abbey kitchen. A stay at Shasta Abbey allows visitors to set aside their usual daily concerns so that they may participate wholeheartedly in the spiritual life of the monastery.

In addition to its monastic and lay training programs, Shasta Abbey offers a Buddhist Supply service and publishes books through Shasta Abbey Press. For more information, call or write Shasta Abbey, 3724 Summit Drive, Mt. Shasta, California, 96067-9102; phone: (530) 926-4208; fax: (530) 926-0428; e-mail: shastaabbey@obcon.org.

O.B.C. website: www.obcon.org